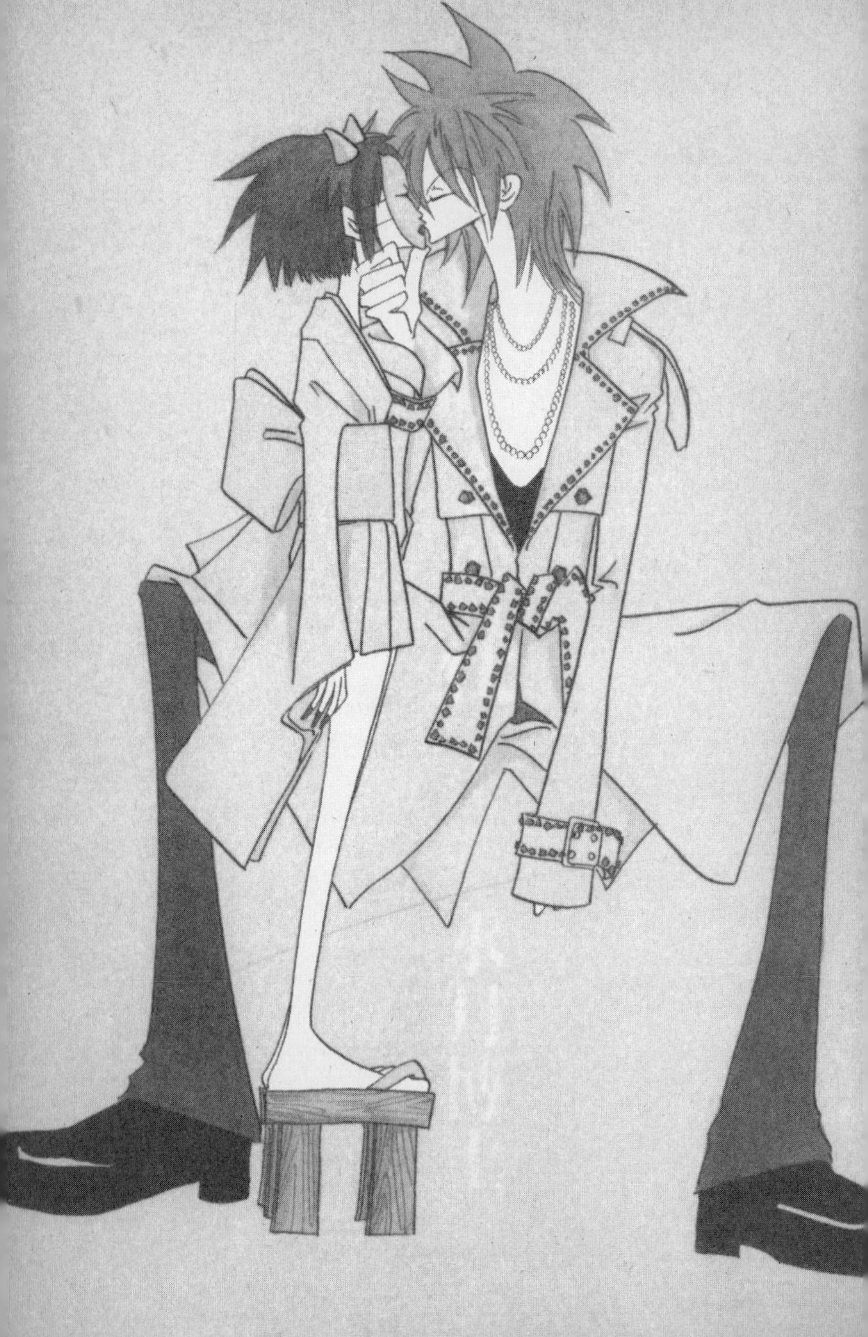

Demon Flowers: Kuruizaki no Hana Volume 1
Created by Mizuki Hakase

Translation - Haruko Furukawa
English Adaptation - Liz Forbes
Retouch and Lettering - Star Print Brokers
Production Artist - Courtney Geter
Graphic Designer - Fawn Lau

Editor - Katherine Schilling
Digital Imaging Manager - Chris Buford
Pre-Production Supervisor - Erika Terriquez
Art Director - Anne Marie Horne
Production Manager - Elisabeth Brizzi
Managing Editor - Vy Nguyen
VP of Production - Ron Klamert
Editor-in-Chief - Rob Tokar
Publisher - Mike Kiley
President and C.O.O. - John Parker
C.E.O. and Chief Creative Officer - Stuart Levy

A **TOKYOPOP**® Manga

TOKYOPOP Inc.
5900 Wilshire Blvd. Suite 2000
Los Angeles, CA 90036

E-mail: info@TOKYOPOP.com
Come visit us online at www.TOKYOPOP.com

ISBN: 978-1-4278-0298-9

First TOKYOPOP printing: September 2007
10 9 8 7 6 5 4 3 2 1
Printed in the USA

DEMON FLOWERS
KURUIZAKI NO HANA

Volume One

By
Mizuki Hakase

HAMBURG // LONDON // LOS ANGELES // TOKYO

MIZUKI HAKASE
Presents
KURUIZAKI NO HANA

CONTENTS

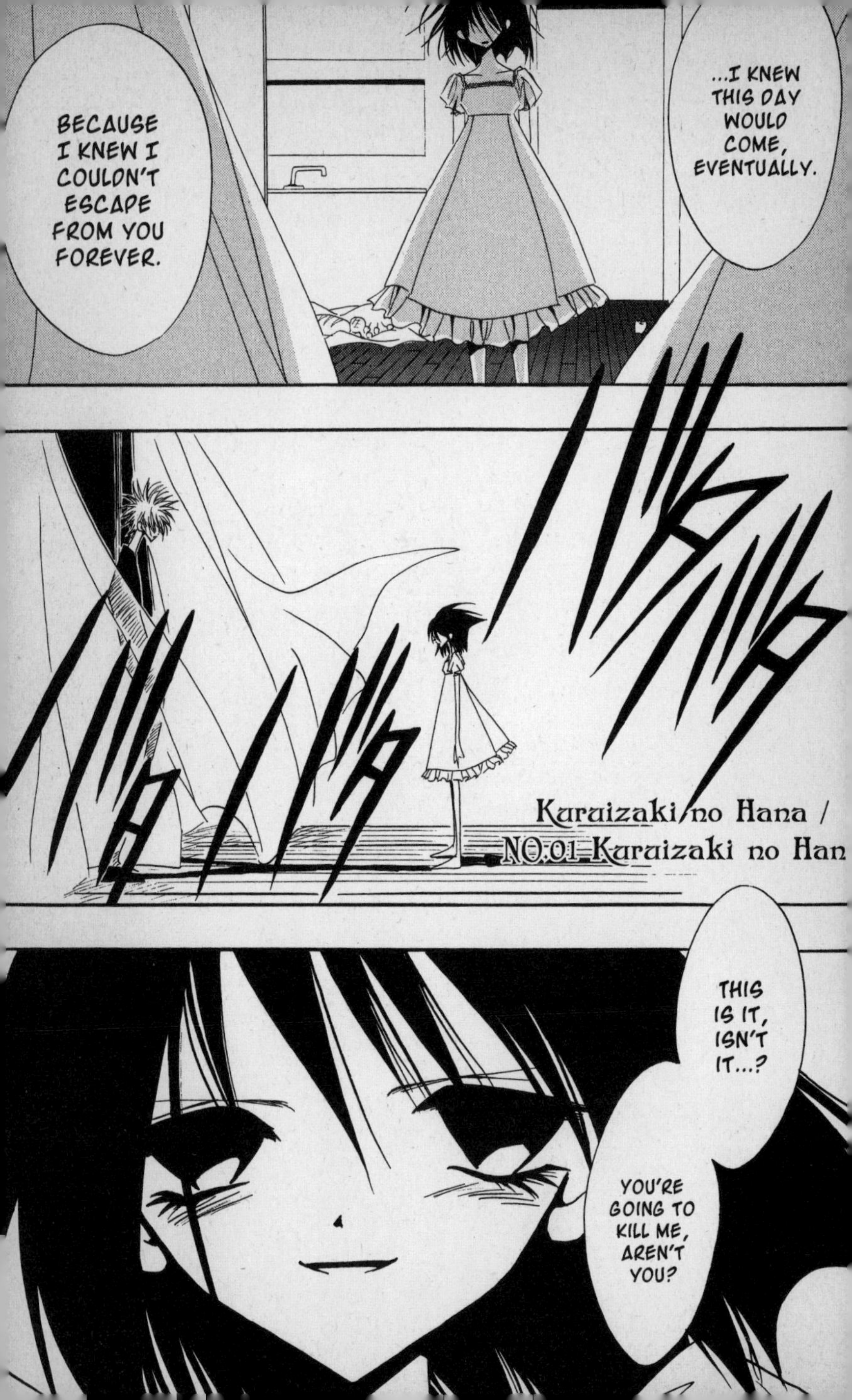
...I KNEW THIS DAY WOULD COME, EVENTUALLY.
BECAUSE I KNEW I COULDN'T ESCAPE FROM YOU FOREVER.
Kuruizaki no Hana /
NO.01 Kuruizaki no Han
THIS IS IT, ISN'T IT...?
YOU'RE GOING TO KILL ME, AREN'T YOU?

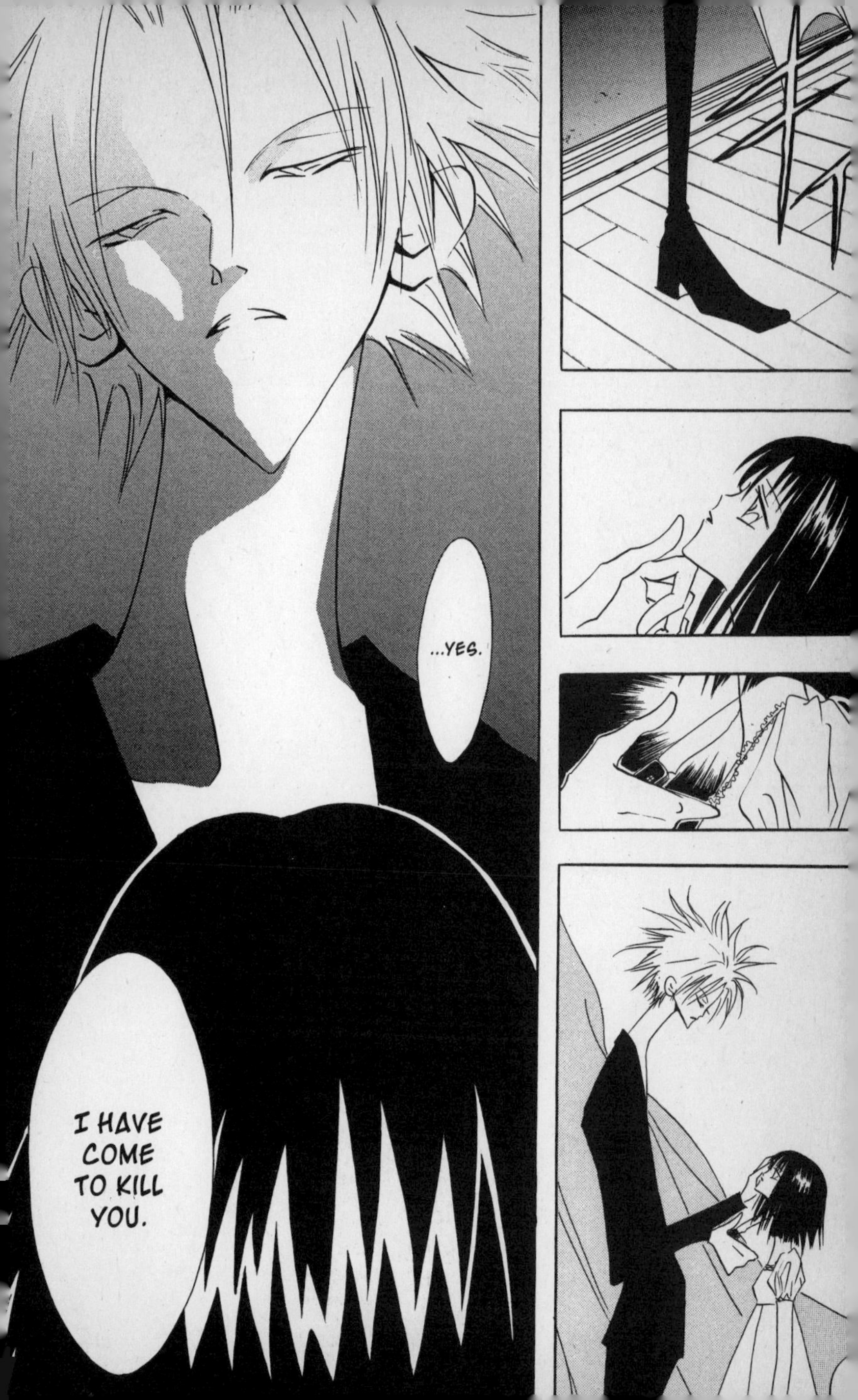
...YES.
I HAVE COME TO KILL YOU.

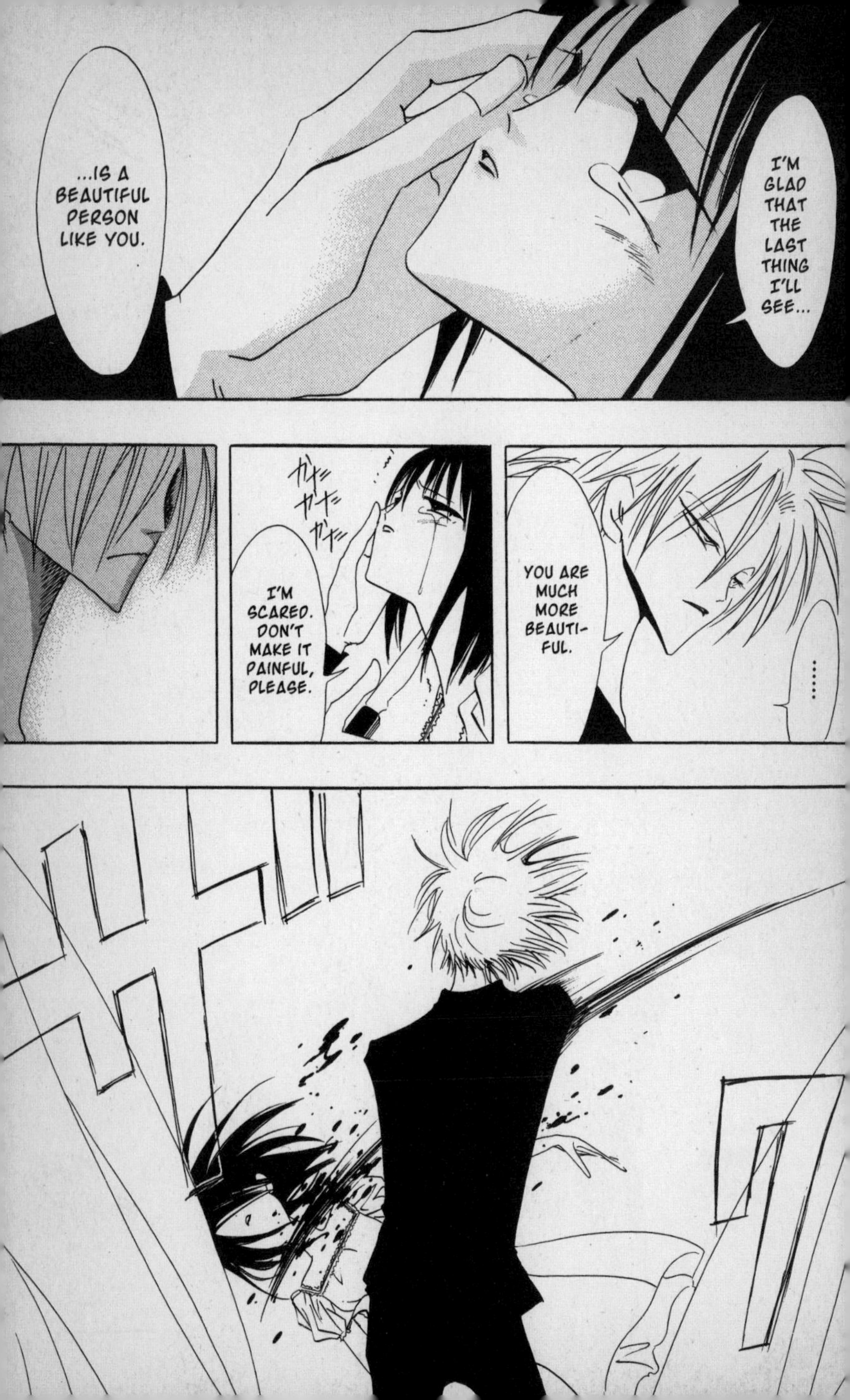
I'M GLAD THAT THE LAST THING I'LL SEE...
...IS A BEAUTIFUL PERSON LIKE YOU.
YOU ARE MUCH MORE BEAUTI-FUL.
......
I'M SCARED. DON'T MAKE IT PAINFUL, PLEASE.

DEMONS DEVOURED THE
GODS THAT ONCE GUARDED
JAPAN AND KEPT IT SAFE.

BY CONSUMING THE FLESH
OF THE GODS, THE DEMONS
ASSIMILATED THEIR POWERS.

THE DEMONS HAVE DISCOVERED
THAT SOME OF THE GODS
BORE HUMAN CHILDREN
WITH SPECIAL POWERS.

THE DEMONS ARE LOOKING
FOR THESE CHILDREN...

TO CONSUME THEM...

TO TAKE THEIR POWERS.

THEY CALL THESE CHILDREN...

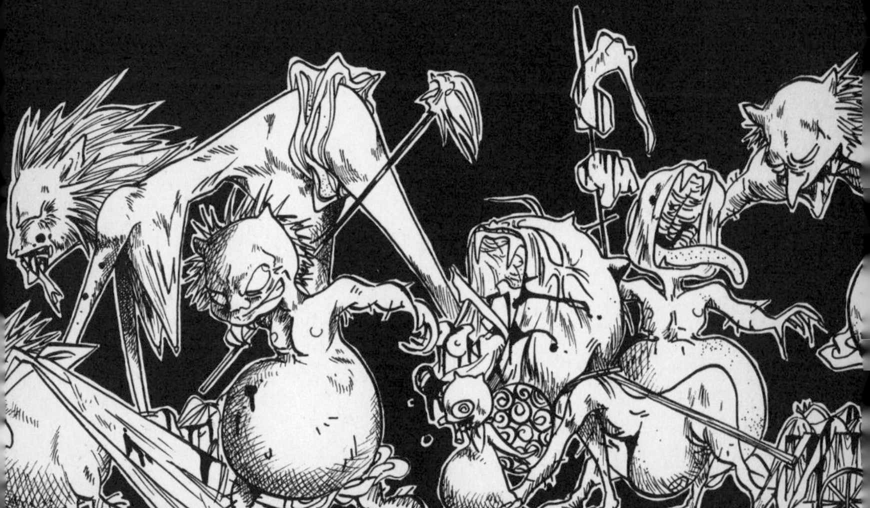

"KURUIZAKI NO HANA"--FLOWERS OUT OF SEASON.

DEMON FLOWERS
KURUIZAKI NO HANA

NO.01 Kuruizaki no Hana

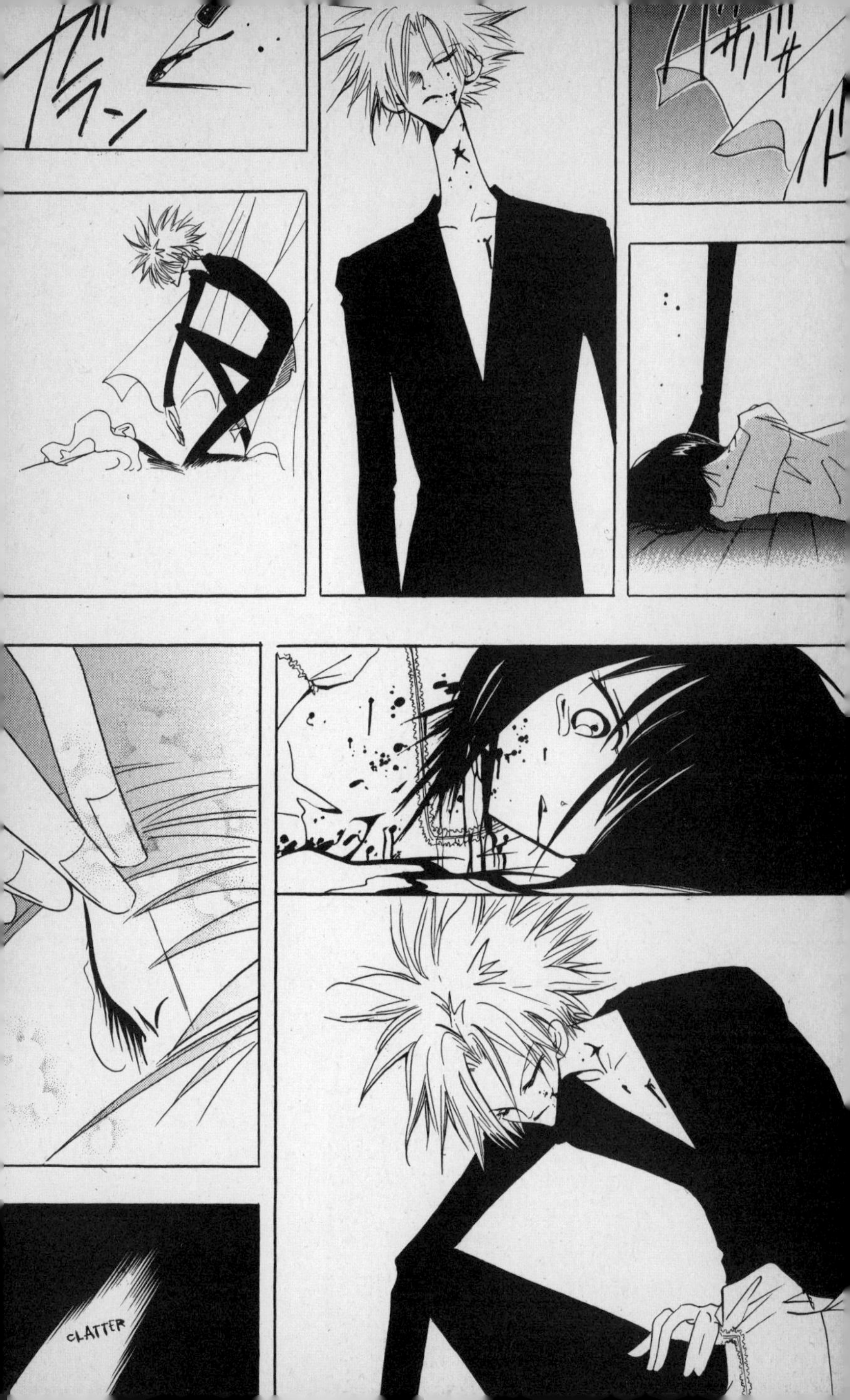
CLATTER

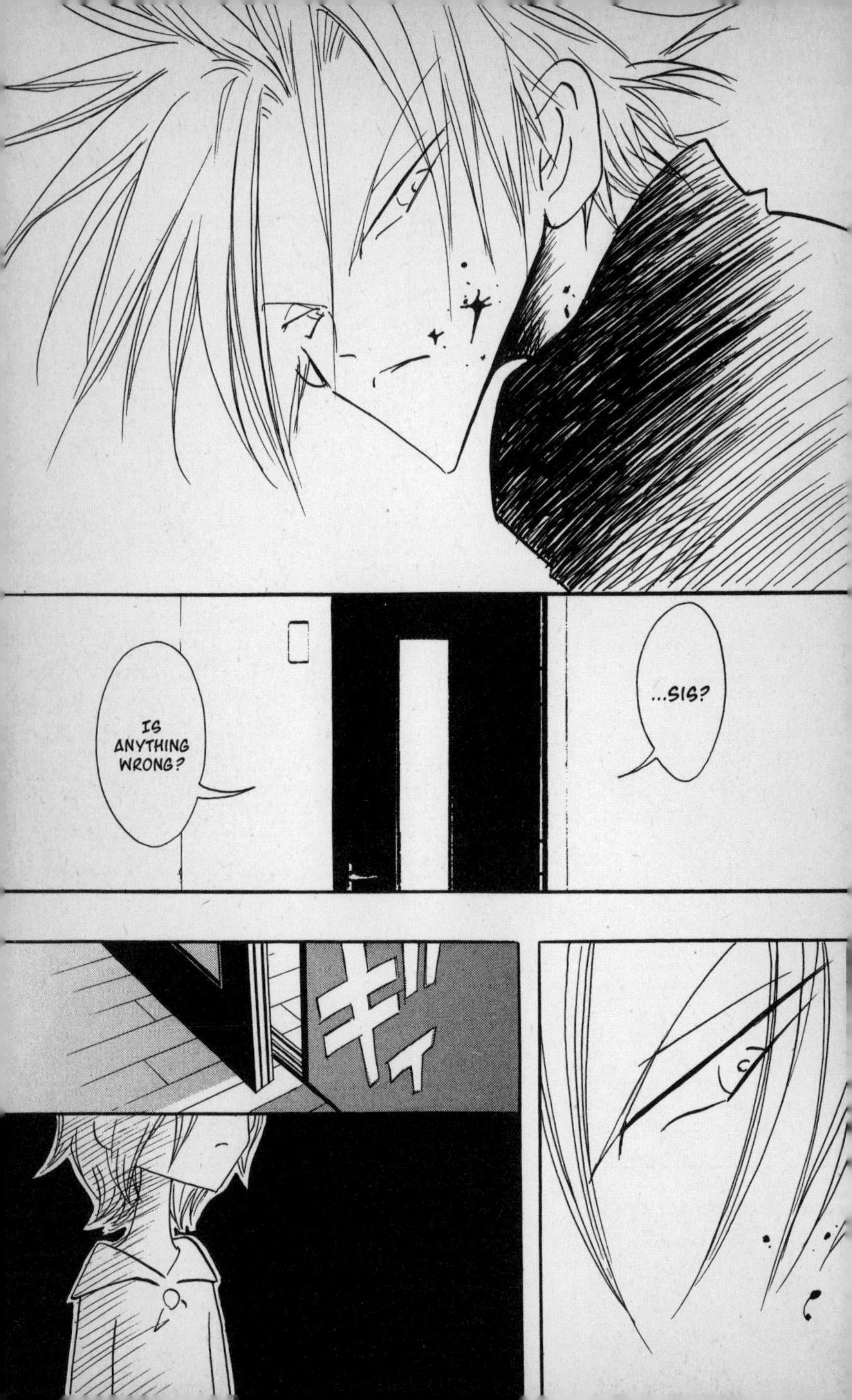
...SIS?
IS ANYTHING WRONG?
ギィ

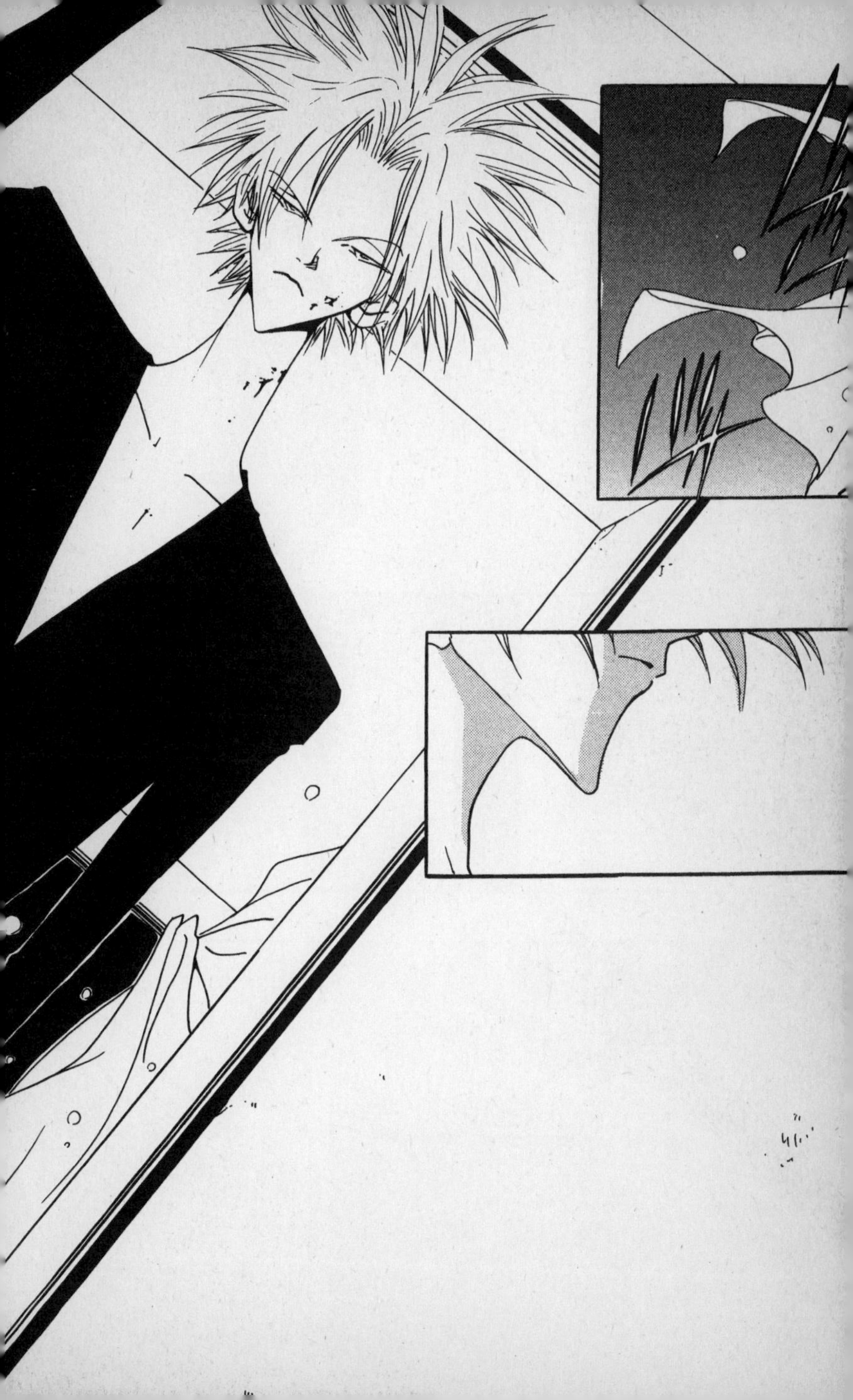

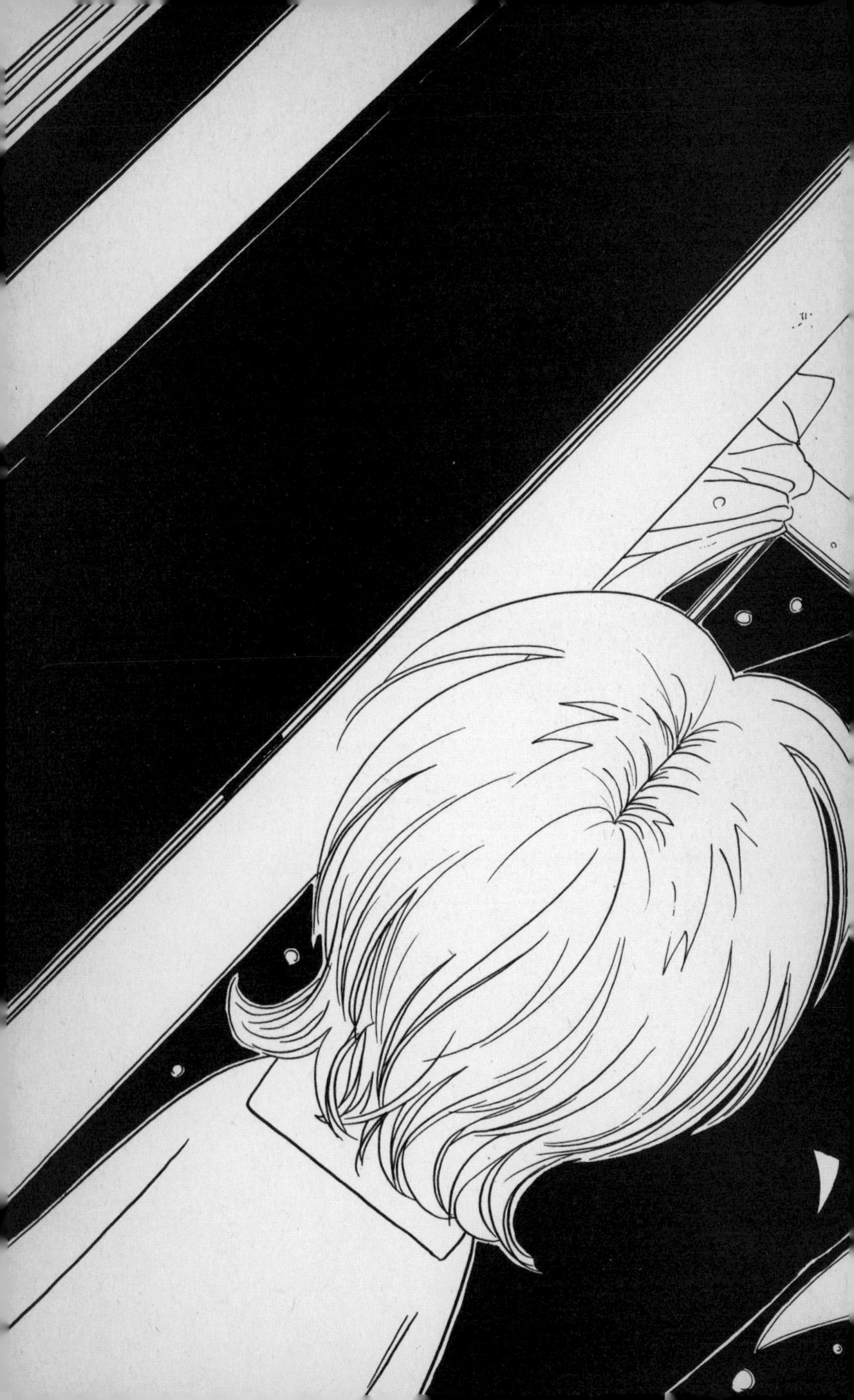

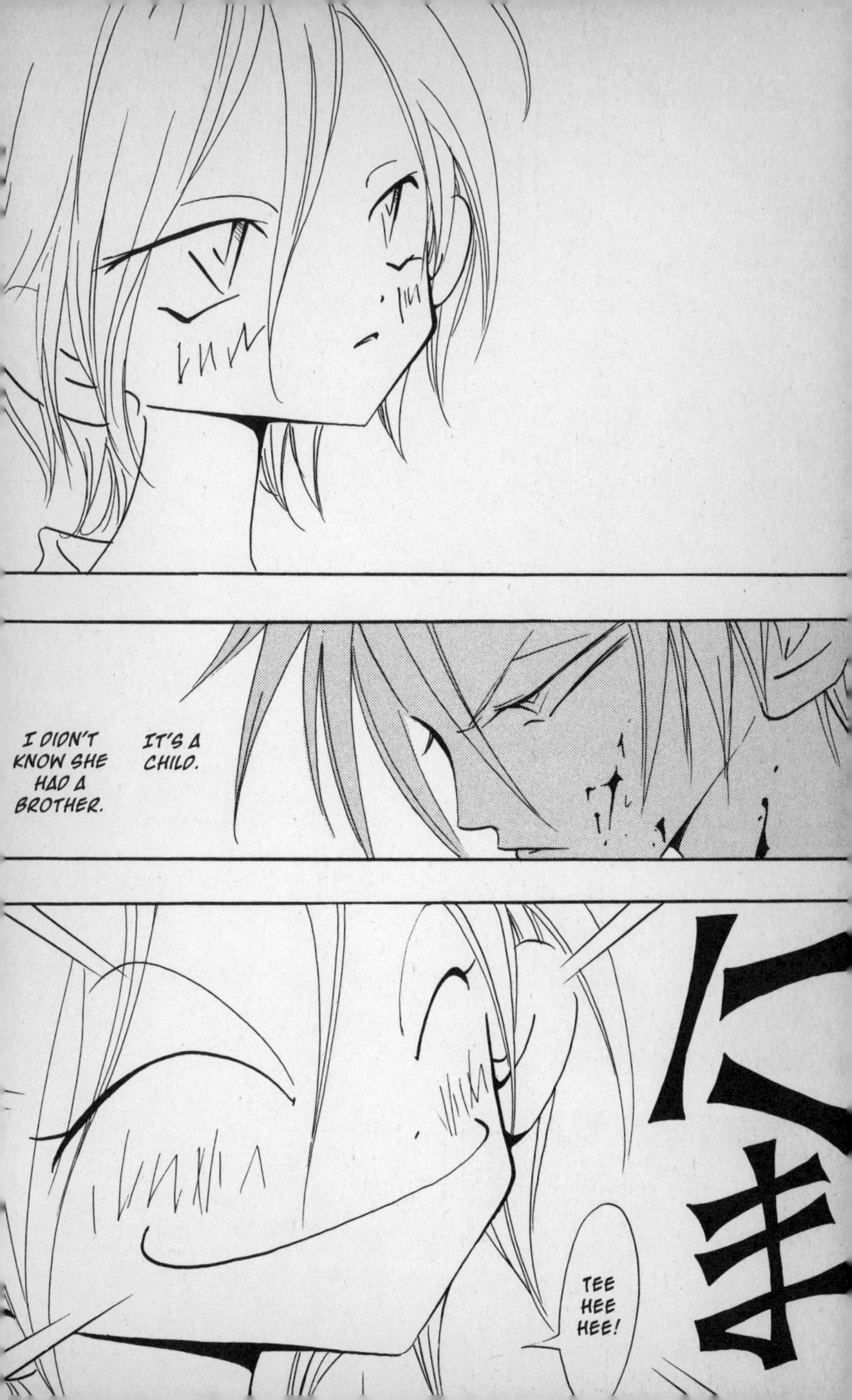
IT'S A CHILD.
I DIDN'T KNOW SHE HAD A BROTHER.
にま
TEE HEE HEE!

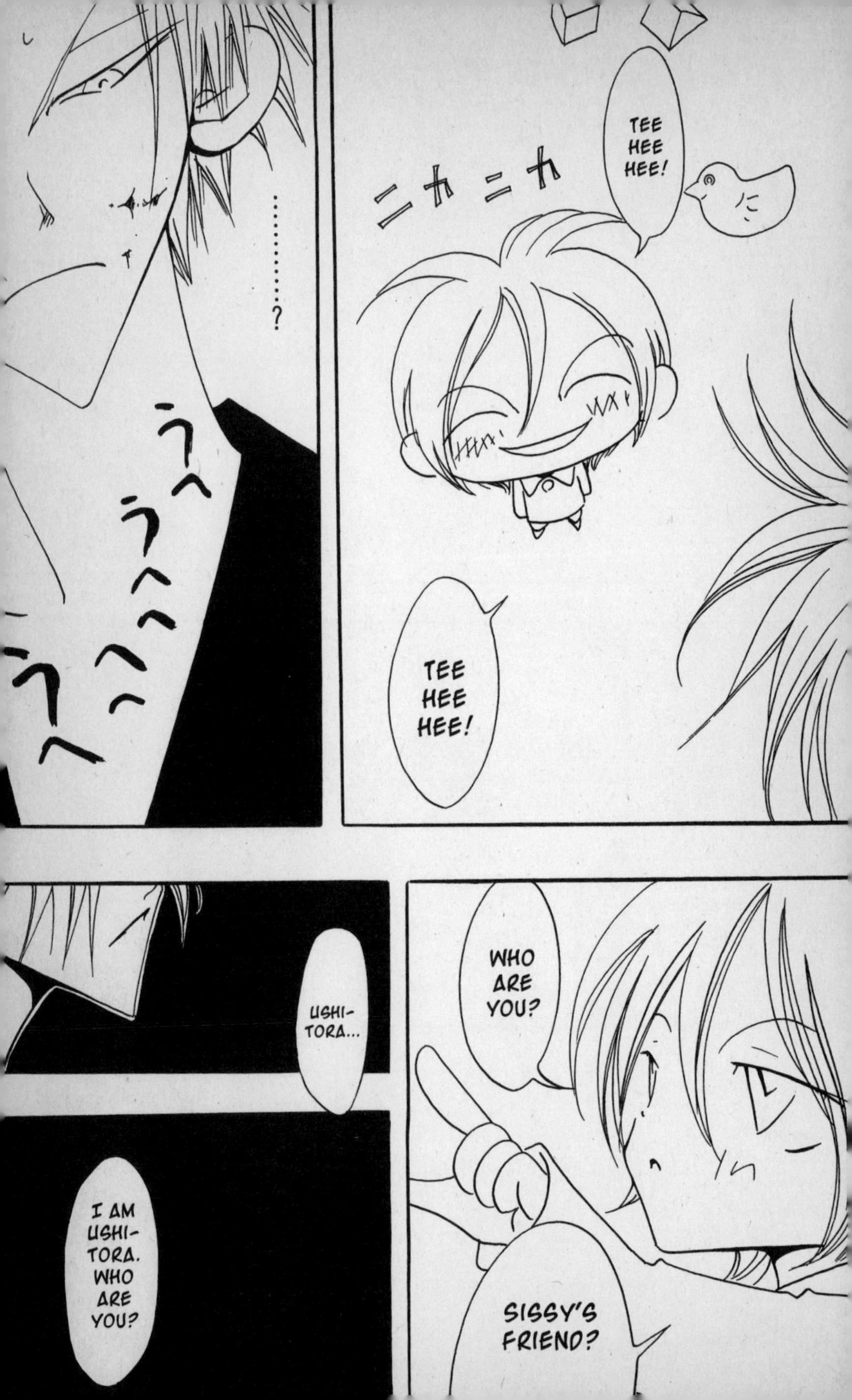
TEE HEE HEE!
ニカニカ
TEE HEE HEE!
……?
WHO ARE YOU?
SISSY'S FRIEND?
USHI-TORA...
I AM USHI-TORA. WHO ARE YOU?

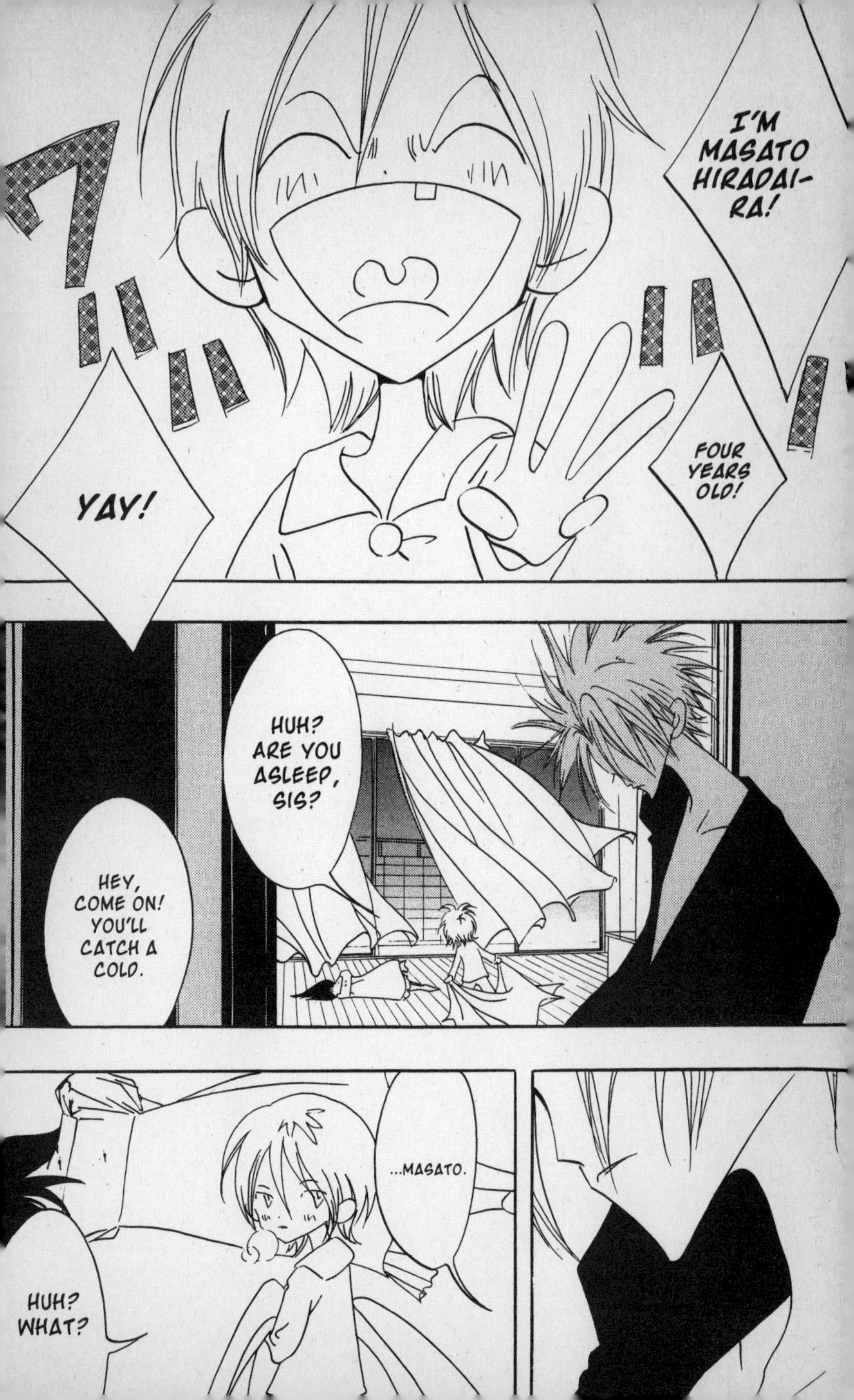
I'M MASATO HIRADAI-RA!
FOUR YEARS OLD!
YAY!
HUH? ARE YOU ASLEEP, SIS?
HEY, COME ON! YOU'LL CATCH A COLD.
...MASATO.
HUH? WHAT?

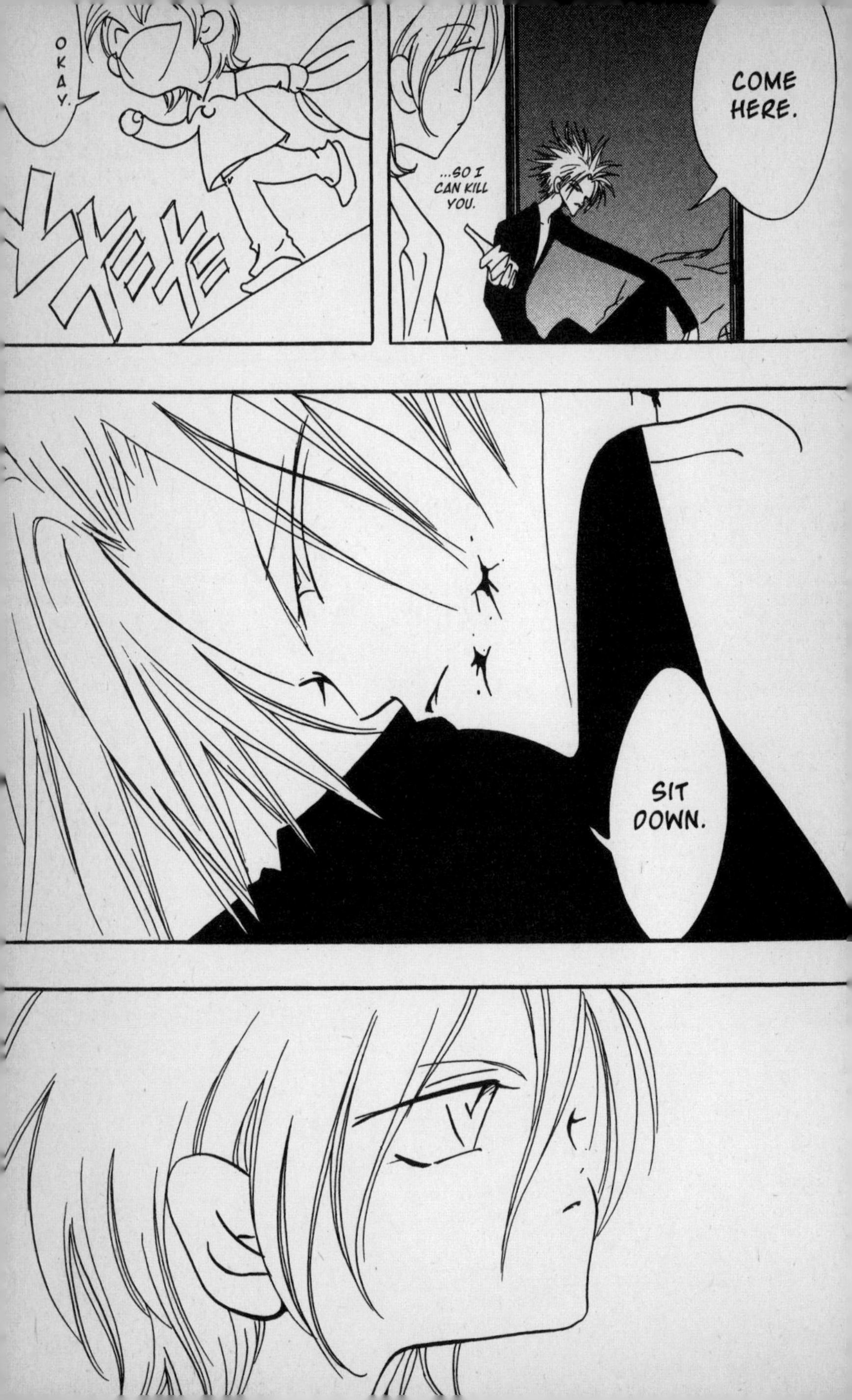
COME HERE.
...SO I CAN KILL YOU.
OKAY.
SIT DOWN.

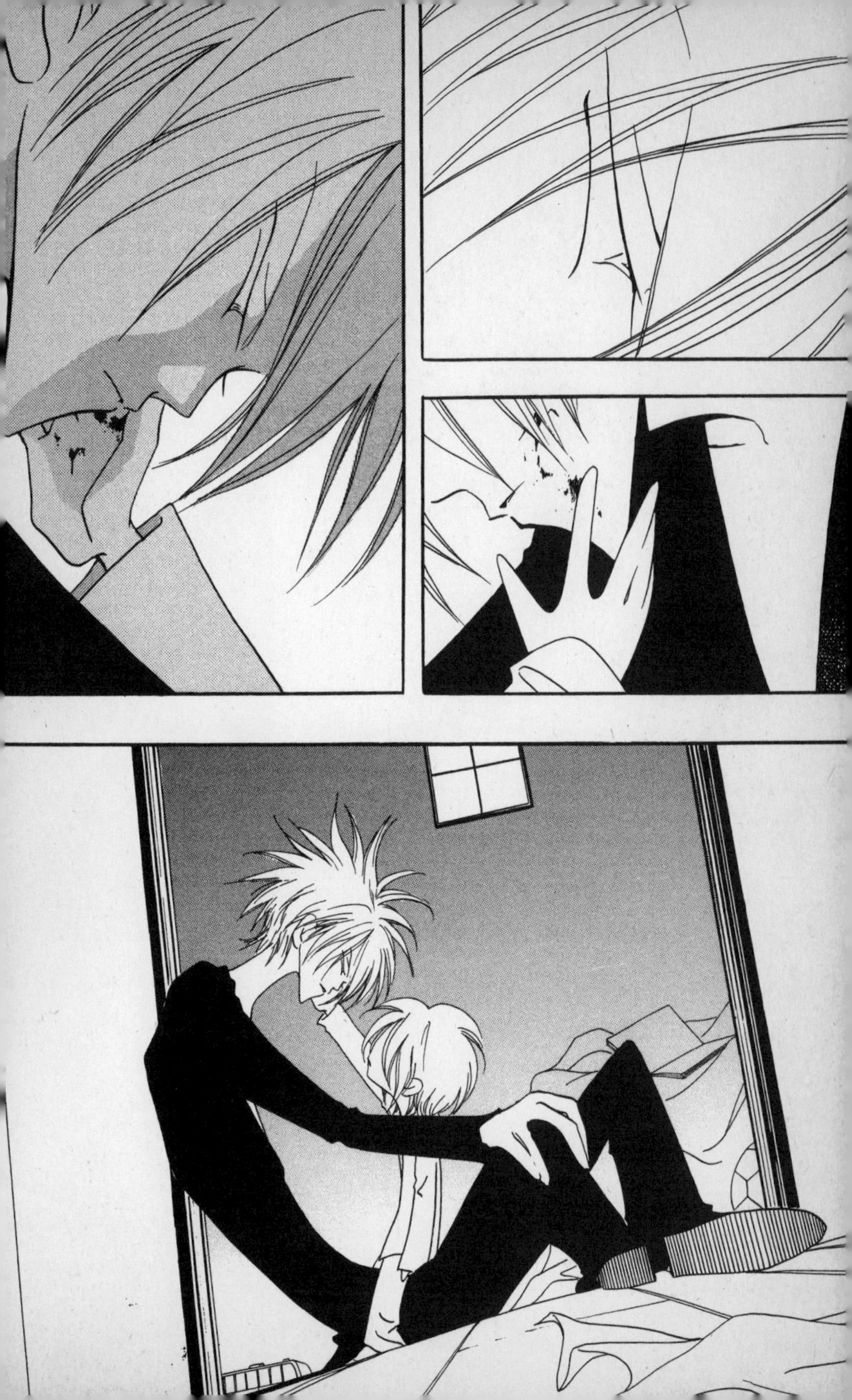

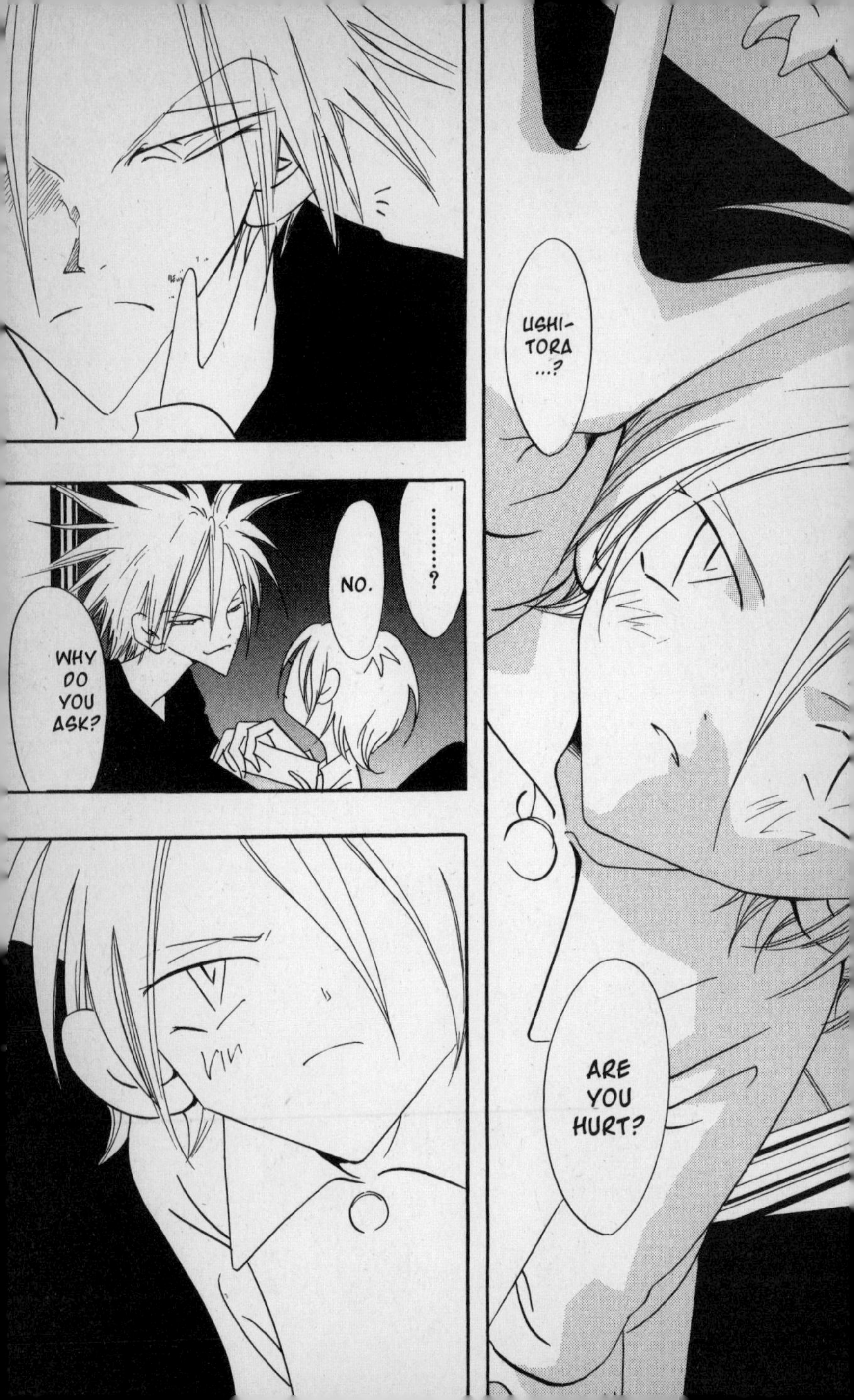
USHI-TORA ...?
ARE YOU HURT?
......?
NO.
WHY DO YOU ASK?

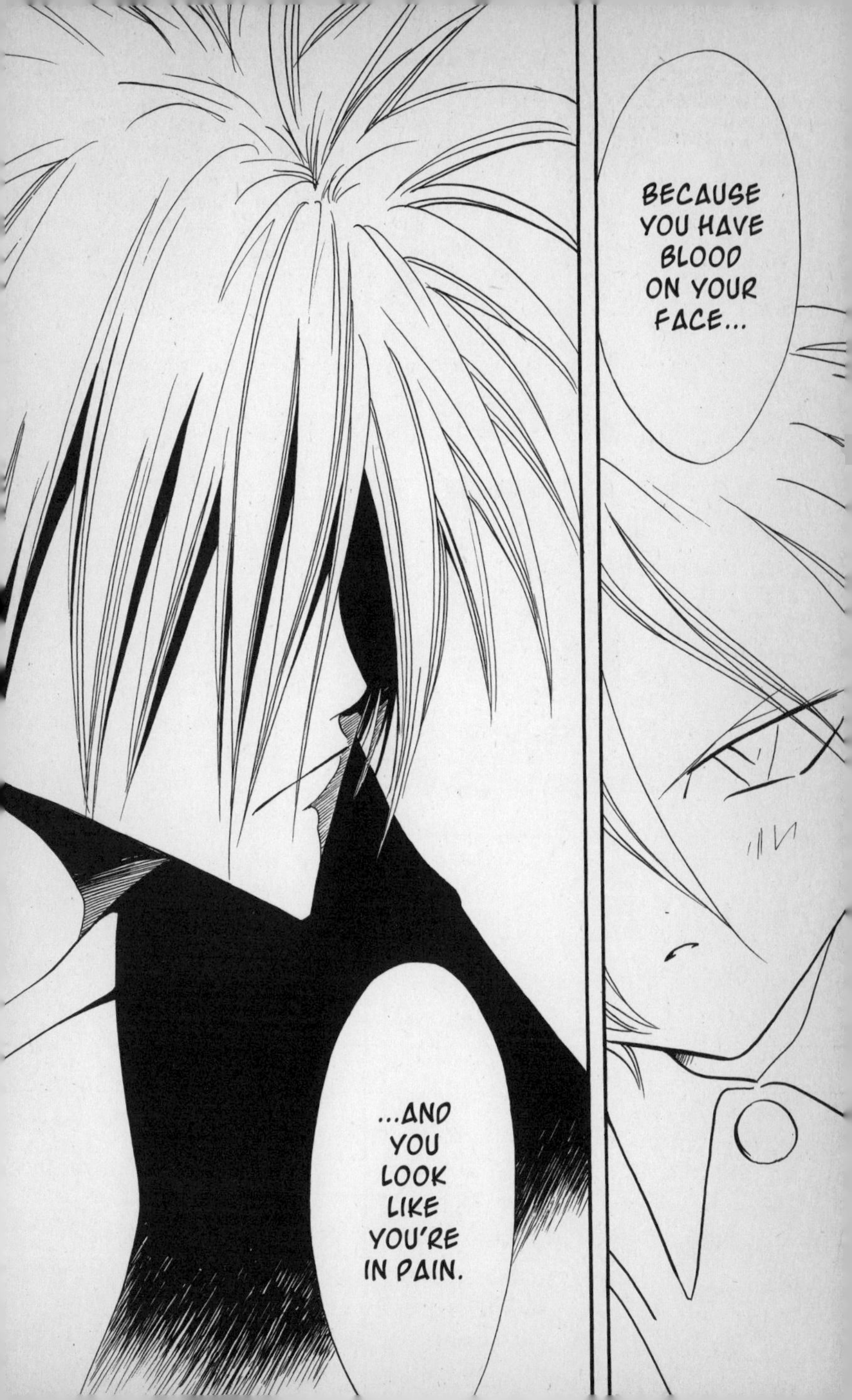
BECAUSE YOU HAVE BLOOD ON YOUR FACE...
...AND YOU LOOK LIKE YOU'RE IN PAIN.

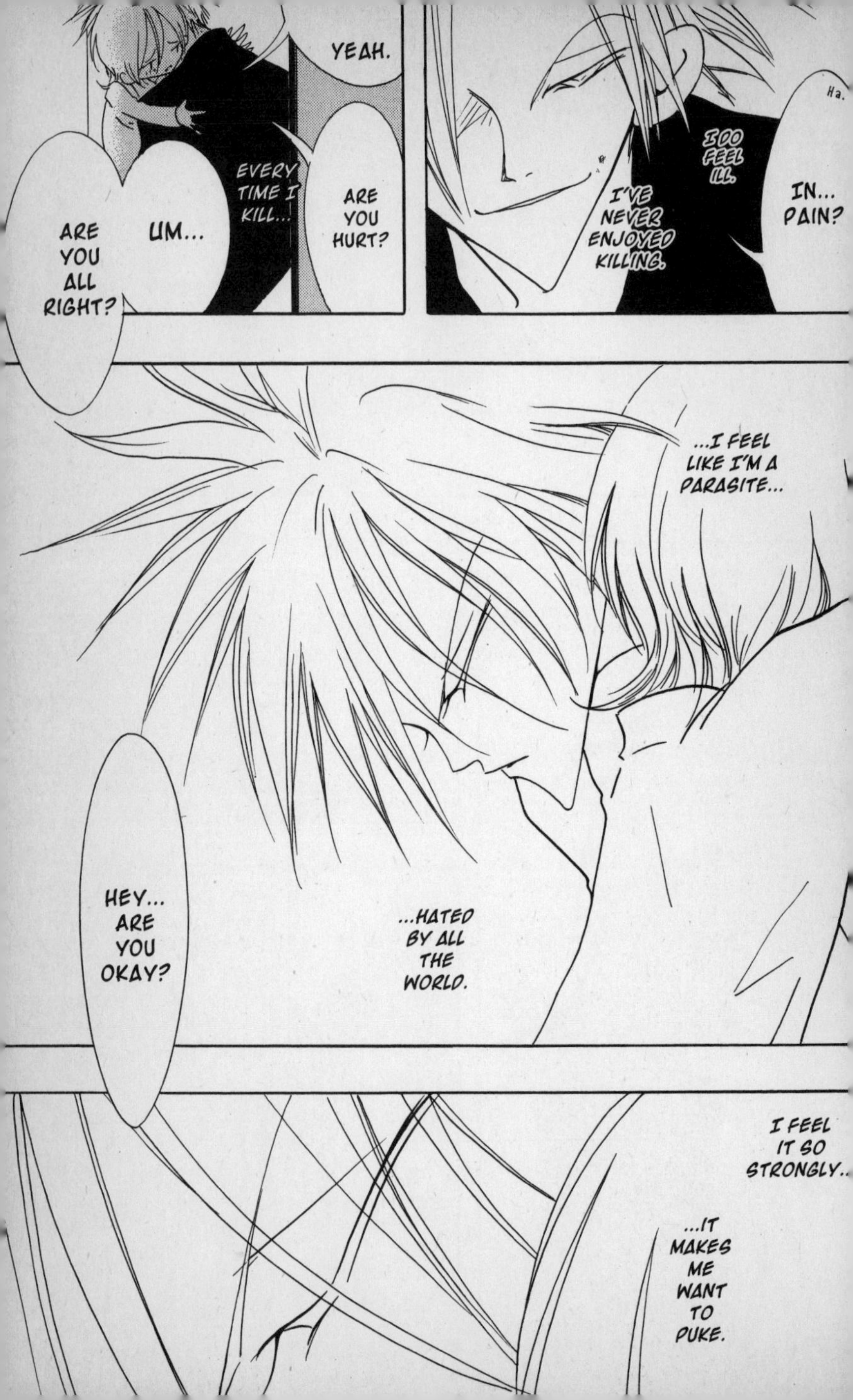
Ha.
IN... PAIN?
I DO FEEL ILL.
I'VE NEVER ENJOYED KILLING.
YEAH.
ARE YOU HURT?
EVERY TIME I KILL...
UM...
ARE YOU ALL RIGHT?
...I FEEL LIKE I'M A PARASITE...
...HATED BY ALL THE WORLD.
HEY... ARE YOU OKAY?
I FEEL IT SO STRONGLY...
...IT MAKES ME WANT TO PUKE.

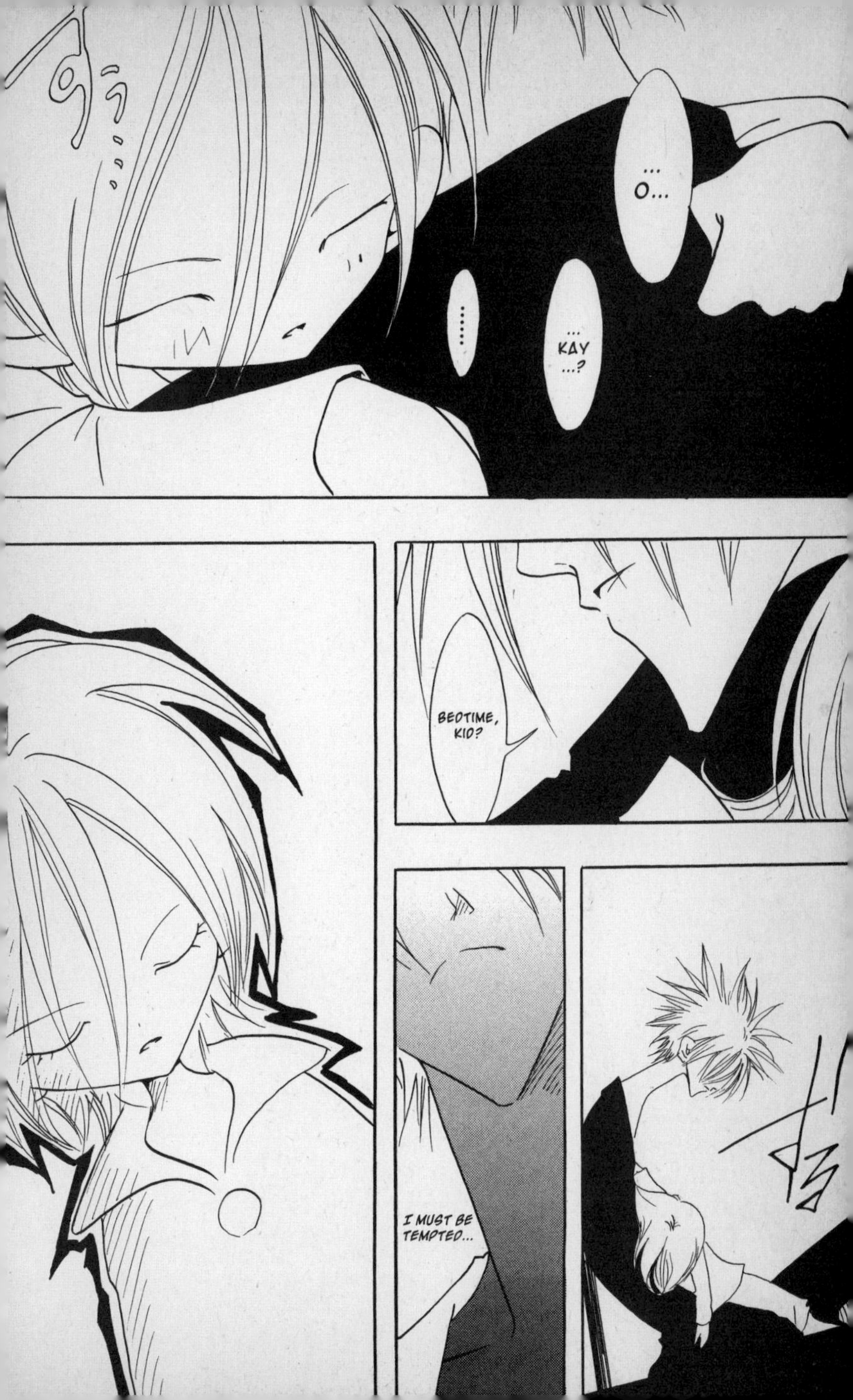
...O...
...KAY...?
......
BEDTIME, KID?
I MUST BE TEMPTED...

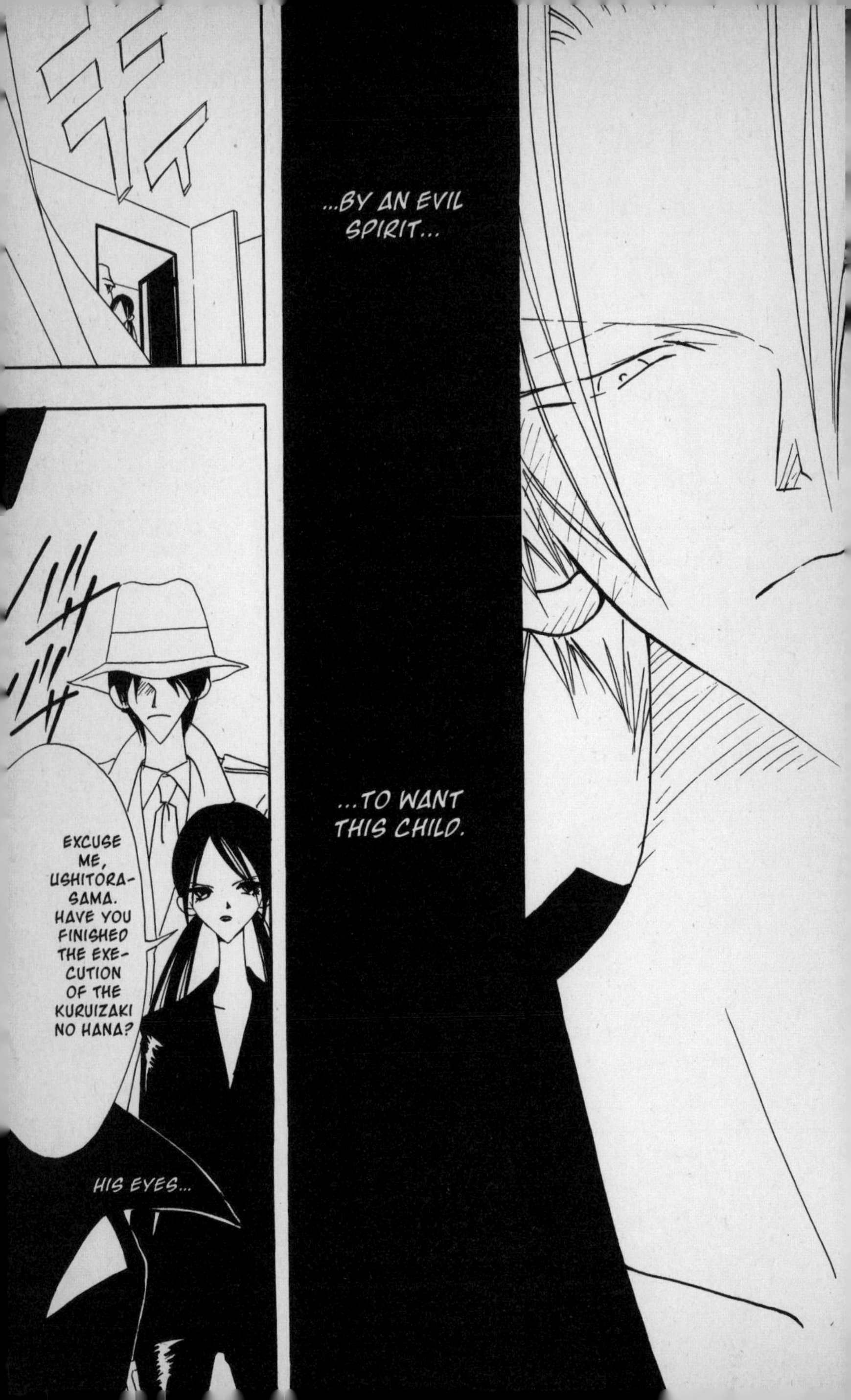
...BY AN EVIL SPIRIT...
...TO WANT THIS CHILD.
EXCUSE ME, USHITORA-SAMA. HAVE YOU FINISHED THE EXECUTION OF THE KURUIZAKI NO HANA?
HIS EYES...

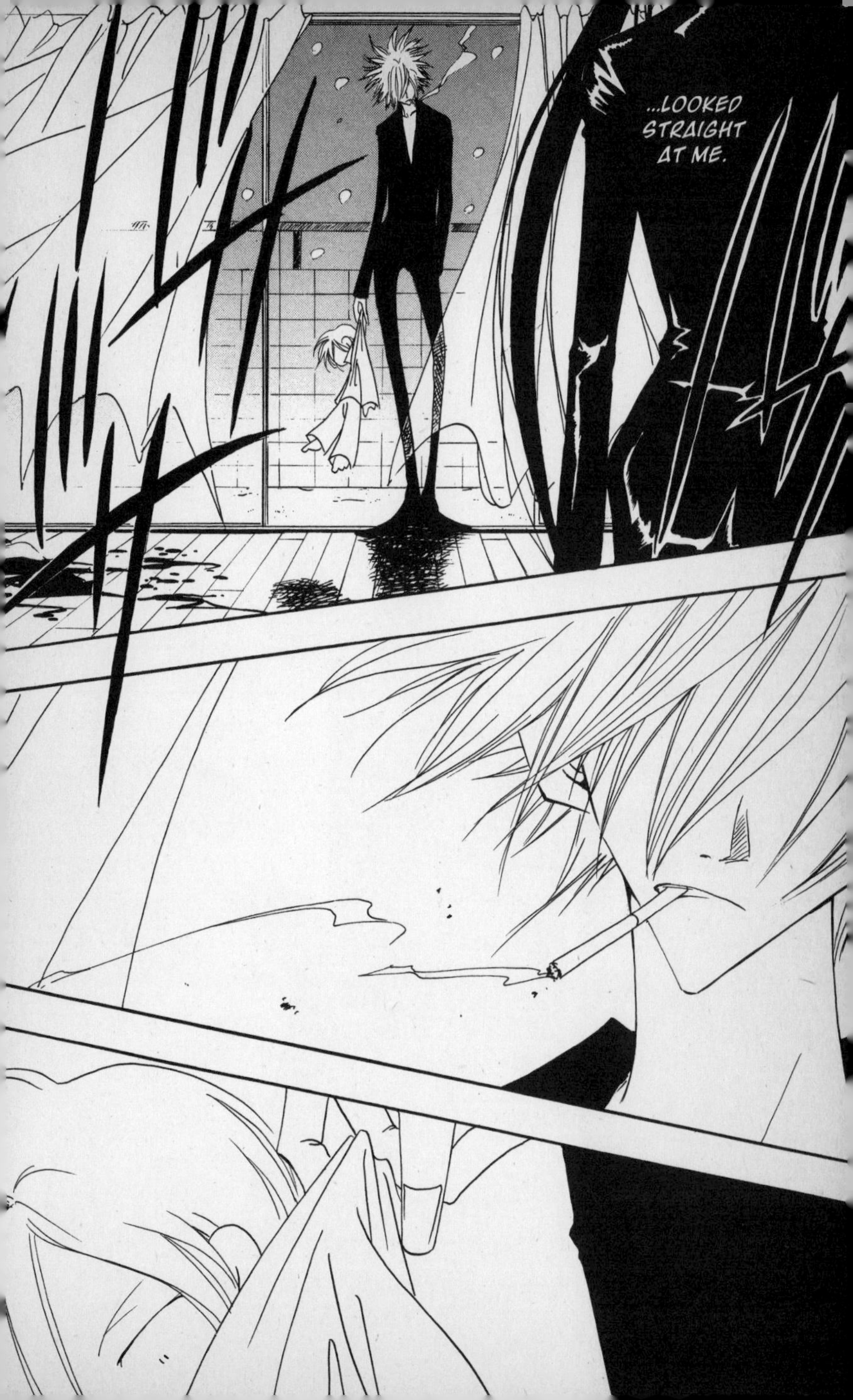
...LOOKED STRAIGHT AT ME.

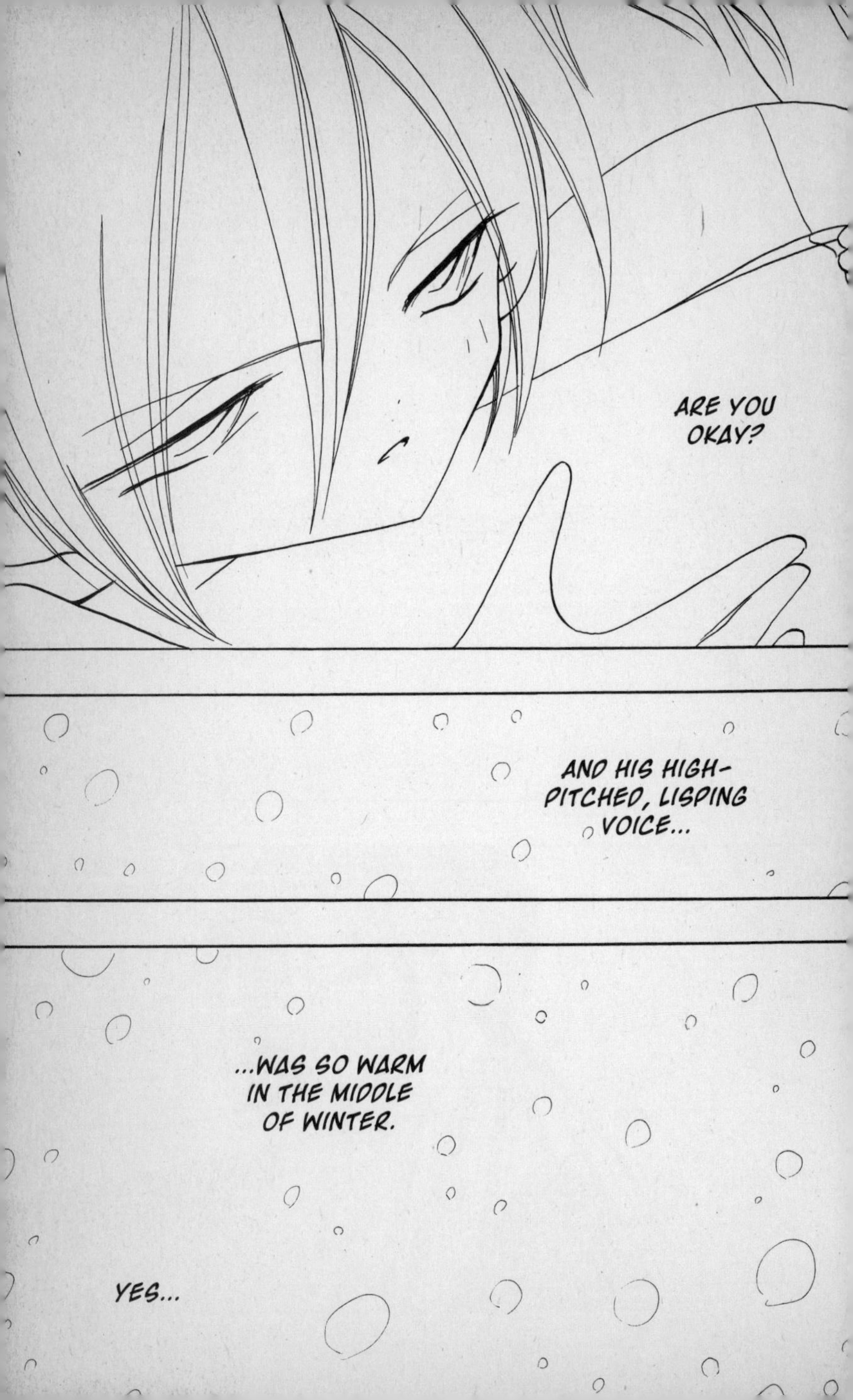
ARE YOU OKAY?
AND HIS HIGH-PITCHED, LISPING VOICE...
...WAS SO WARM IN THE MIDDLE OF WINTER.
YES...

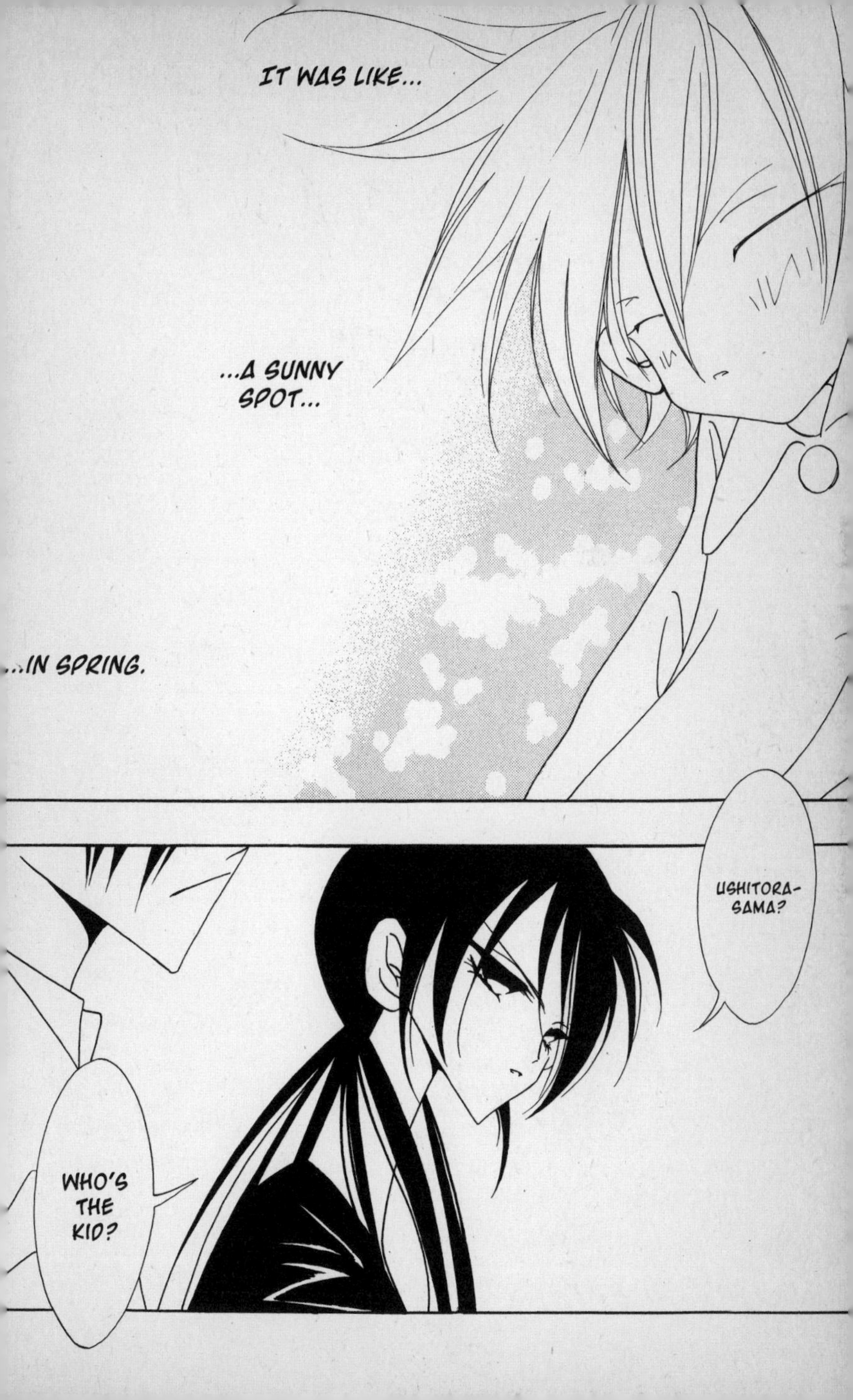
IT WAS LIKE...
...A SUNNY SPOT...
...IN SPRING.
USHITORA-SAMA?
WHO'S THE KID?

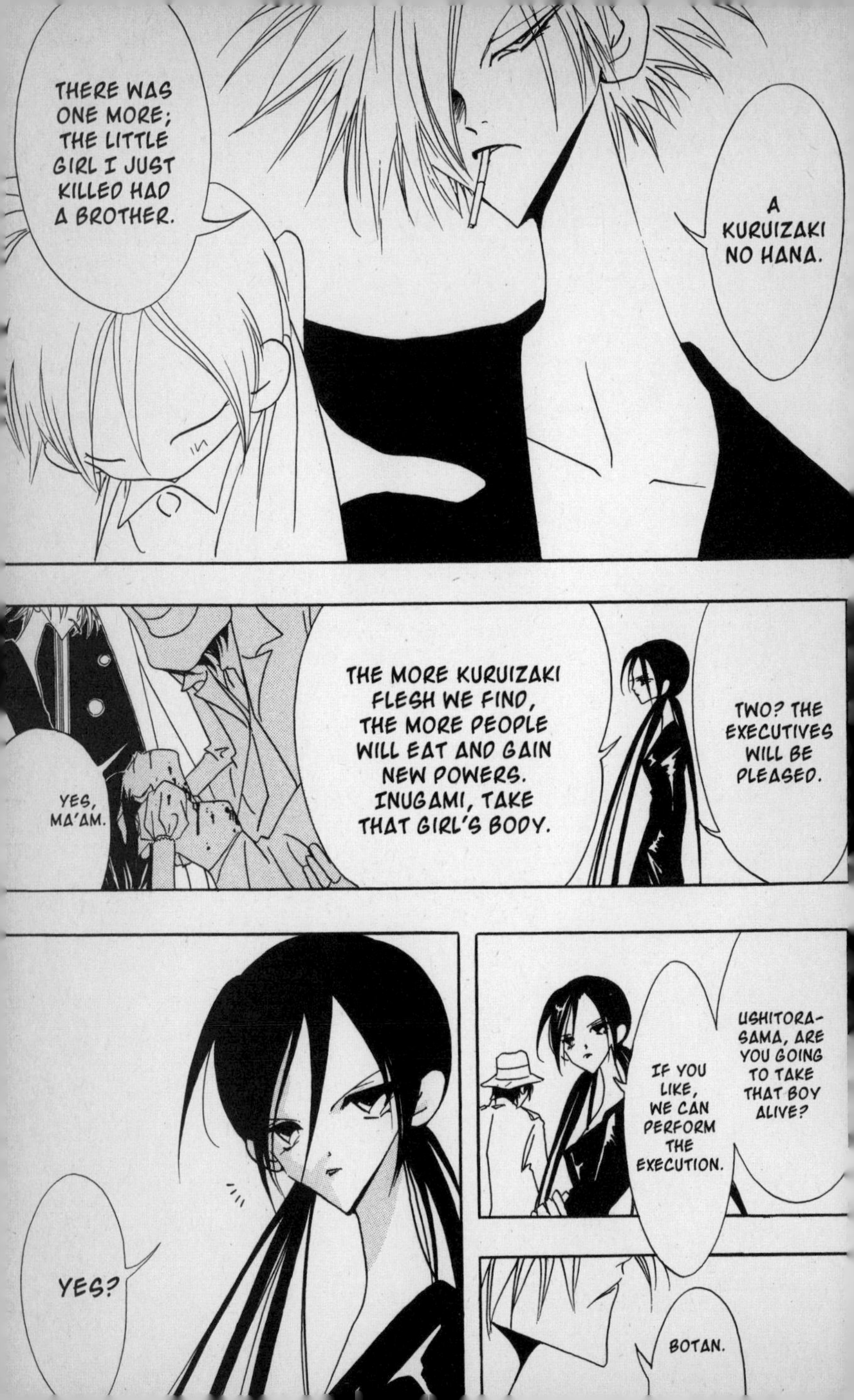
A KURUIZAKI NO HANA.
THERE WAS ONE MORE; THE LITTLE GIRL I JUST KILLED HAD A BROTHER.
TWO? THE EXECUTIVES WILL BE PLEASED.
THE MORE KURUIZAKI FLESH WE FIND, THE MORE PEOPLE WILL EAT AND GAIN NEW POWERS. INUGAMI, TAKE THAT GIRL'S BODY.
YES, MA'AM.
USHITORA-SAMA, ARE YOU GOING TO TAKE THAT BOY ALIVE?
IF YOU LIKE, WE CAN PERFORM THE EXECUTION.
BOTAN.
YES?

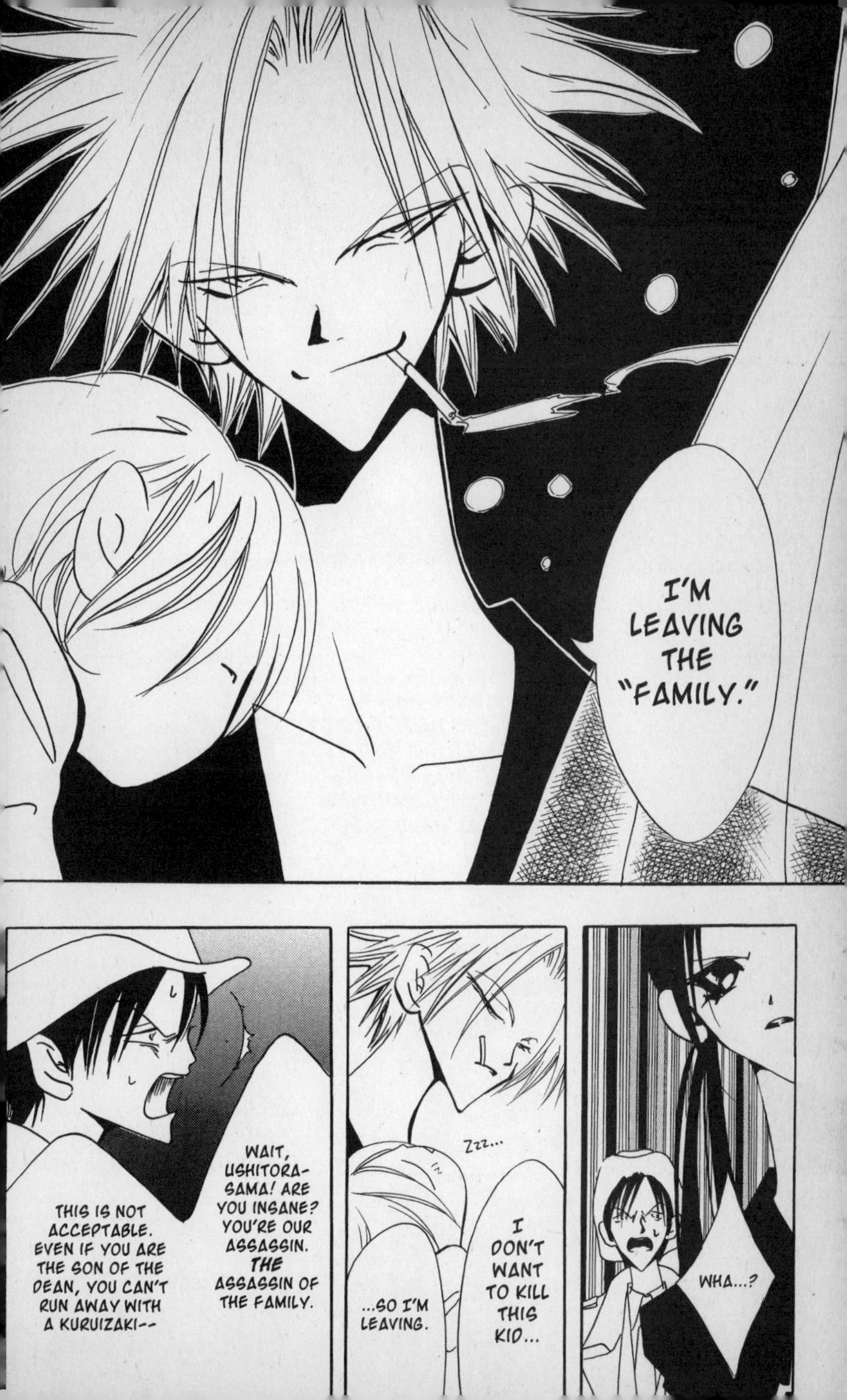
I'M LEAVING THE "FAMILY."
WHA...?
Zzz...
I DON'T WANT TO KILL THIS KID...
...SO I'M LEAVING.
WAIT, USHITORA-SAMA! ARE YOU INSANE? YOU'RE OUR ASSASSIN. *THE* ASSASSIN OF THE FAMILY.
THIS IS NOT ACCEPTABLE. EVEN IF YOU ARE THE SON OF THE DEAN, YOU CAN'T RUN AWAY WITH A KURUIZAKI--

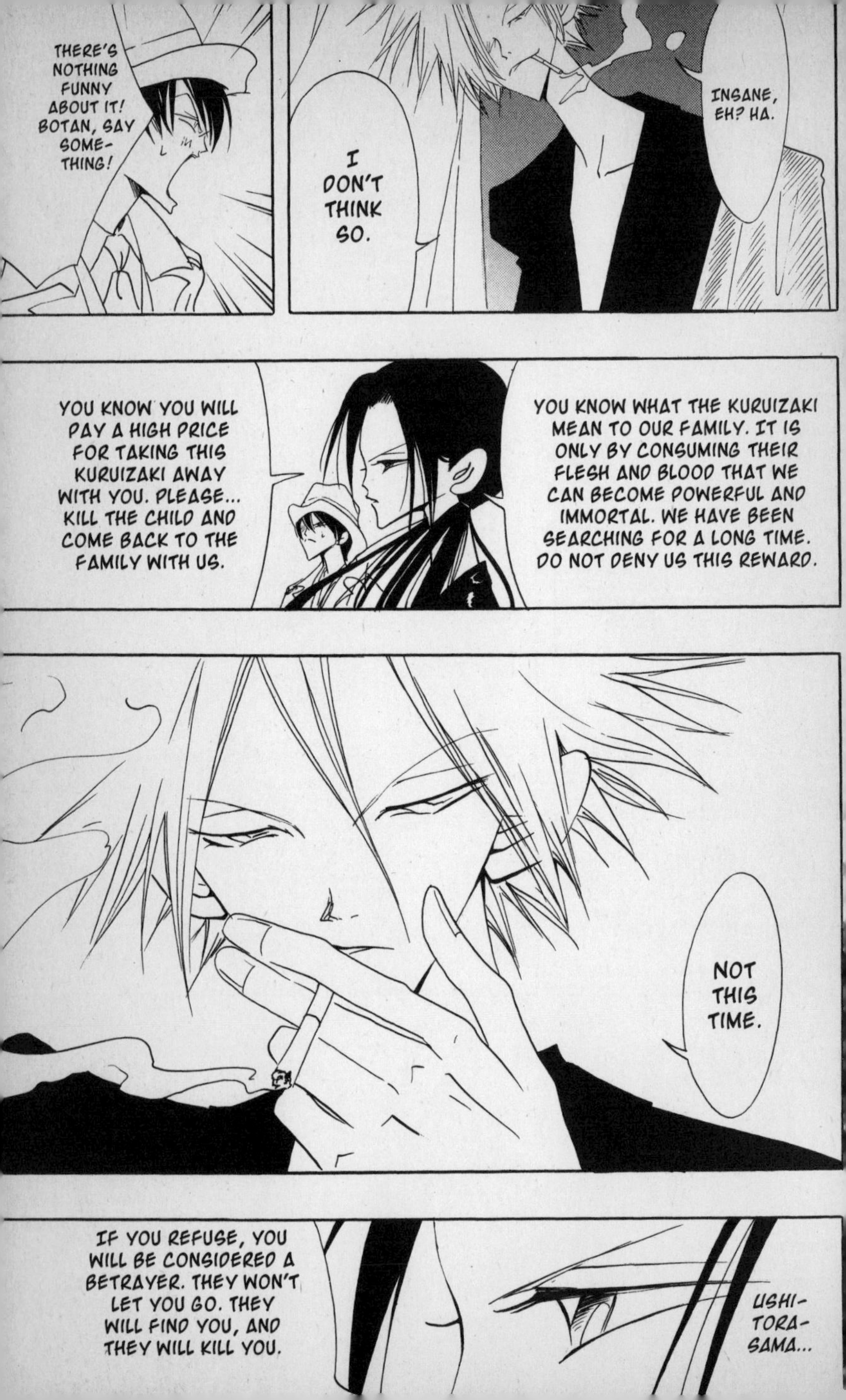
INSANE, EH? HA.
I DON'T THINK SO.
THERE'S NOTHING FUNNY ABOUT IT! BOTAN, SAY SOME-THING!
YOU KNOW WHAT THE KURUIZAKI MEAN TO OUR FAMILY. IT IS ONLY BY CONSUMING THEIR FLESH AND BLOOD THAT WE CAN BECOME POWERFUL AND IMMORTAL. WE HAVE BEEN SEARCHING FOR A LONG TIME. DO NOT DENY US THIS REWARD.
YOU KNOW YOU WILL PAY A HIGH PRICE FOR TAKING THIS KURUIZAKI AWAY WITH YOU. PLEASE... KILL THE CHILD AND COME BACK TO THE FAMILY WITH US.
NOT THIS TIME.
USHI-TORA-SAMA...
IF YOU REFUSE, YOU WILL BE CONSIDERED A BETRAYER. THEY WON'T LET YOU GO. THEY WILL FIND YOU, AND THEY WILL KILL YOU.

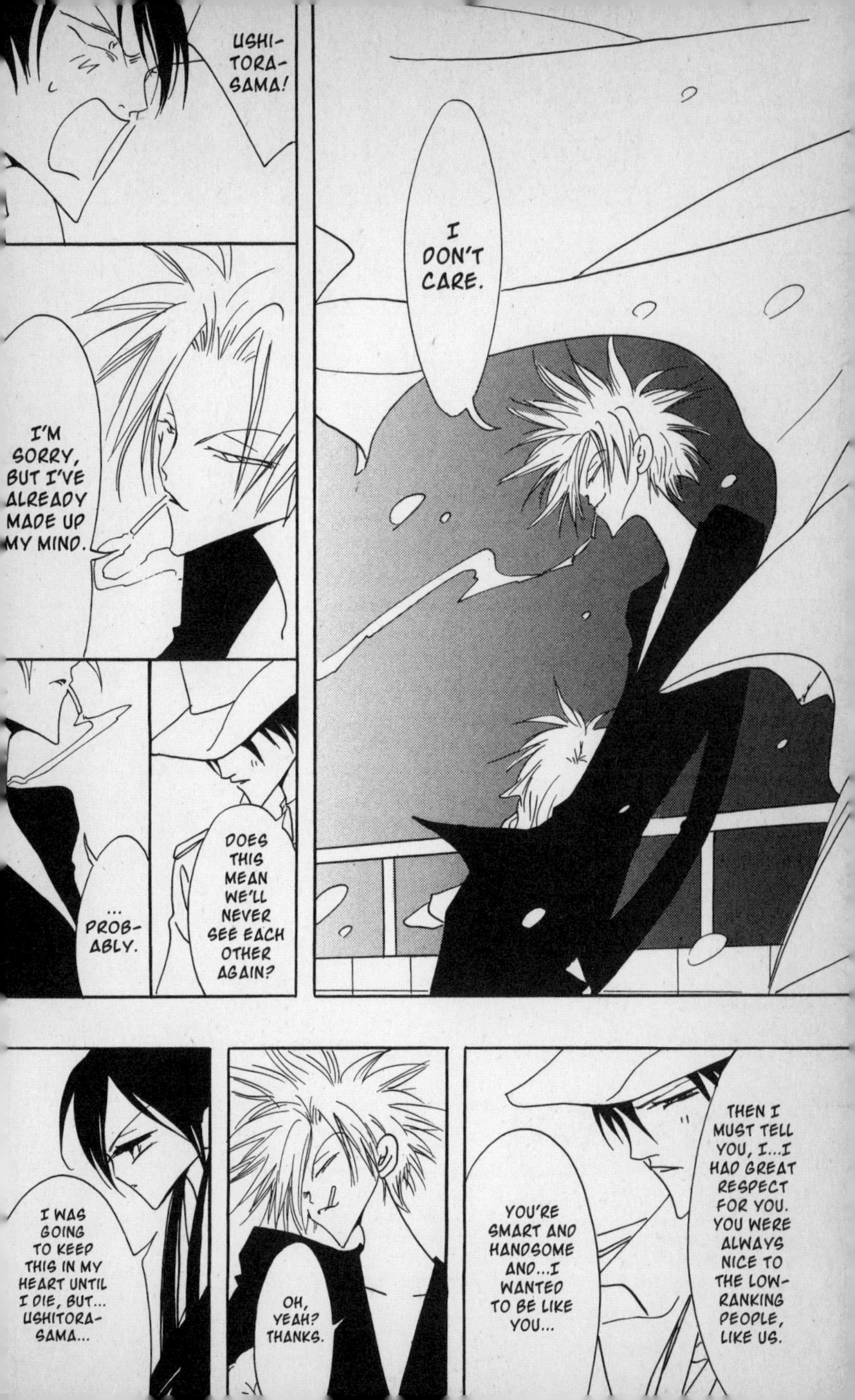
I DON'T CARE.
USHI-TORA-SAMA!
I'M SORRY, BUT I'VE ALREADY MADE UP MY MIND.
DOES THIS MEAN WE'LL NEVER SEE EACH OTHER AGAIN?
...PROB-ABLY.
THEN I MUST TELL YOU, I...I HAD GREAT RESPECT FOR YOU. YOU WERE ALWAYS NICE TO THE LOW-RANKING PEOPLE, LIKE US.
YOU'RE SMART AND HANDSOME AND...I WANTED TO BE LIKE YOU...
OH, YEAH? THANKS.
I WAS GOING TO KEEP THIS IN MY HEART UNTIL I DIE, BUT... USHITORA-SAMA...

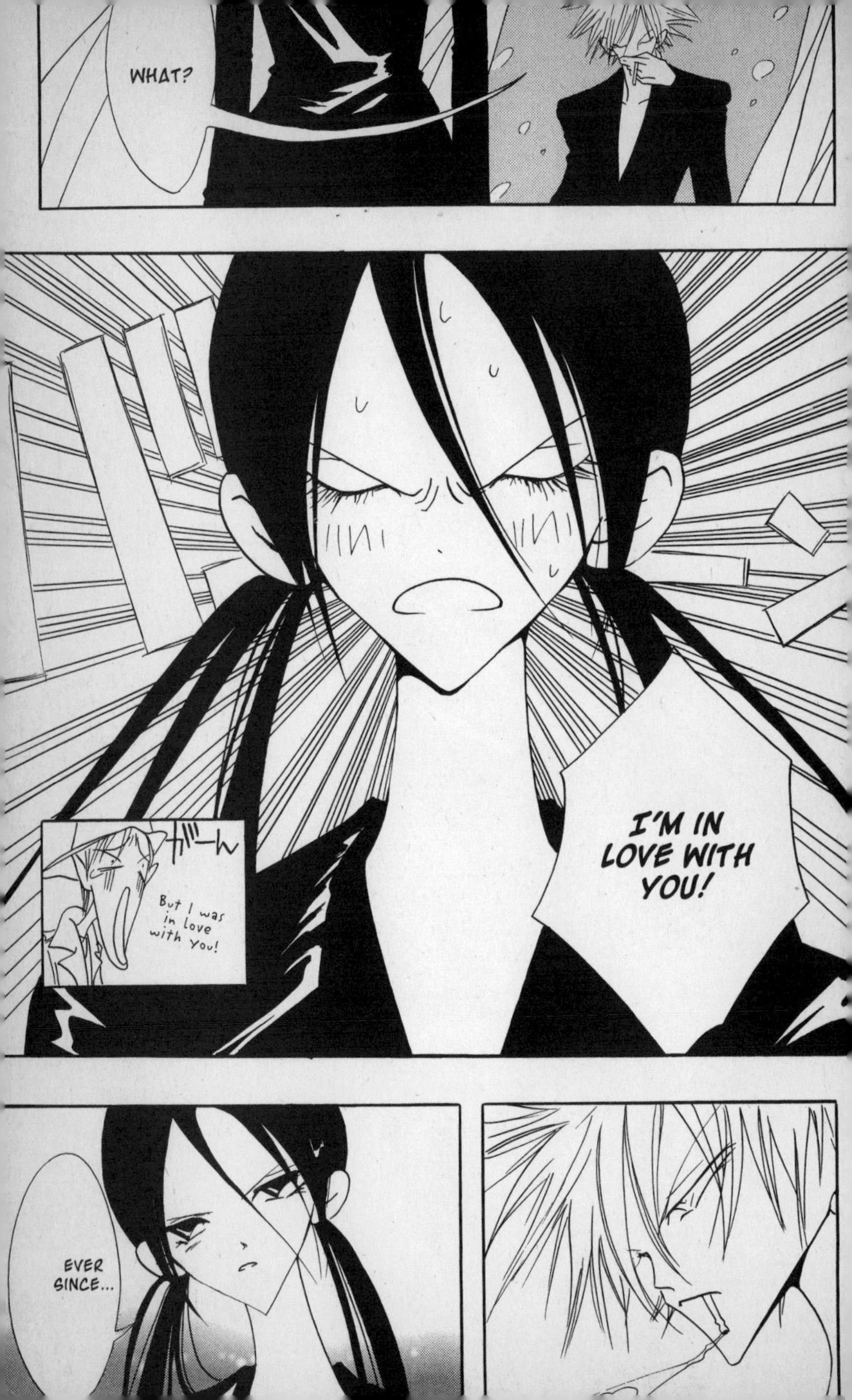
WHAT?
I'M IN LOVE WITH YOU!
ガーん
But I was in love with you!
EVER SINCE...

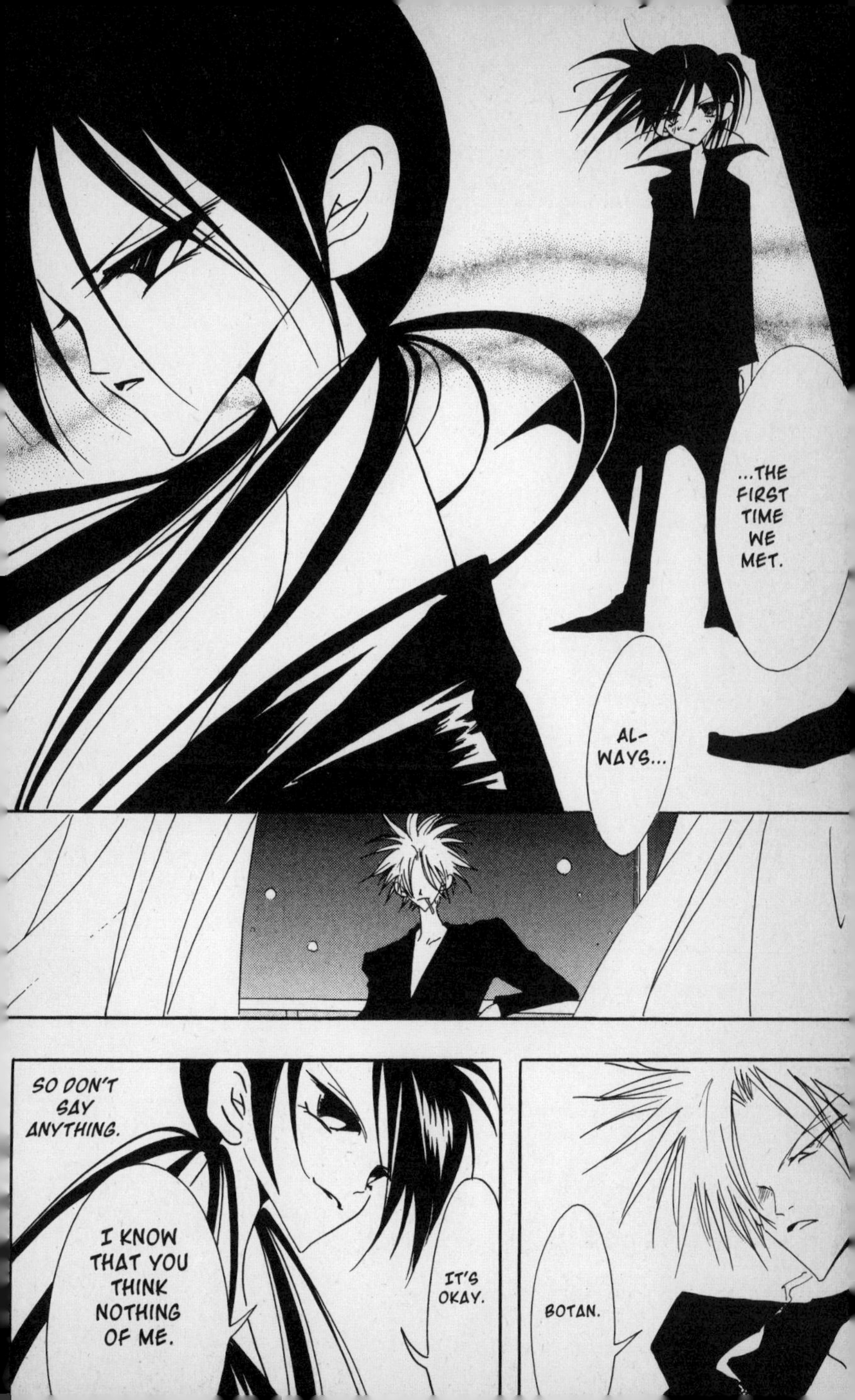
...THE FIRST TIME WE MET.
AL-WAYS...
BOTAN.
IT'S OKAY.
I KNOW THAT YOU THINK NOTHING OF ME.
SO DON'T SAY ANYTHING.

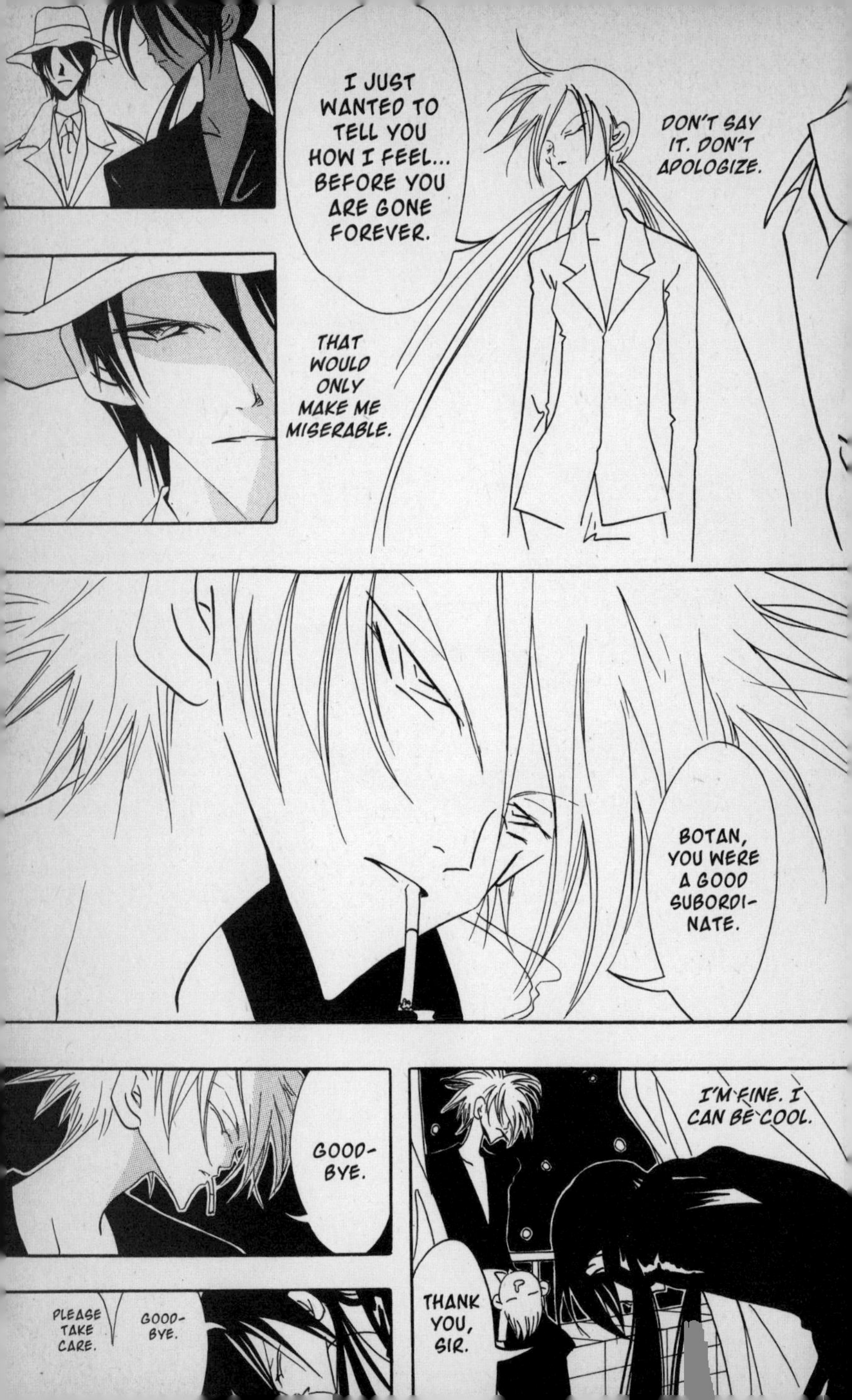

I JUST WANTED TO TELL YOU HOW I FEEL... BEFORE YOU ARE GONE FOREVER.
DON'T SAY IT. DON'T APOLOGIZE.
THAT WOULD ONLY MAKE ME MISERABLE.
BOTAN, YOU WERE A GOOD SUBORDI-NATE.
I'M FINE. I CAN BE COOL.
THANK YOU, SIR.
GOOD-BYE.
GOOD-BYE.
PLEASE TAKE CARE.

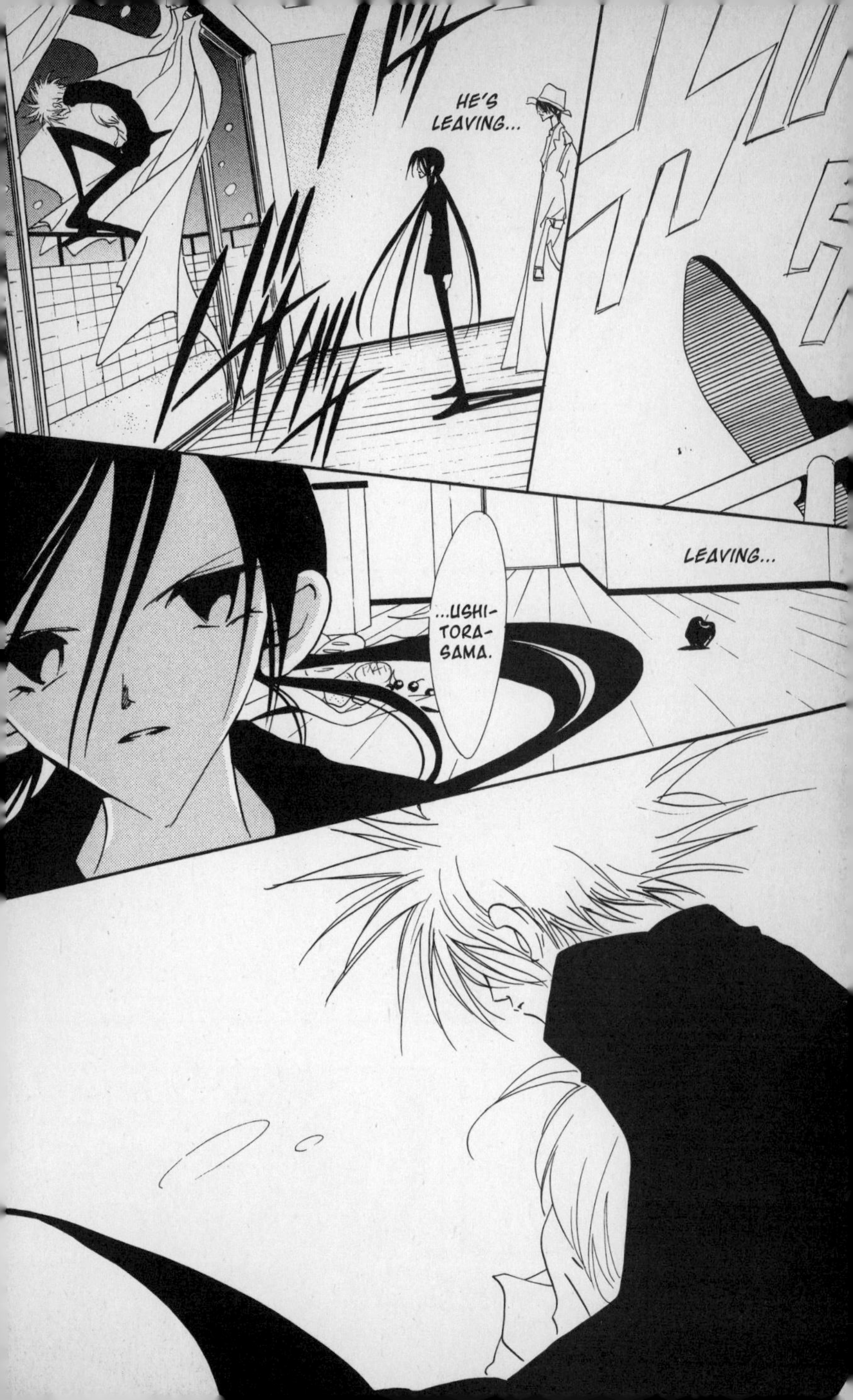
HE'S LEAVING...
LEAVING...
...USHI-TORA-SAMA.

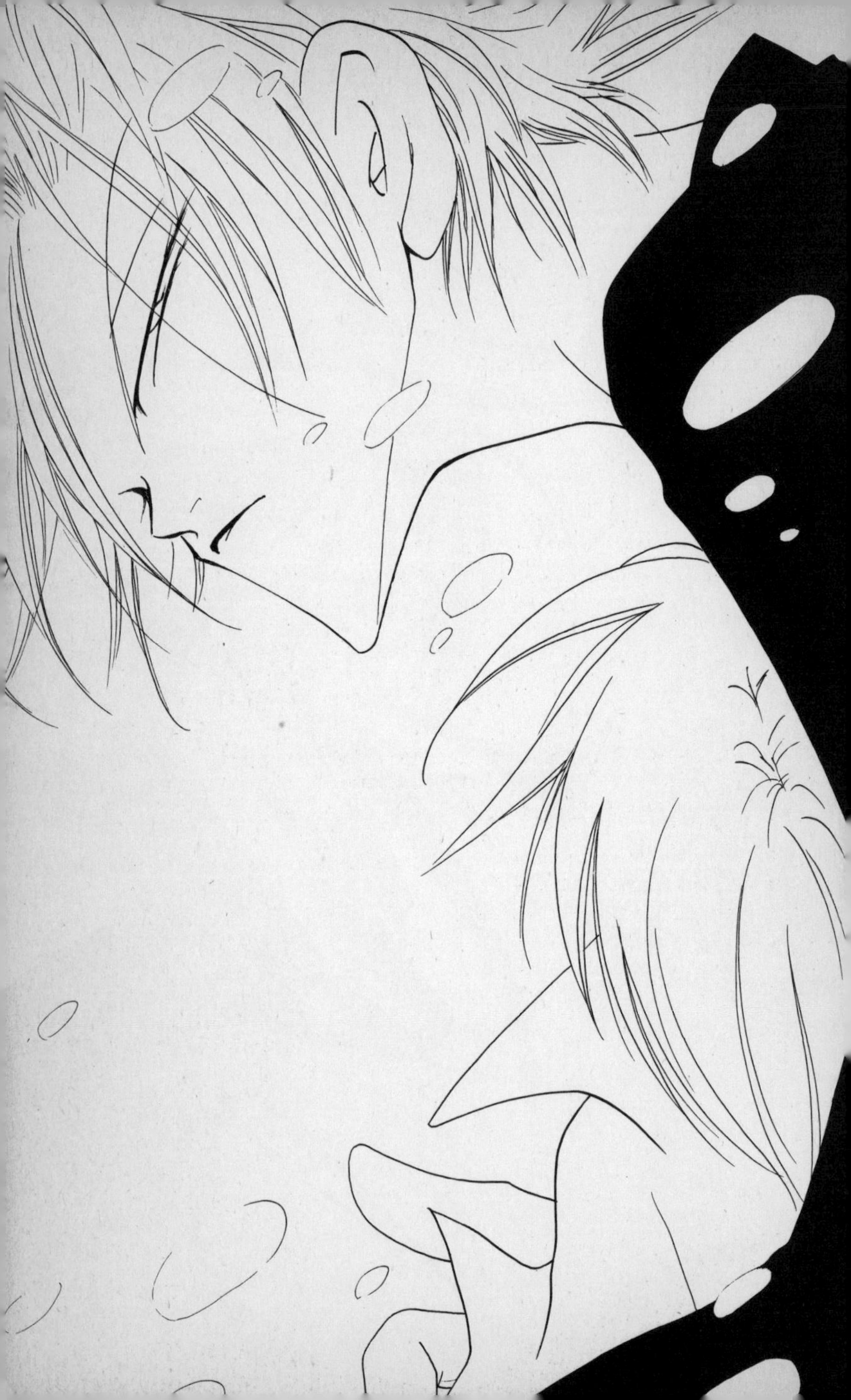

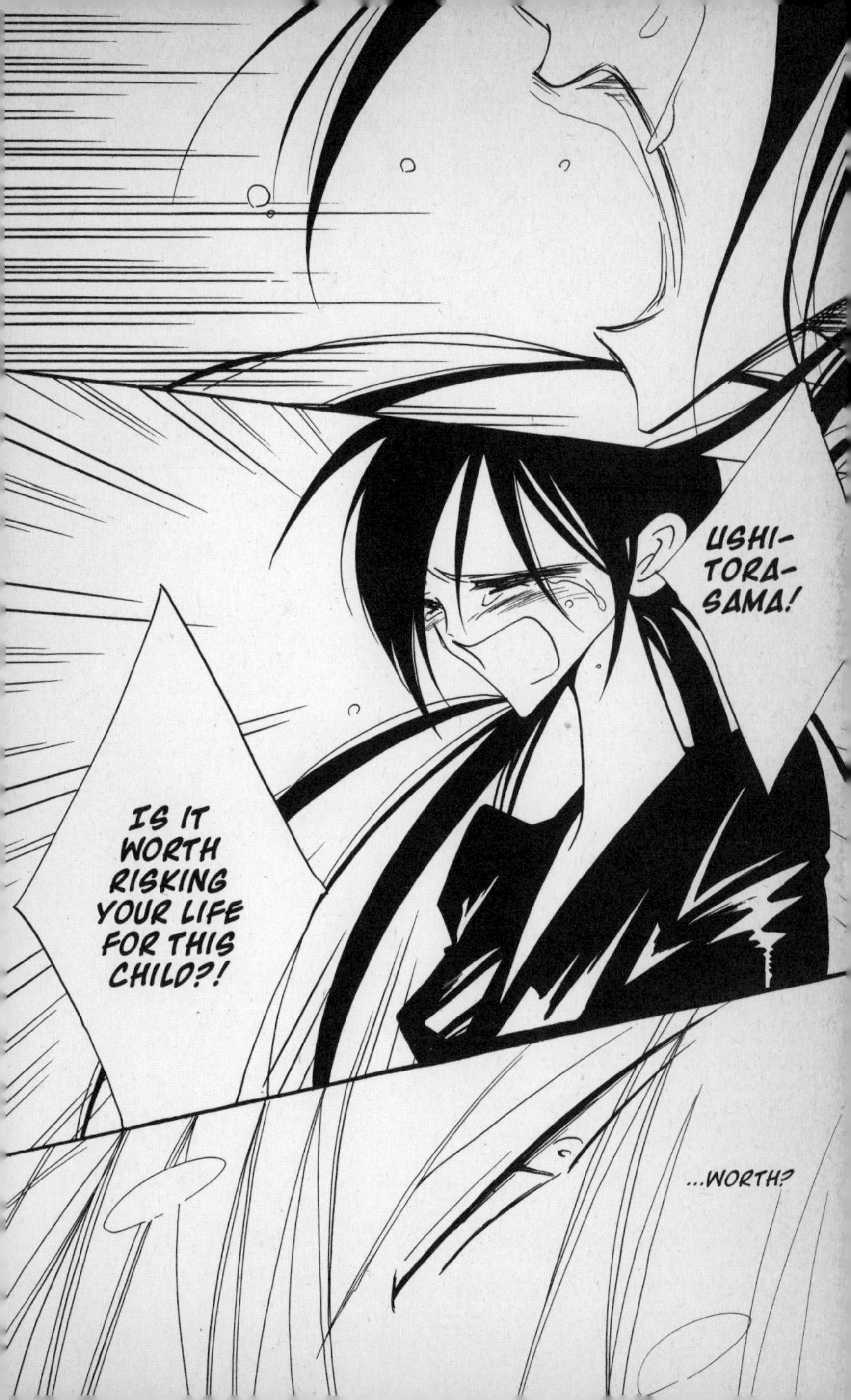
USHI-TORA-SAMA!
IS IT WORTH RISKING YOUR LIFE FOR THIS CHILD?!
...WORTH?

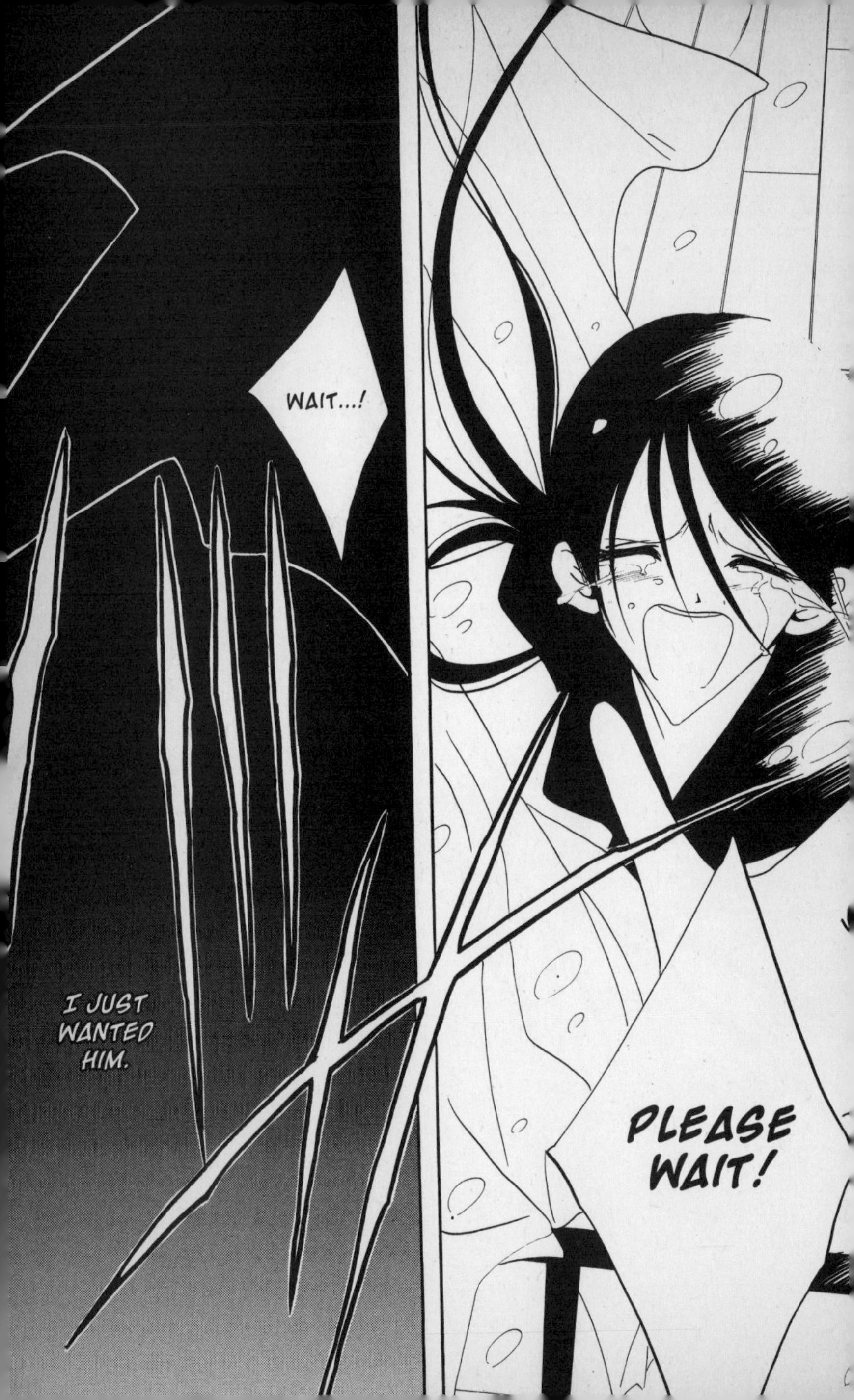
PLEASE WAIT!
WAIT...!
I JUST WANTED HIM.

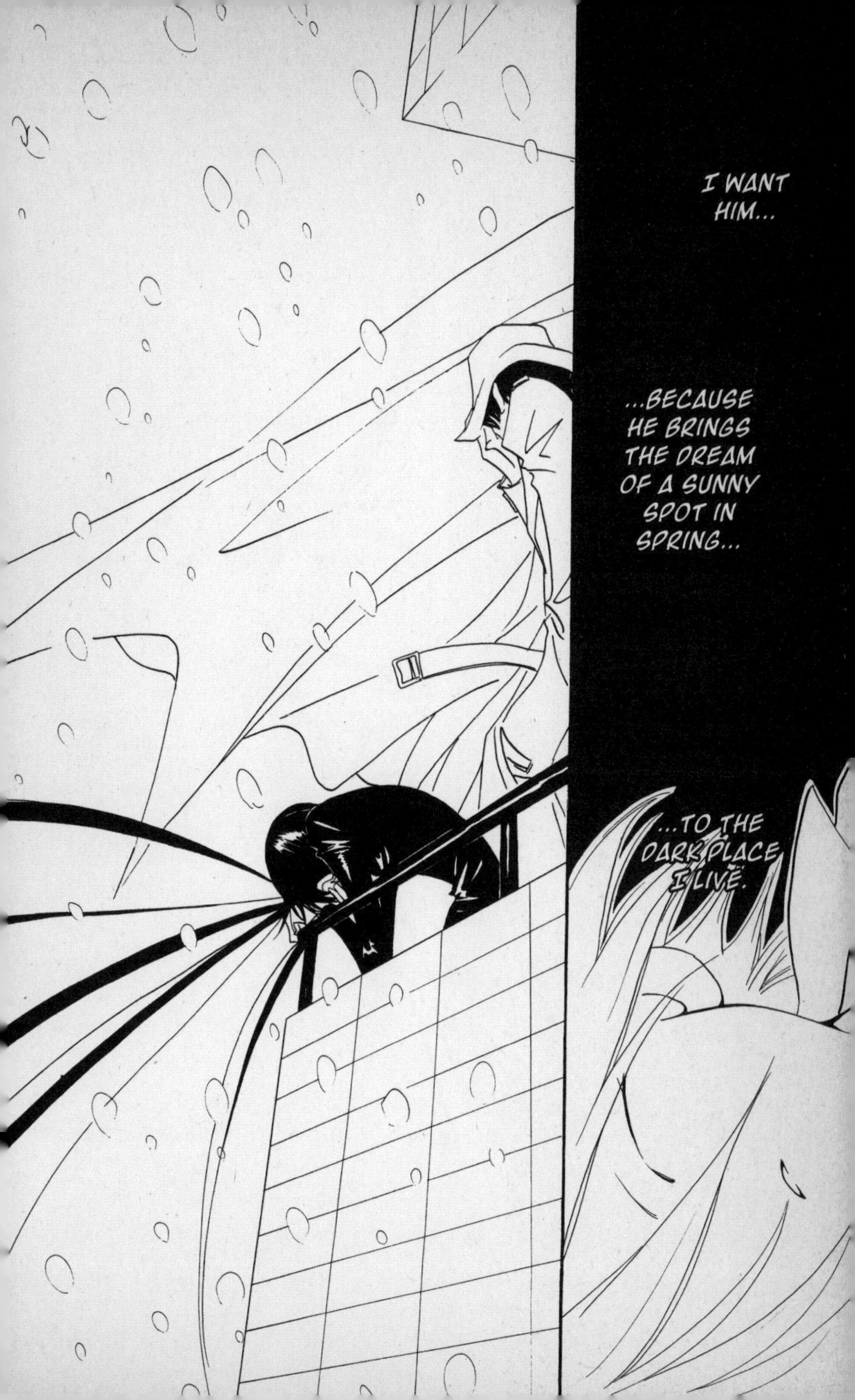
I WANT HIM...
...BECAUSE HE BRINGS THE DREAM OF A SUNNY SPOT IN SPRING...
...TO THE DARK PLACE I LIVE.

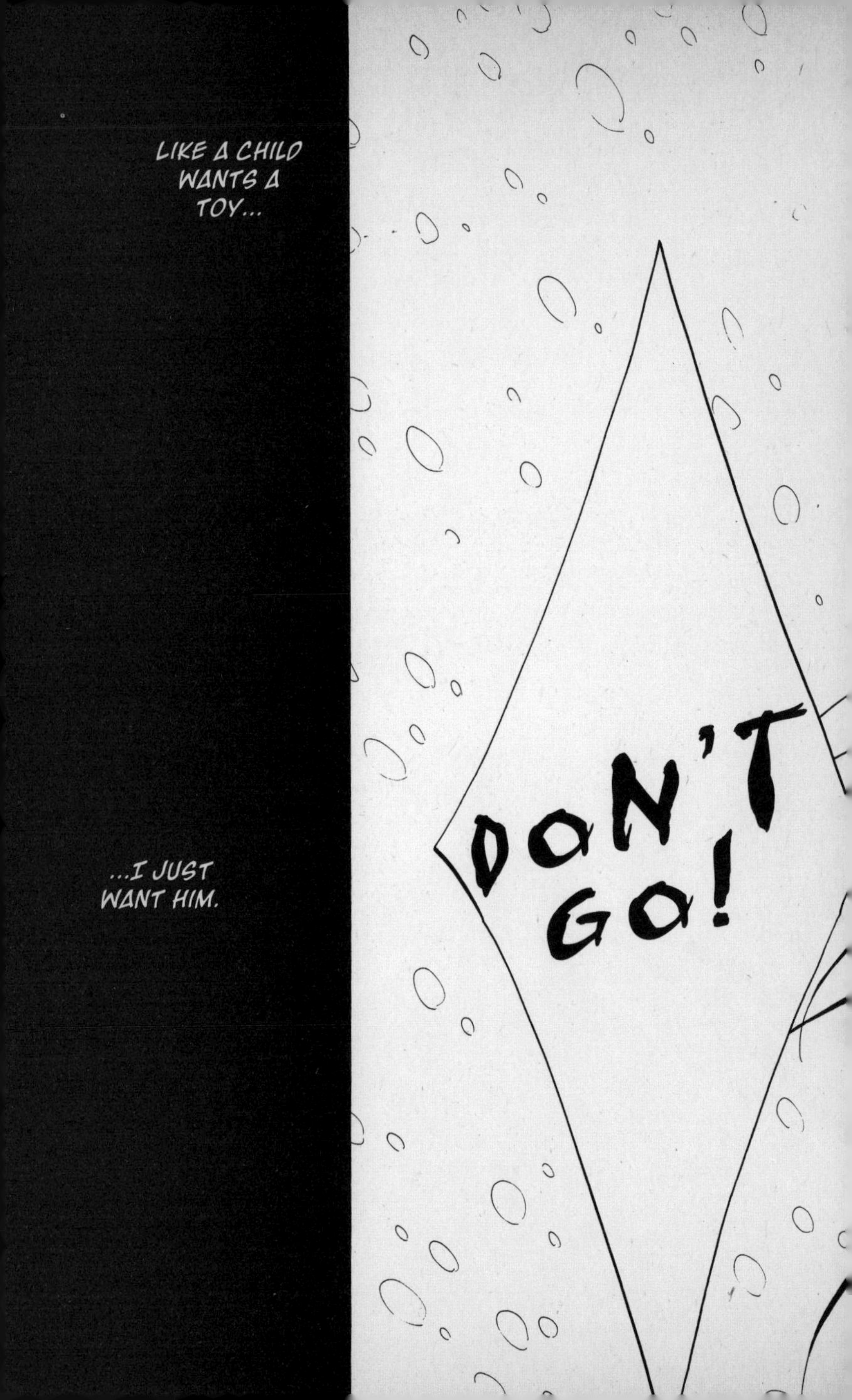
DON'T GO!
LIKE A CHILD WANTS A TOY...
...I JUST WANT HIM.

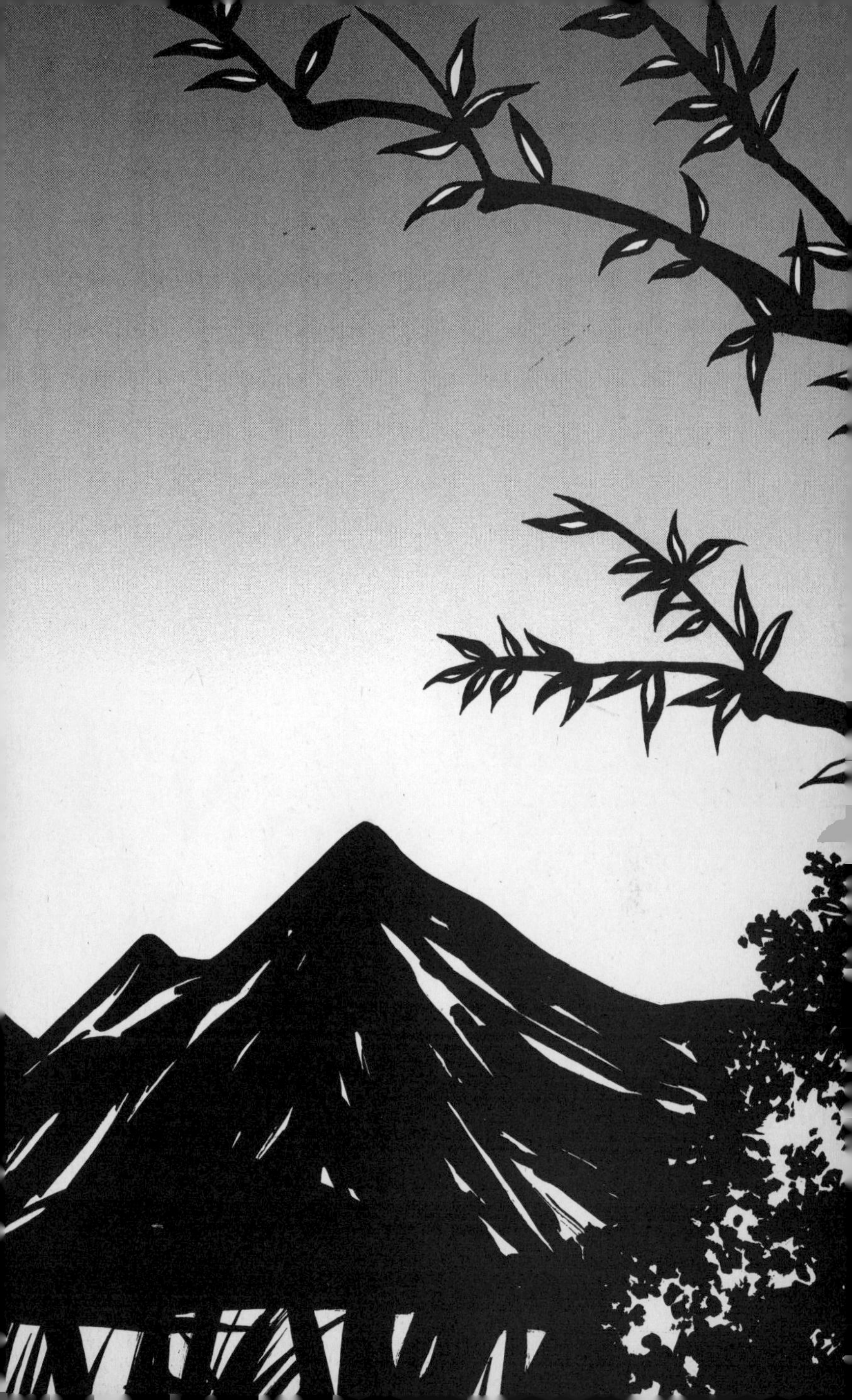

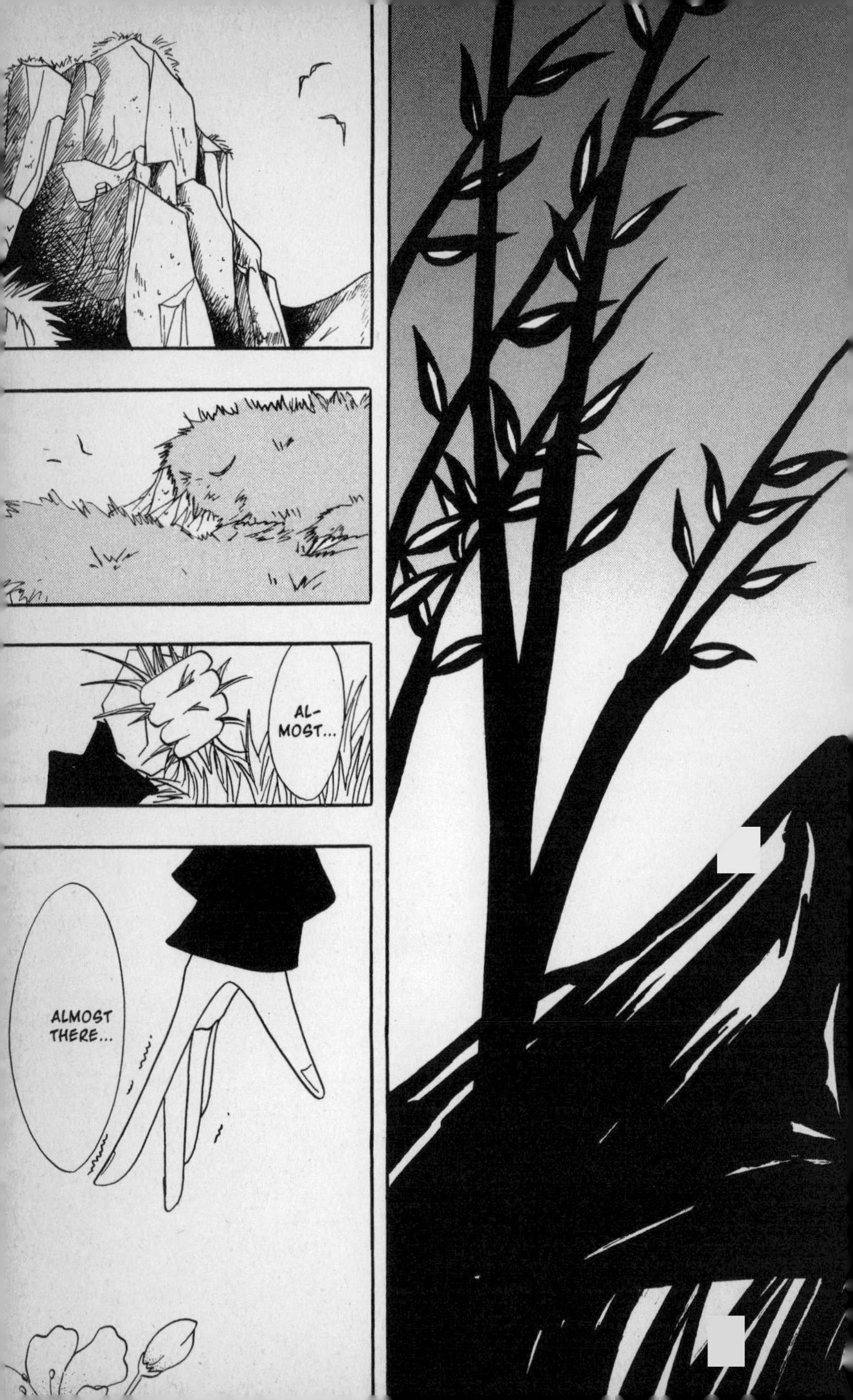
AL-
MOST...
ALMOST
THERE...

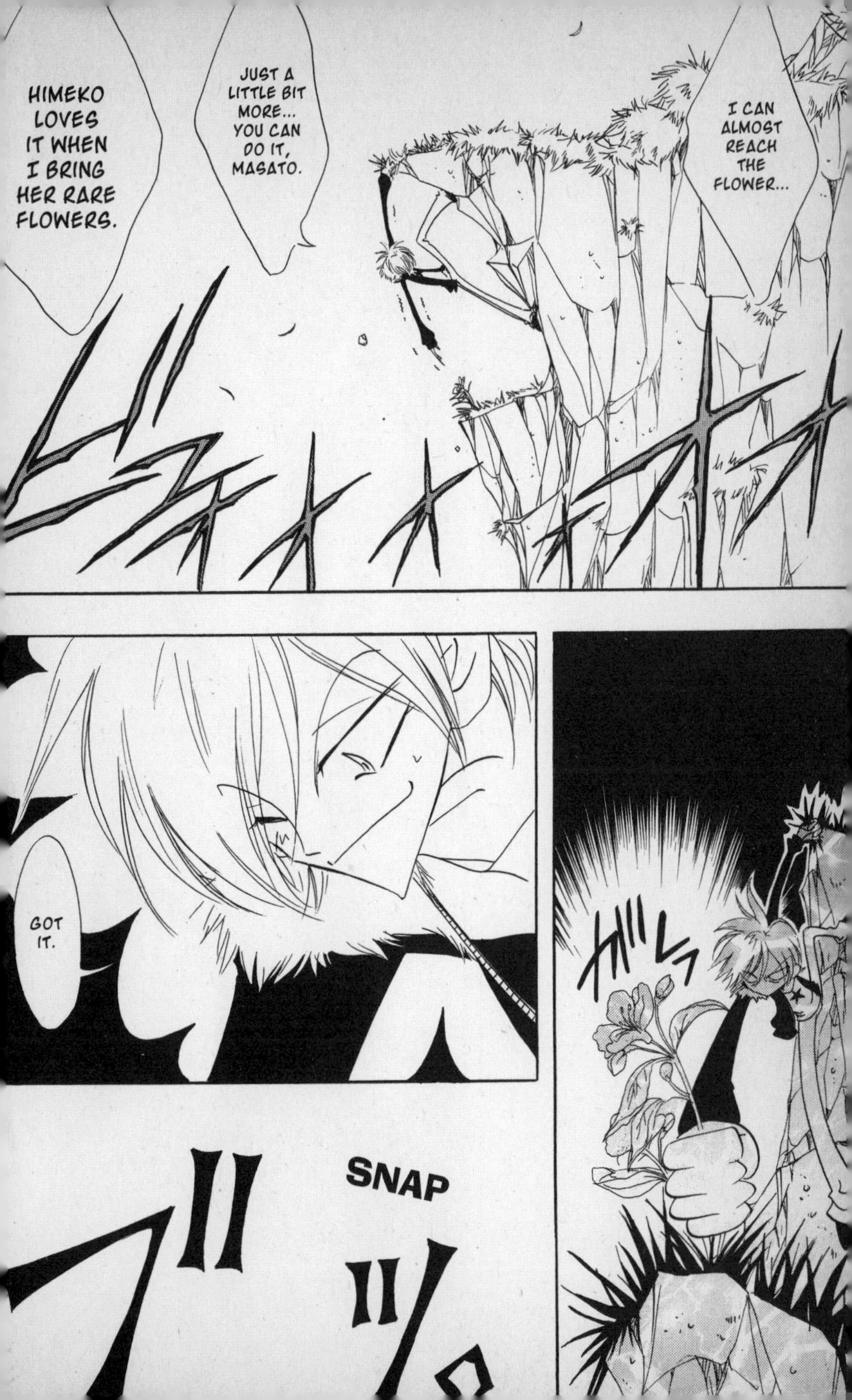
I CAN ALMOST REACH THE FLOWER...
JUST A LITTLE BIT MORE... YOU CAN DO IT, MASATO.
HIMEKO LOVES IT WHEN I BRING HER RARE FLOWERS.
GOT IT.
SNAP

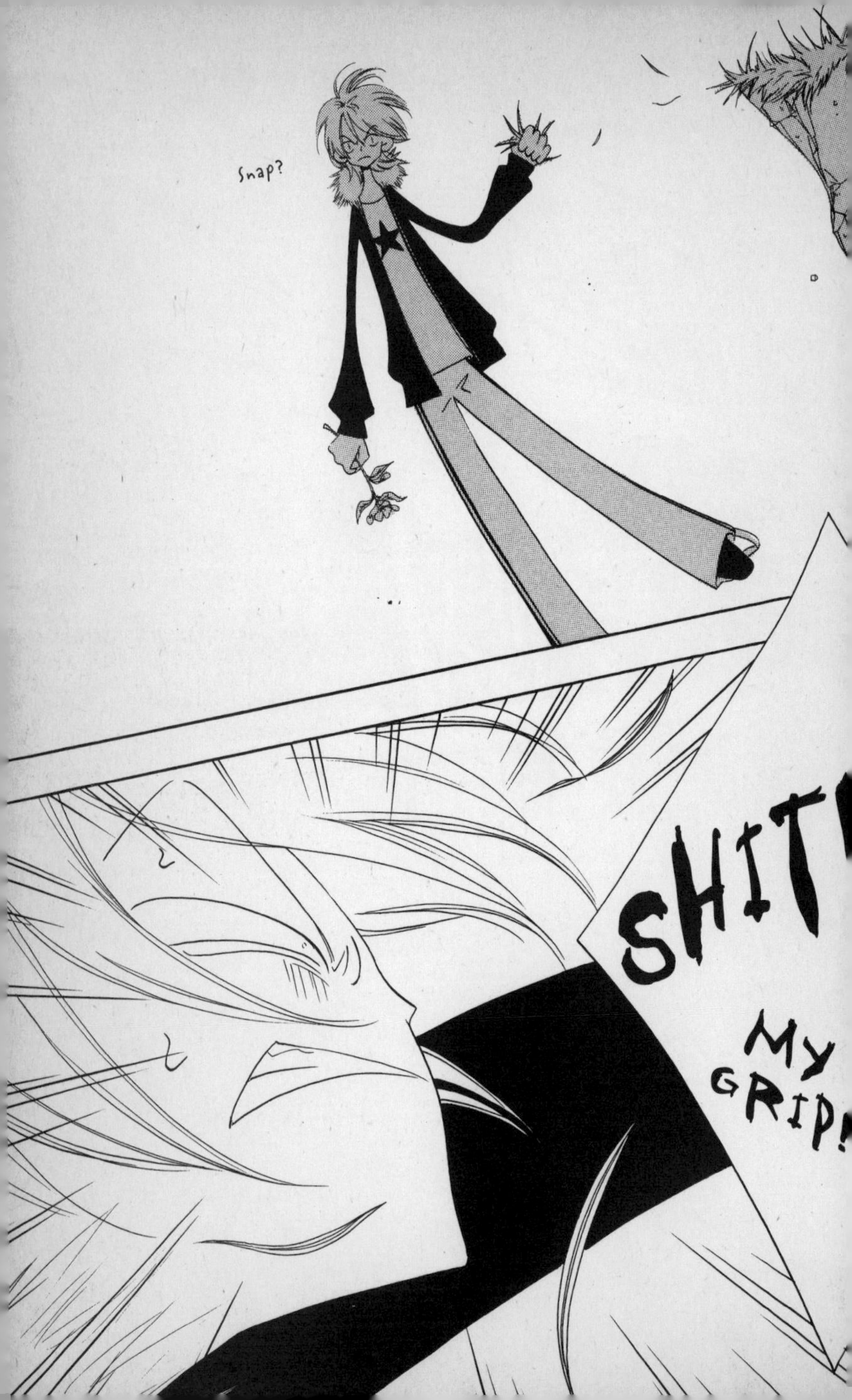
Snap?
SHIT!
MY GRIP!

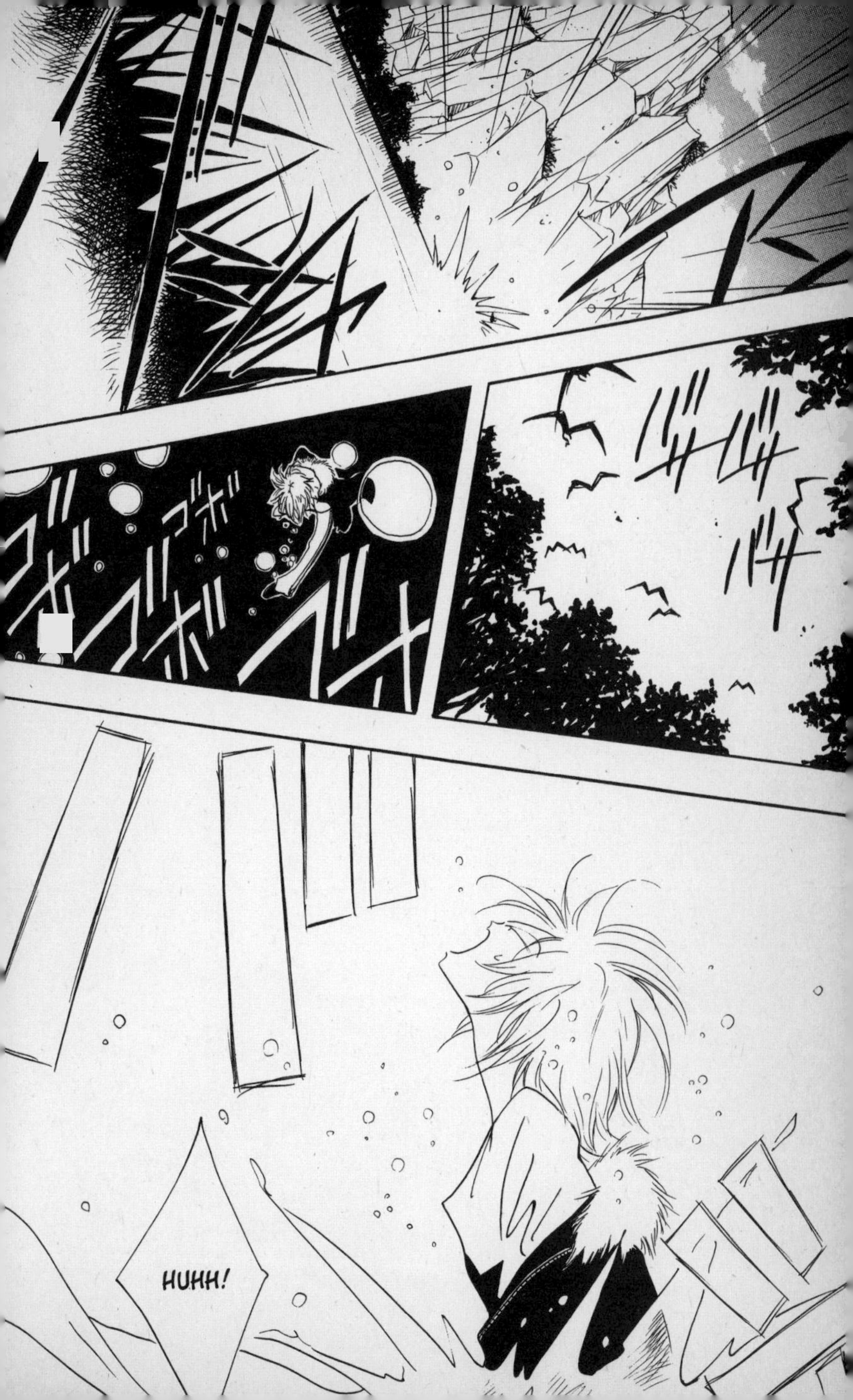
HUHH!

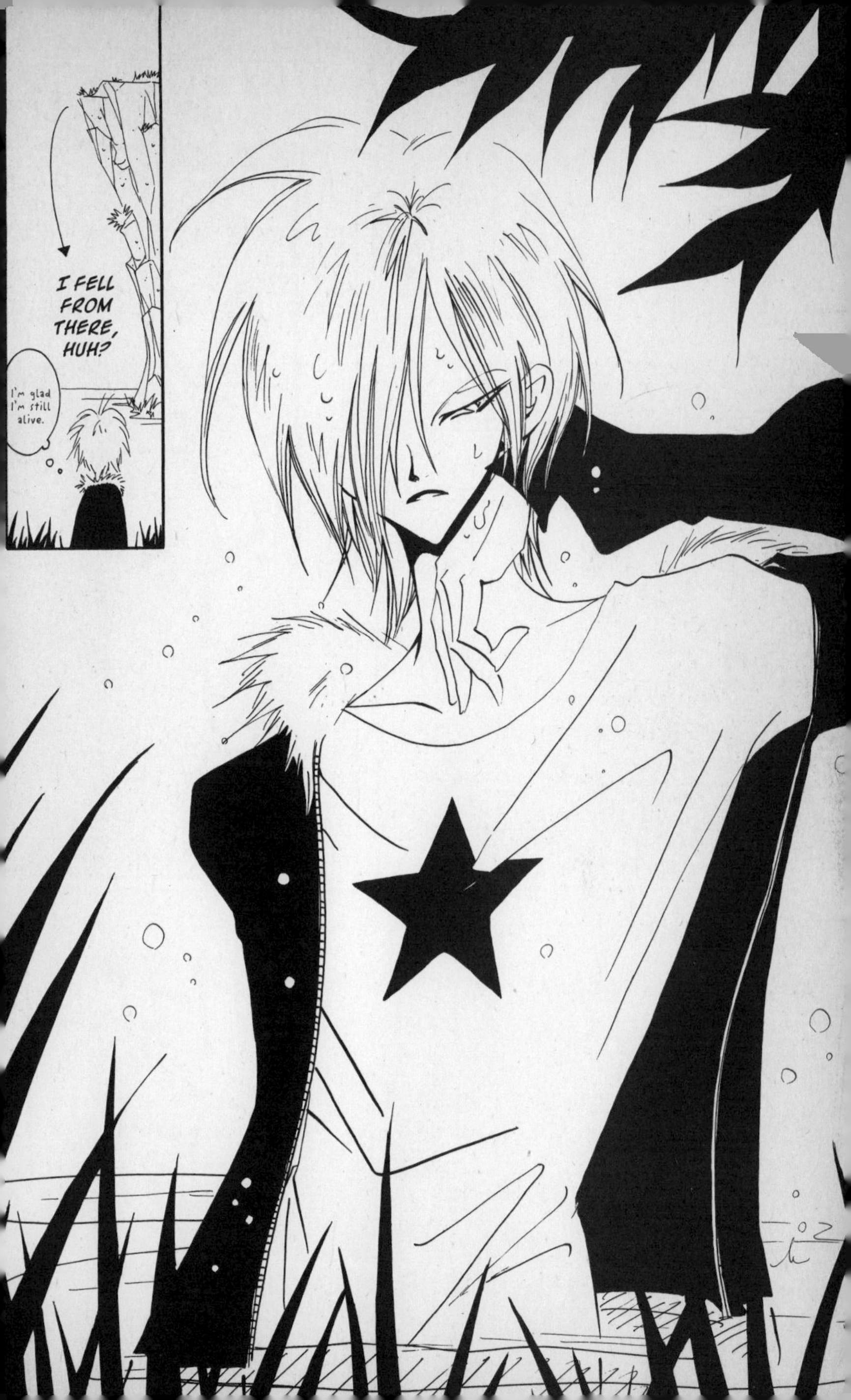
I FELL FROM THERE, HUH?
I'm glad I'm still alive.

PHEW...

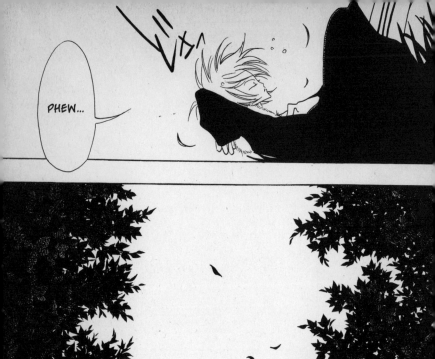

tweet
tweet
tweet

chirp
chirp...

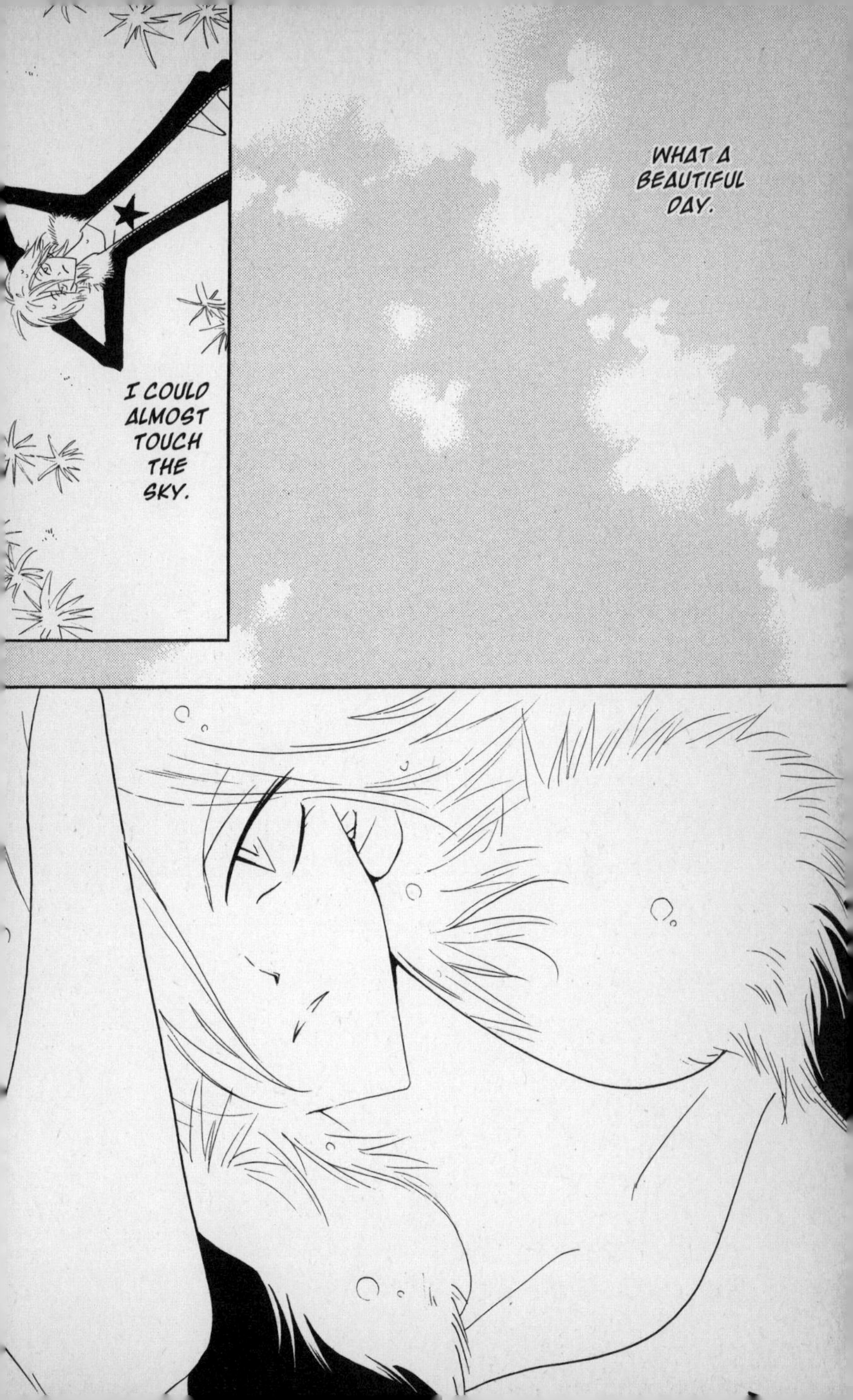
WHAT A BEAUTIFUL DAY.
I COULD ALMOST TOUCH THE SKY.

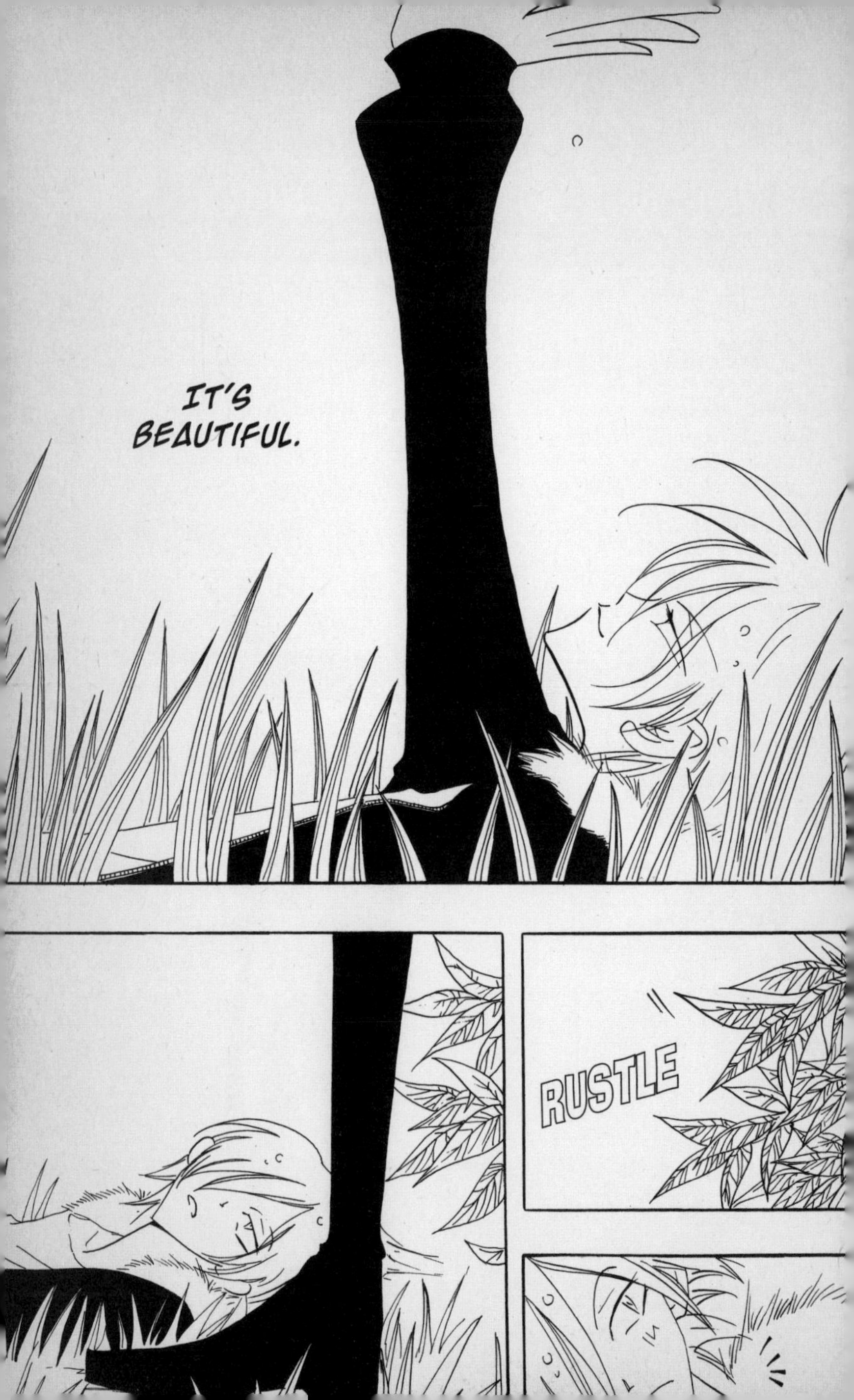
IT'S BEAUTIFUL.
RUSTLE

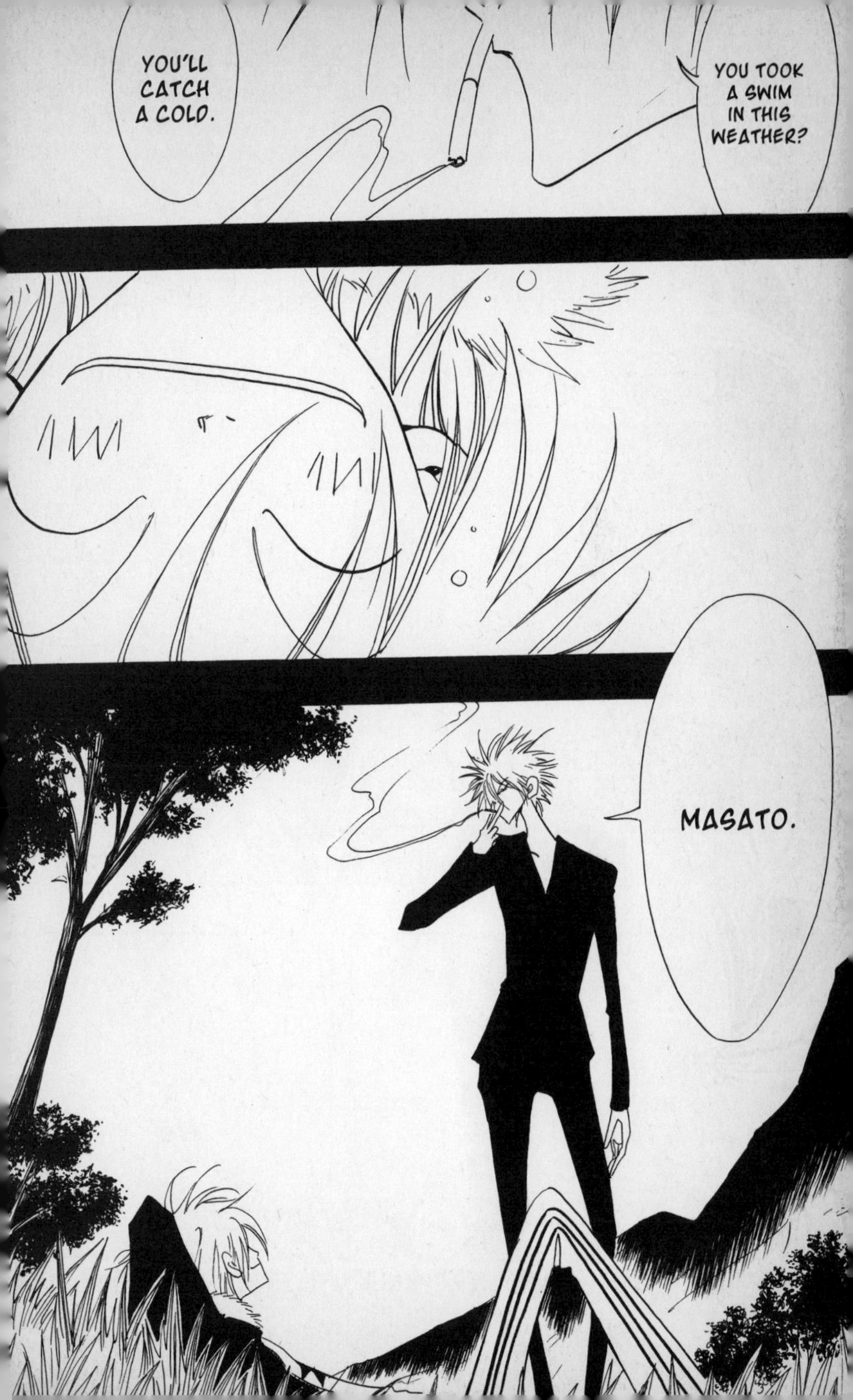
YOU TOOK A SWIM IN THIS WEATHER?
YOU'LL CATCH A COLD.
MASATO.

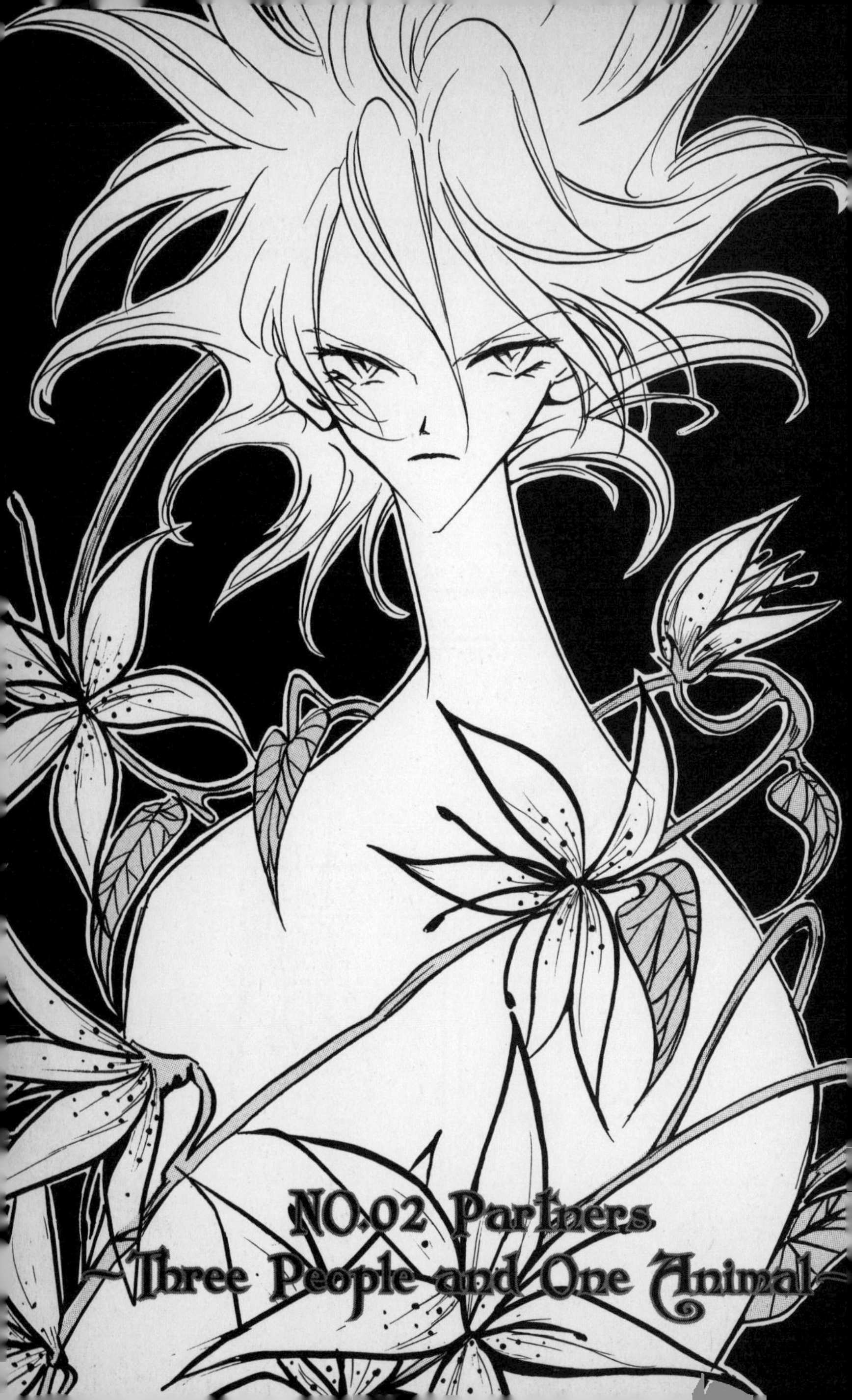
NO.02 Partners
~Three People and One Animal~

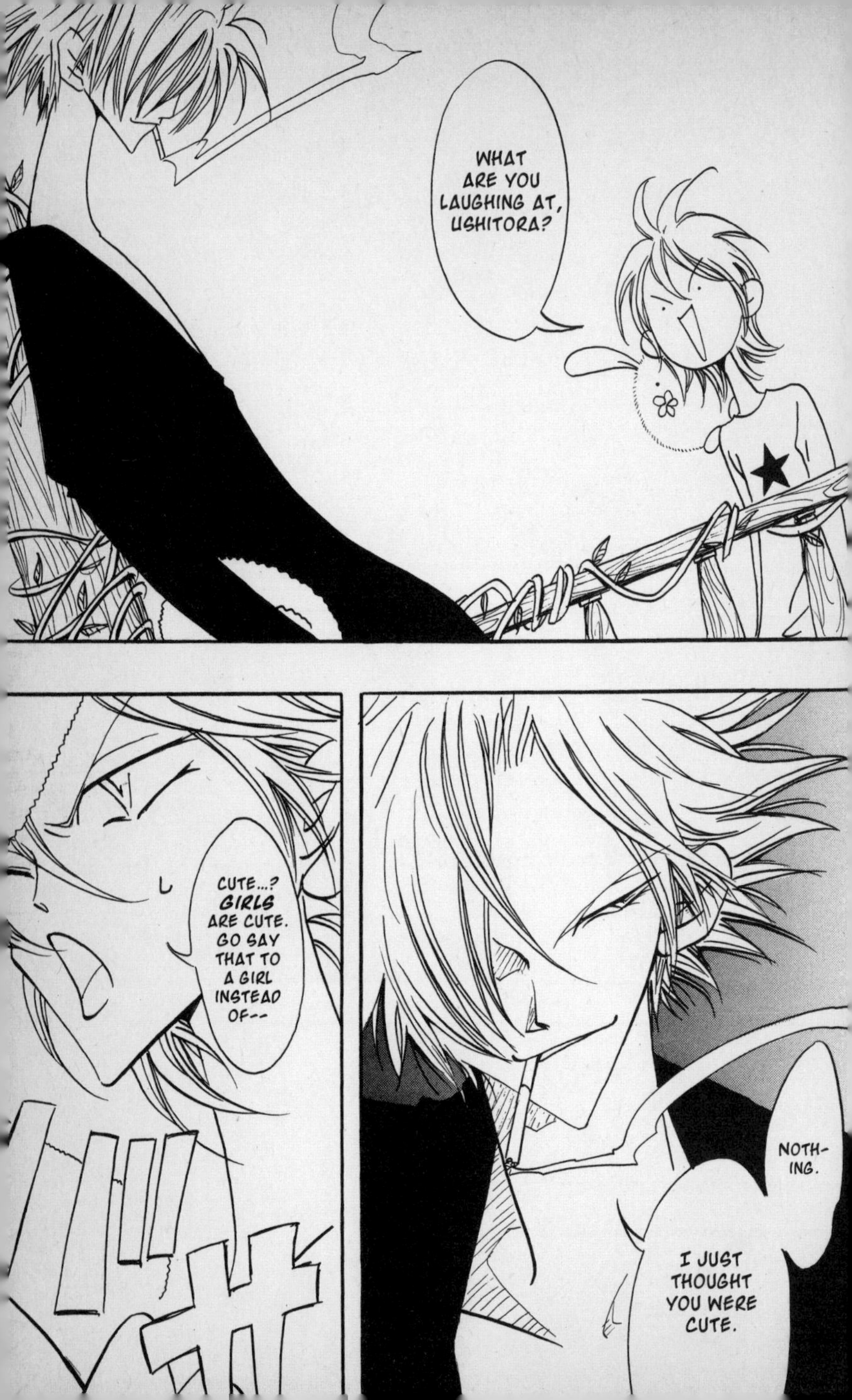
WHAT ARE YOU LAUGHING AT, USHITORA?
NOTH-ING.
I JUST THOUGHT YOU WERE CUTE.
CUTE...? GIRLS ARE CUTE. GO SAY THAT TO A GIRL INSTEAD OF--

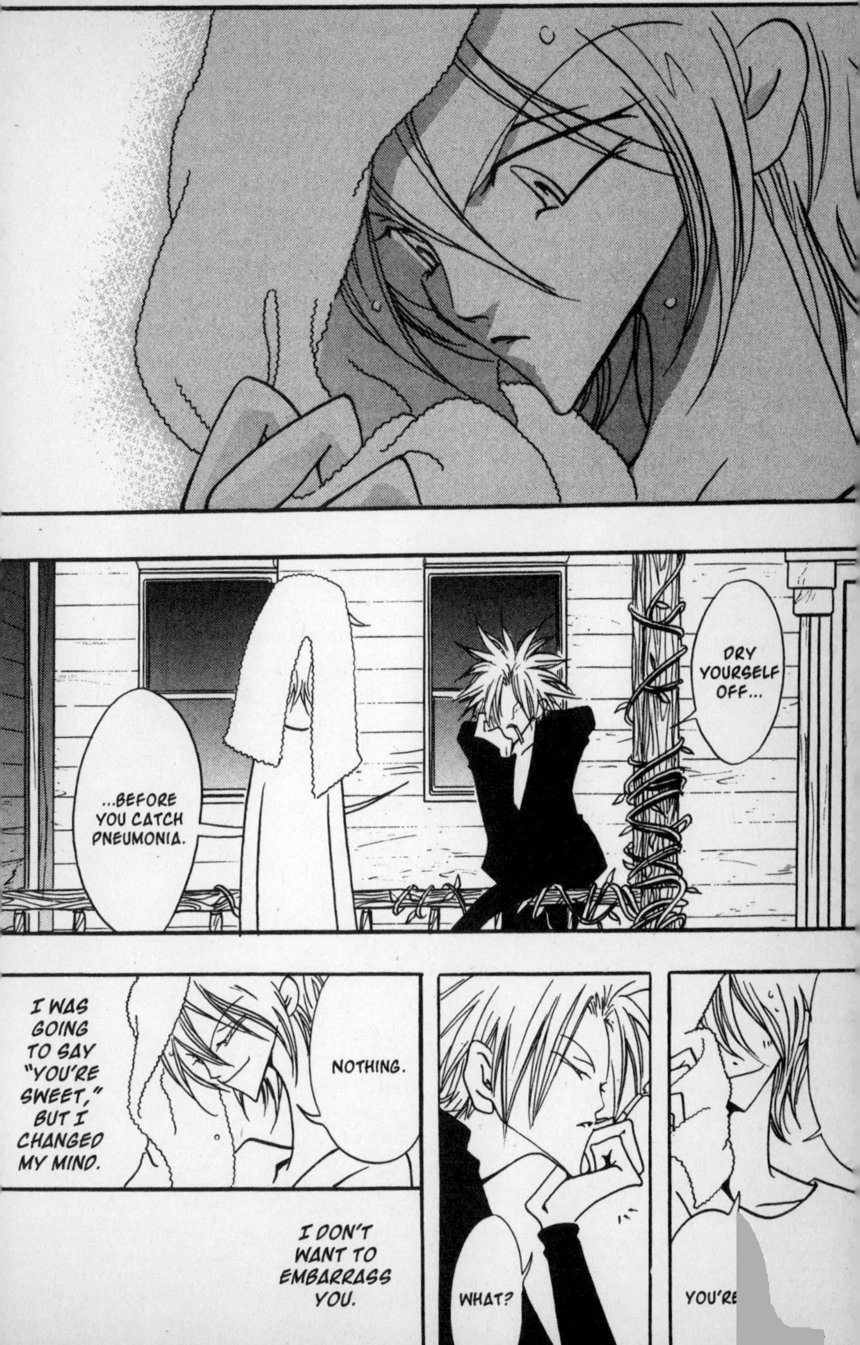
DRY YOURSELF OFF...
...BEFORE YOU CATCH PNEUMONIA.
YOU'RE
WHAT?
NOTHING.
I WAS GOING TO SAY "YOU'RE SWEET," BUT I CHANGED MY MIND.
I DON'T WANT TO EMBARRASS YOU.

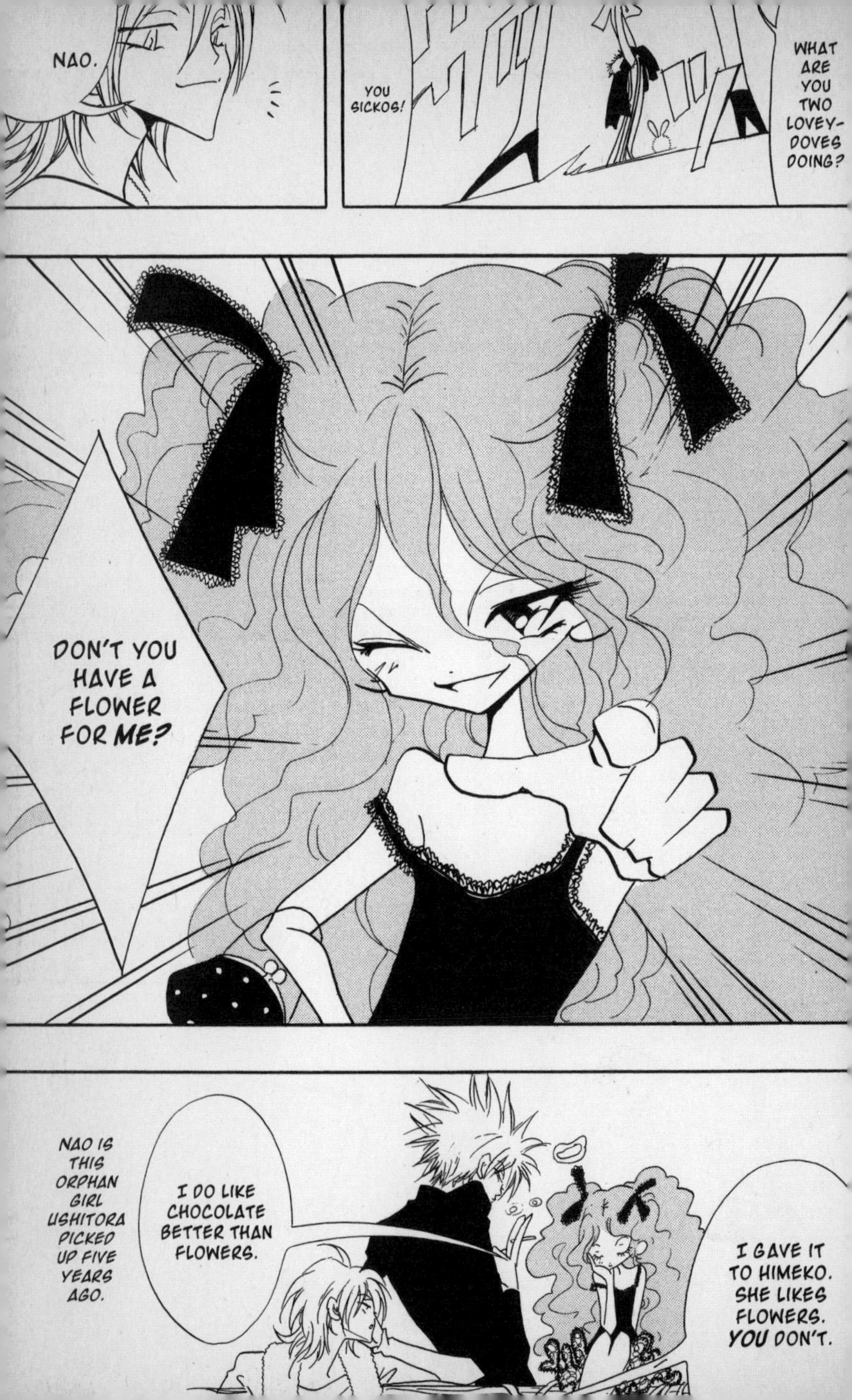
WHAT ARE YOU TWO LOVEY-DOVES DOING?
YOU SICKOS!
NAO.
DON'T YOU HAVE A FLOWER FOR **ME?**
I GAVE IT TO HIMEKO. SHE LIKES FLOWERS. ***YOU*** DON'T.
I DO LIKE CHOCOLATE BETTER THAN FLOWERS.
NAO IS THIS ORPHAN GIRL USHITORA PICKED UP FIVE YEARS AGO.

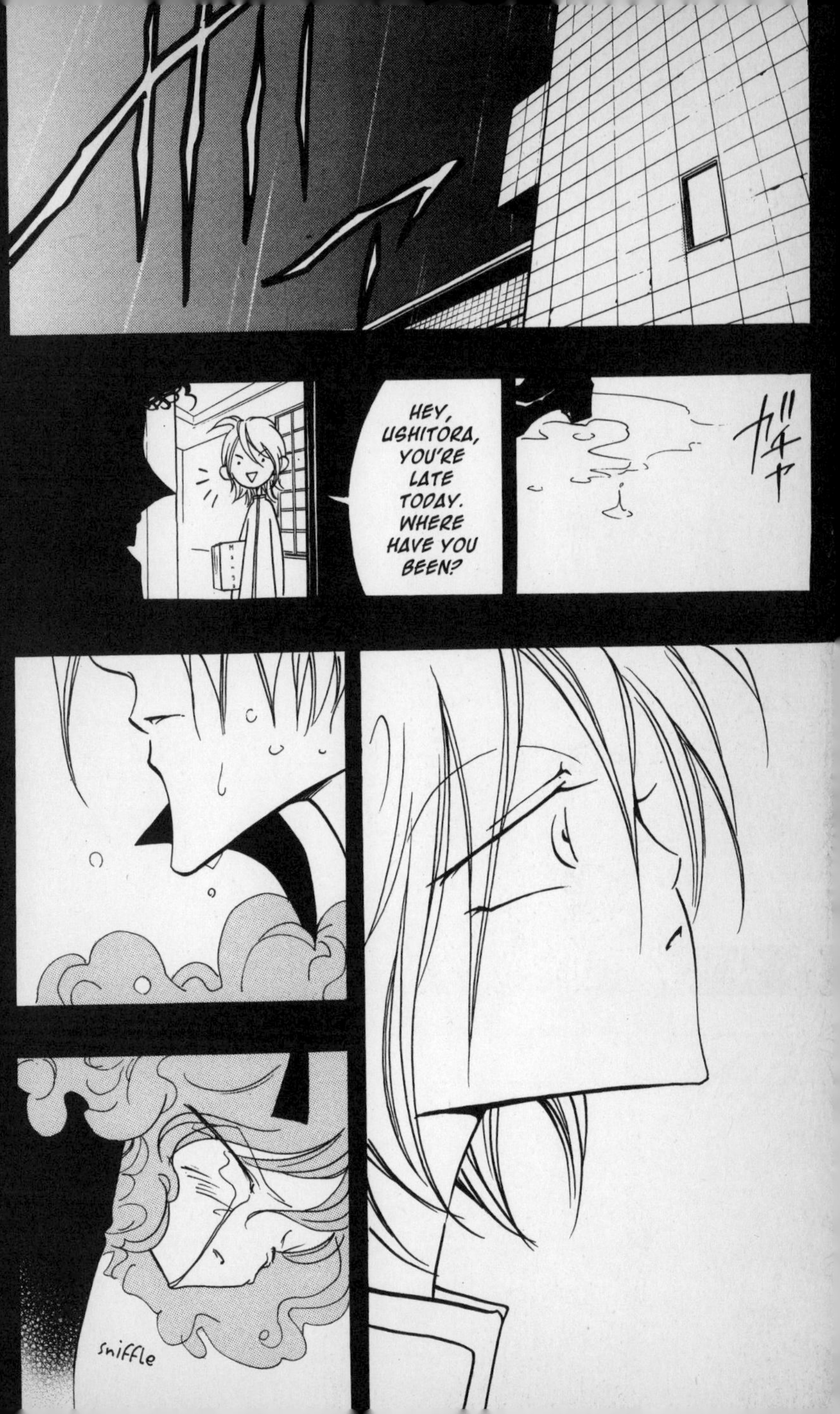
ガチャ
HEY, USHITORA, YOU'RE LATE TODAY. WHERE HAVE YOU BEEN?
sniffle

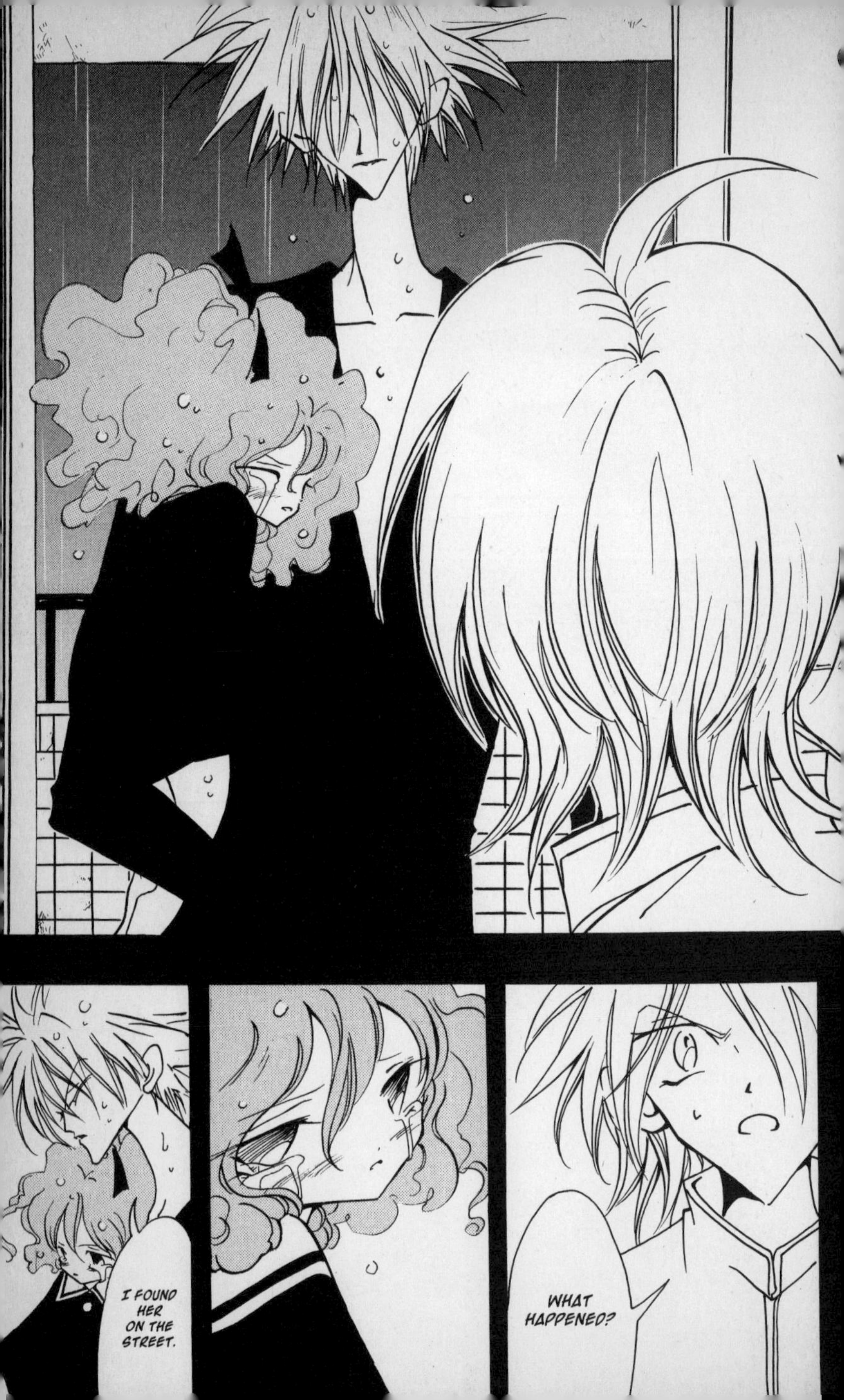
WHAT HAPPENED?
I FOUND HER ON THE STREET.

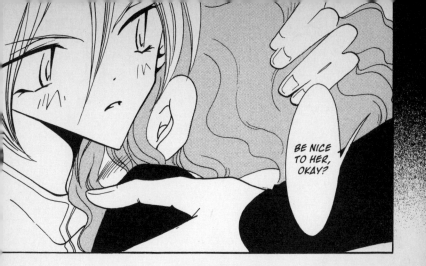

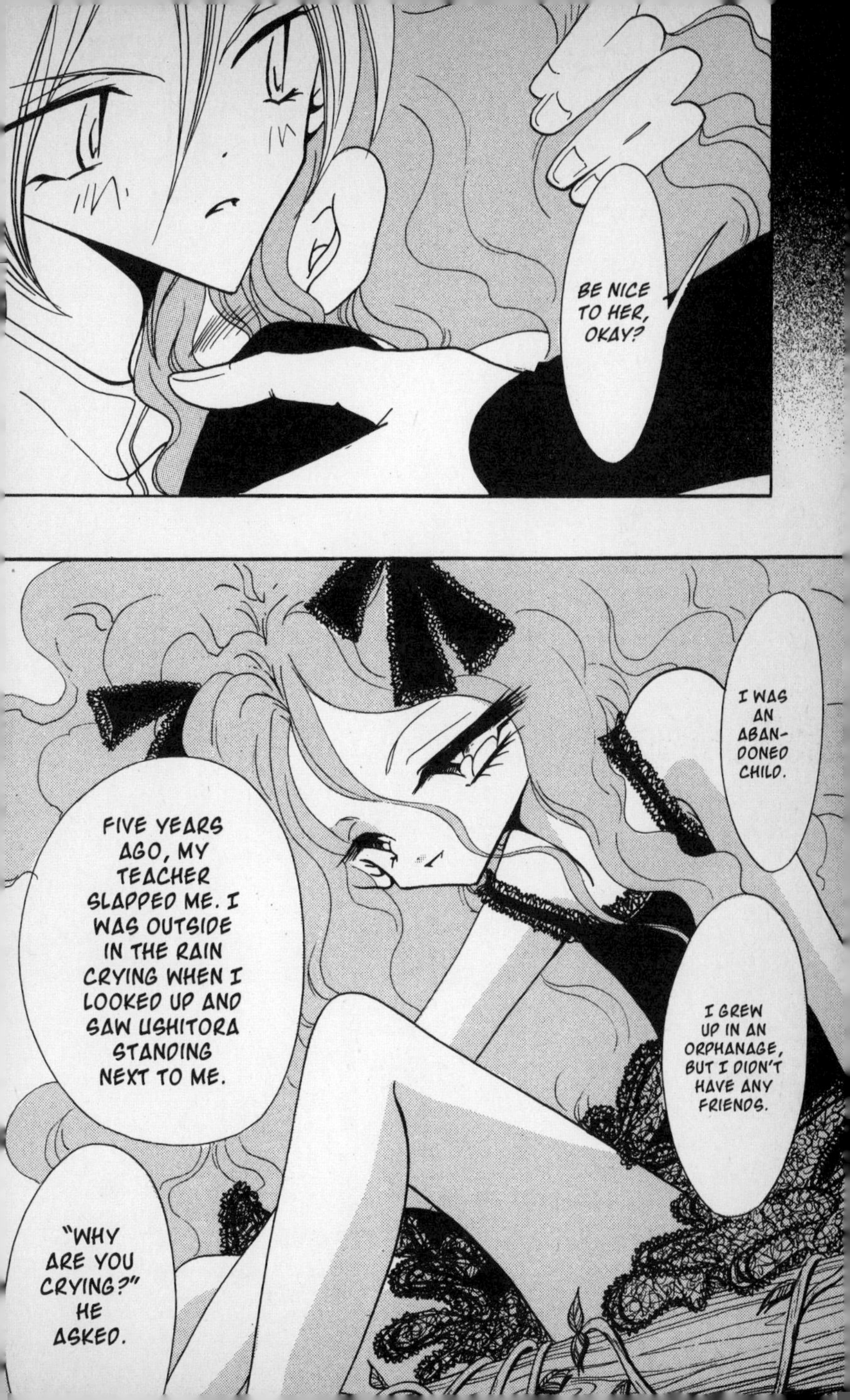
BE NICE TO HER, OKAY?
I WAS AN ABAN-DONED CHILD.
I GREW UP IN AN ORPHANAGE, BUT I DIDN'T HAVE ANY FRIENDS.
FIVE YEARS AGO, MY TEACHER SLAPPED ME. I WAS OUTSIDE IN THE RAIN CRYING WHEN I LOOKED UP AND SAW USHITORA STANDING NEXT TO ME.
"WHY ARE YOU CRYING?" HE ASKED.

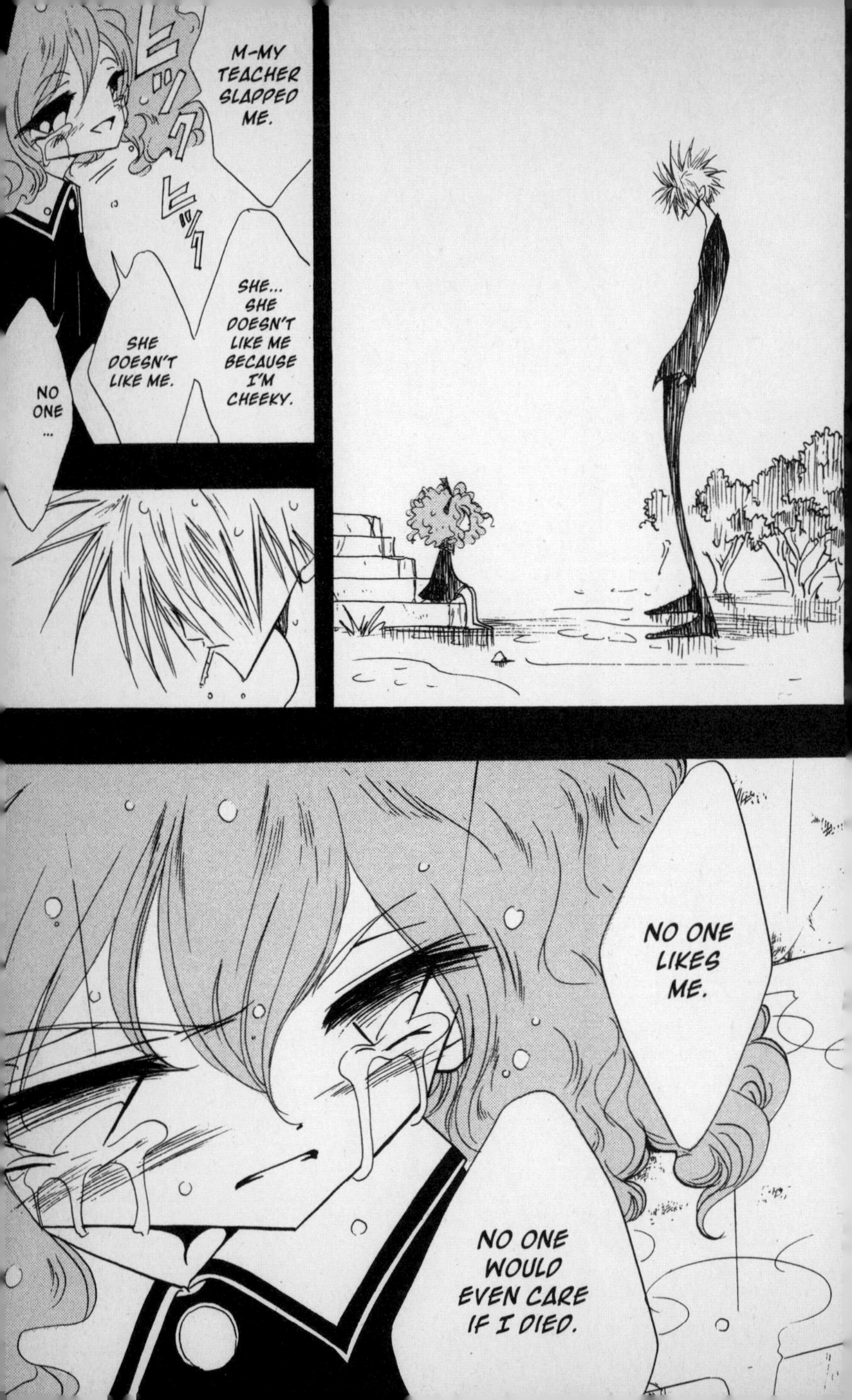
M-MY TEACHER SLAPPED ME.
ヒック
ヒック
SHE... SHE DOESN'T LIKE ME BECAUSE I'M CHEEKY.
SHE DOESN'T LIKE ME.
NO ONE ...
NO ONE LIKES ME.
NO ONE WOULD EVEN CARE IF I DIED.

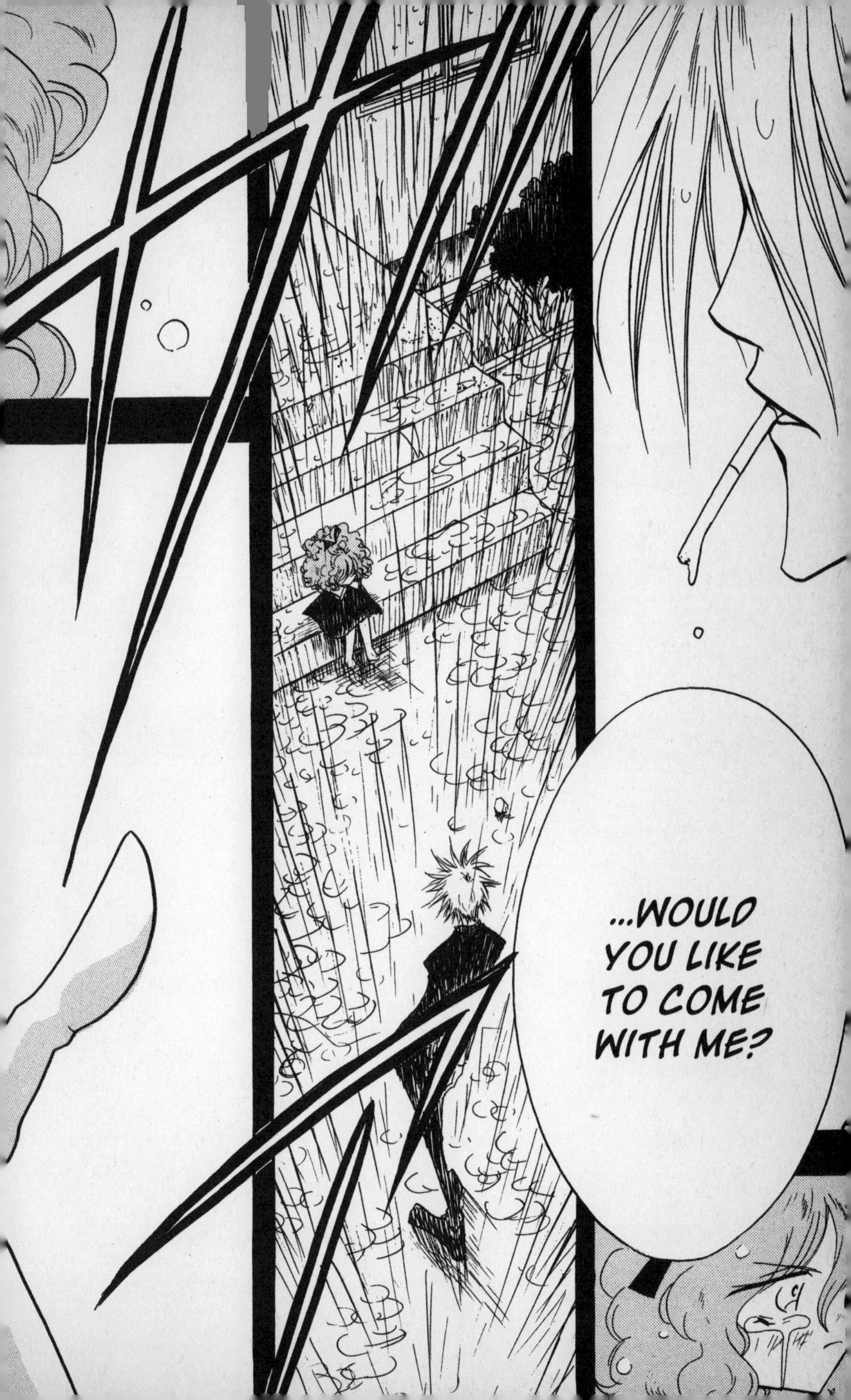
...WOULD YOU LIKE TO COME WITH ME?

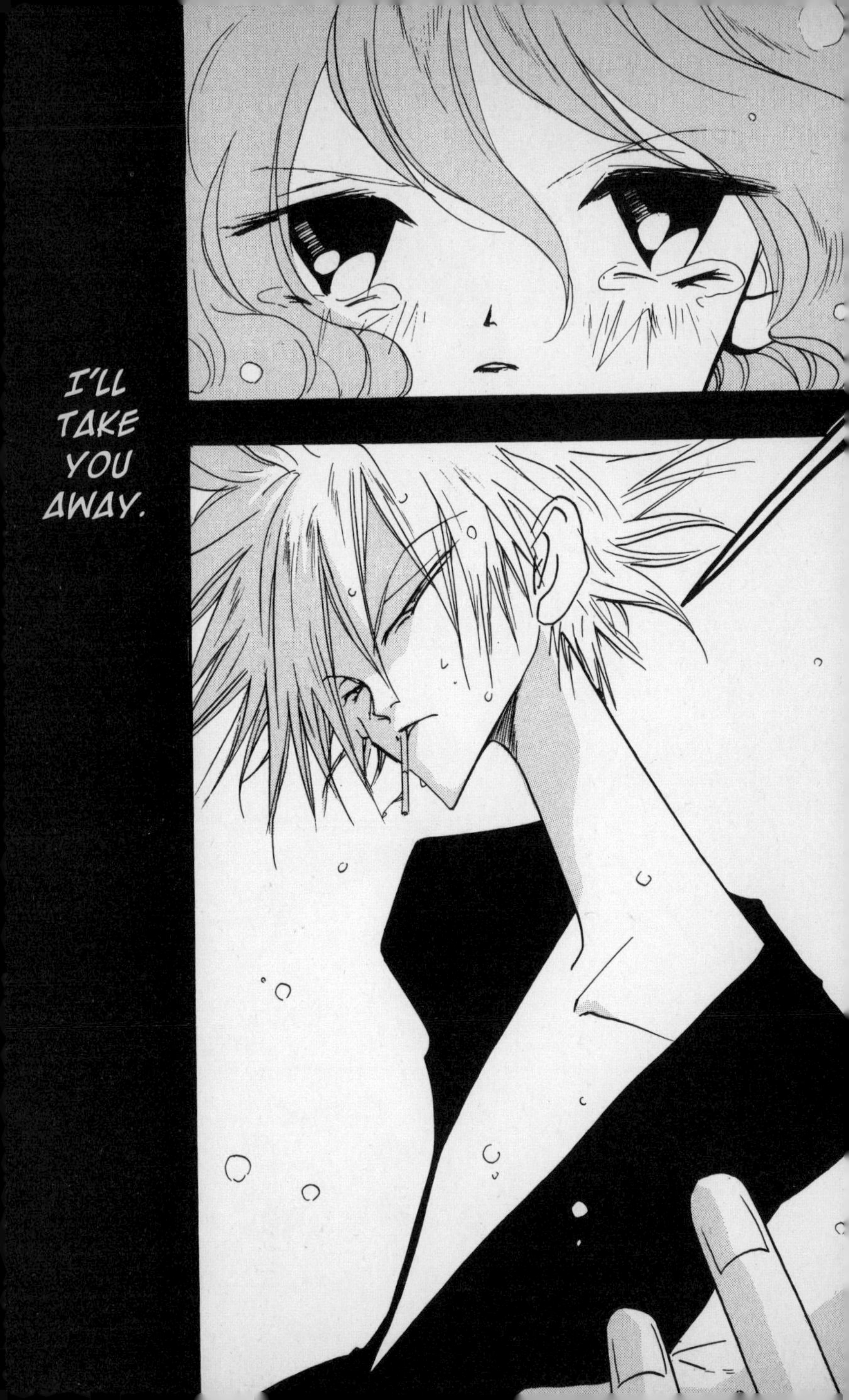
I'LL TAKE YOU AWAY.

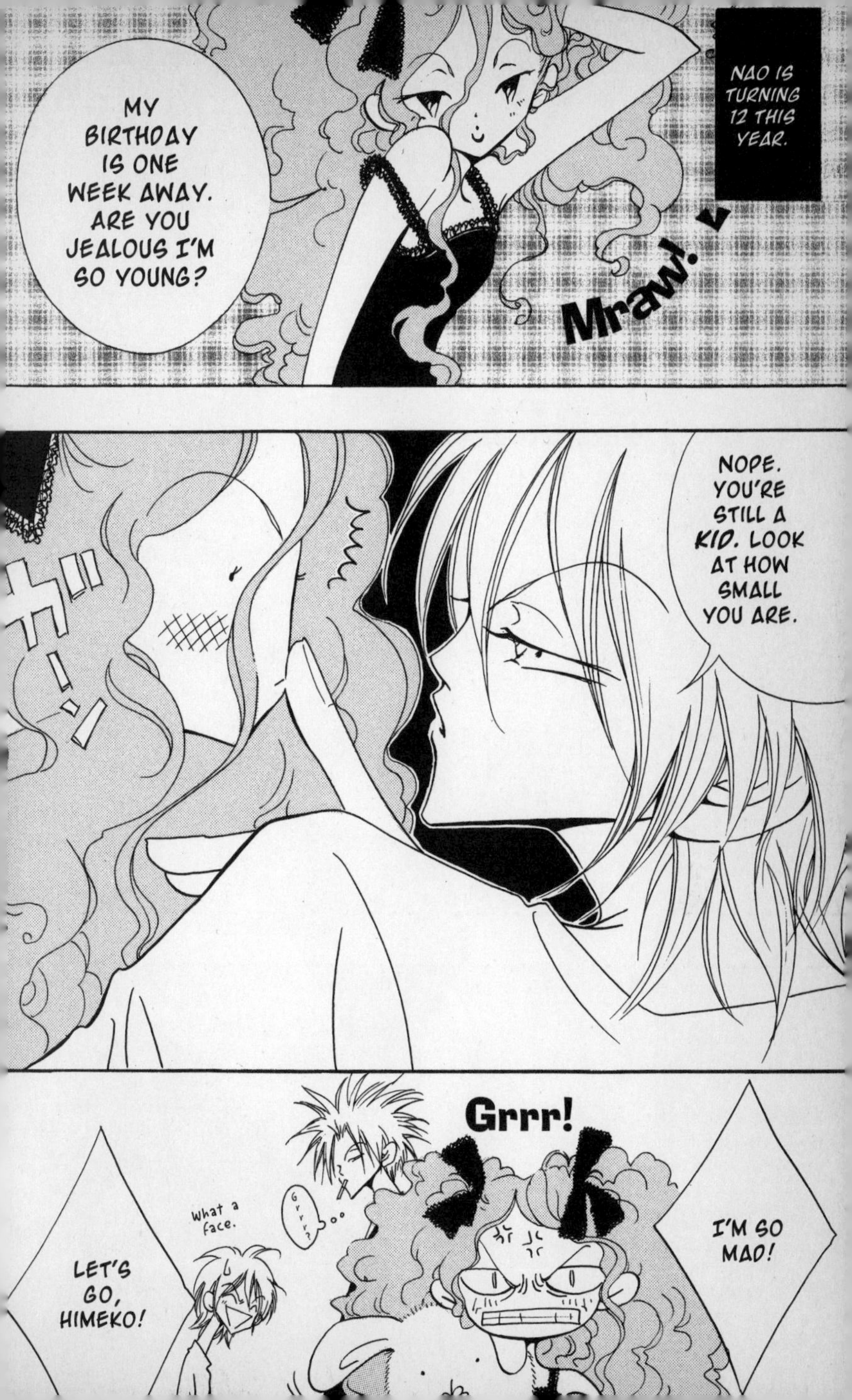
NAO IS TURNING 12 THIS YEAR.
Mraw!
MY BIRTHDAY IS ONE WEEK AWAY. ARE YOU JEALOUS I'M SO YOUNG?
NOPE. YOU'RE STILL A KID. LOOK AT HOW SMALL YOU ARE.
ガーン
Grrr!
I'M SO MAD!
Grrr?
What a face.
LET'S GO, HIMEKO!

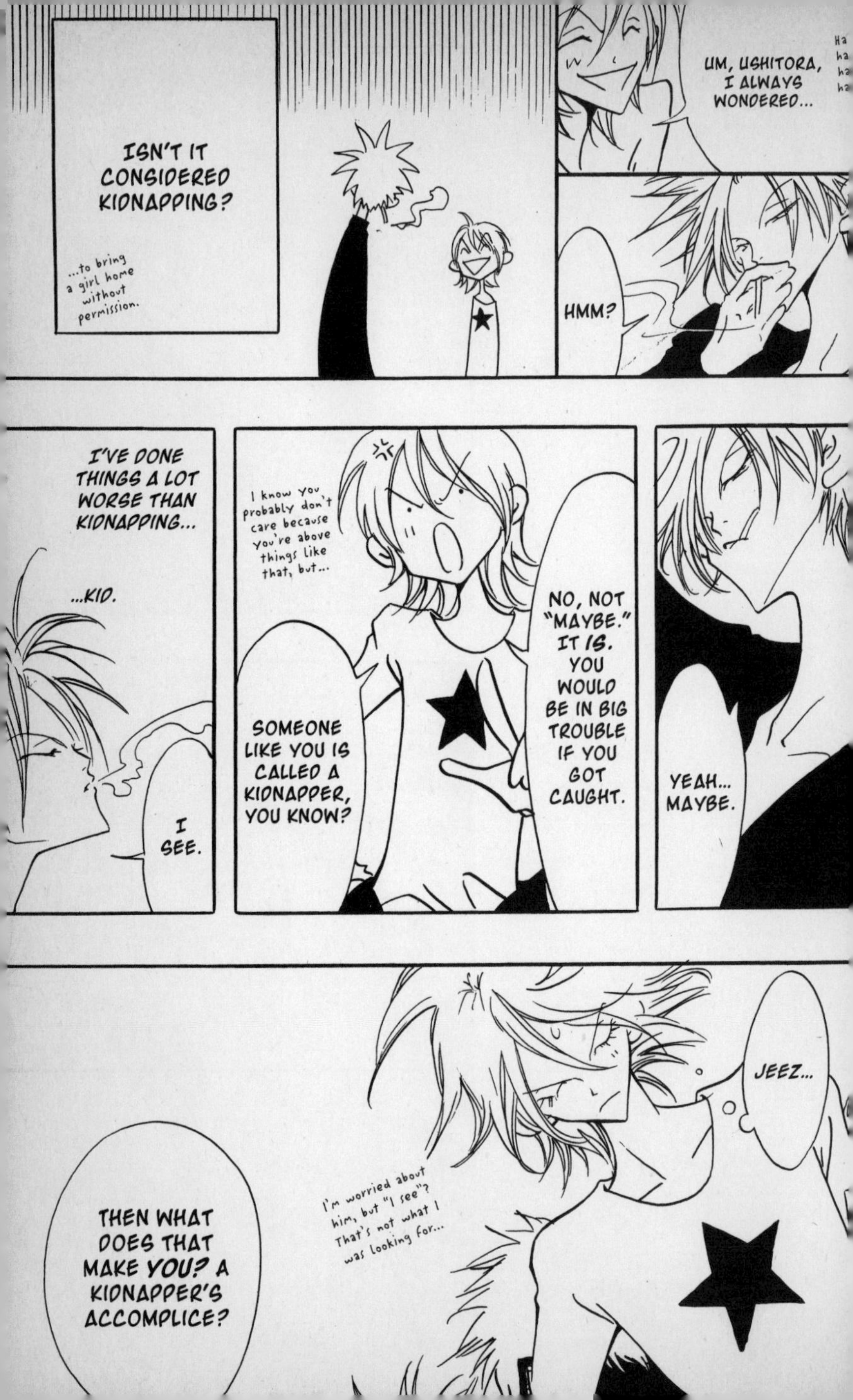

Ha ha ha ha
UM, USHITORA, I ALWAYS WONDERED...
HMM?
ISN'T IT CONSIDERED KIDNAPPING?
...to bring a girl home without permission.
YEAH... MAYBE.
NO, NOT "MAYBE." IT IS. YOU WOULD BE IN BIG TROUBLE IF YOU GOT CAUGHT.
I know you probably don't care because you're above things like that, but...
SOMEONE LIKE YOU IS CALLED A KIDNAPPER, YOU KNOW?
I SEE.
I'VE DONE THINGS A LOT WORSE THAN KIDNAPPING...
...KID.
JEEZ...
I'm worried about him, but "I see"? That's not what I was looking for...
THEN WHAT DOES THAT MAKE YOU? A KIDNAPPER'S ACCOMPLICE?

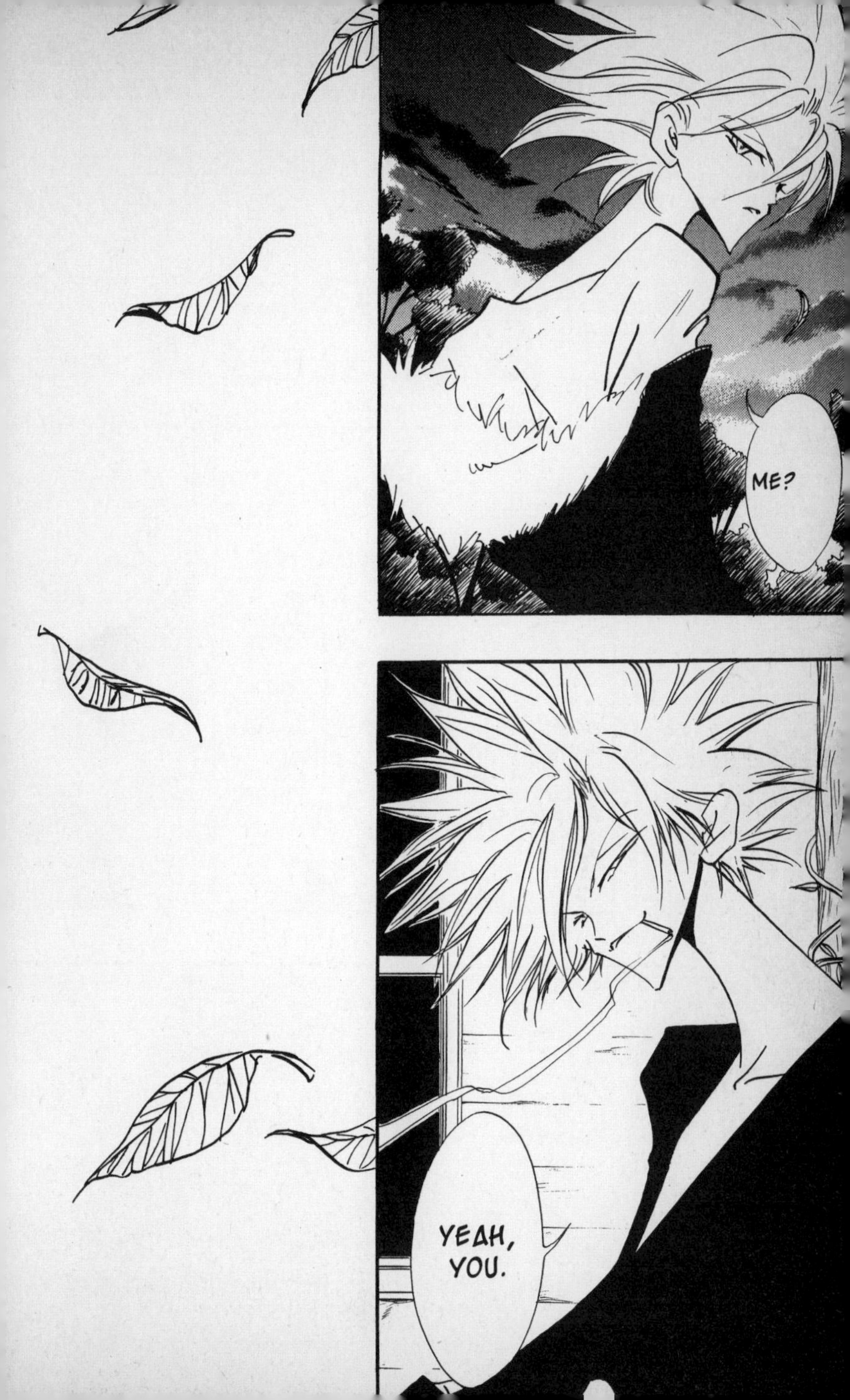

ME?
YEAH, YOU.

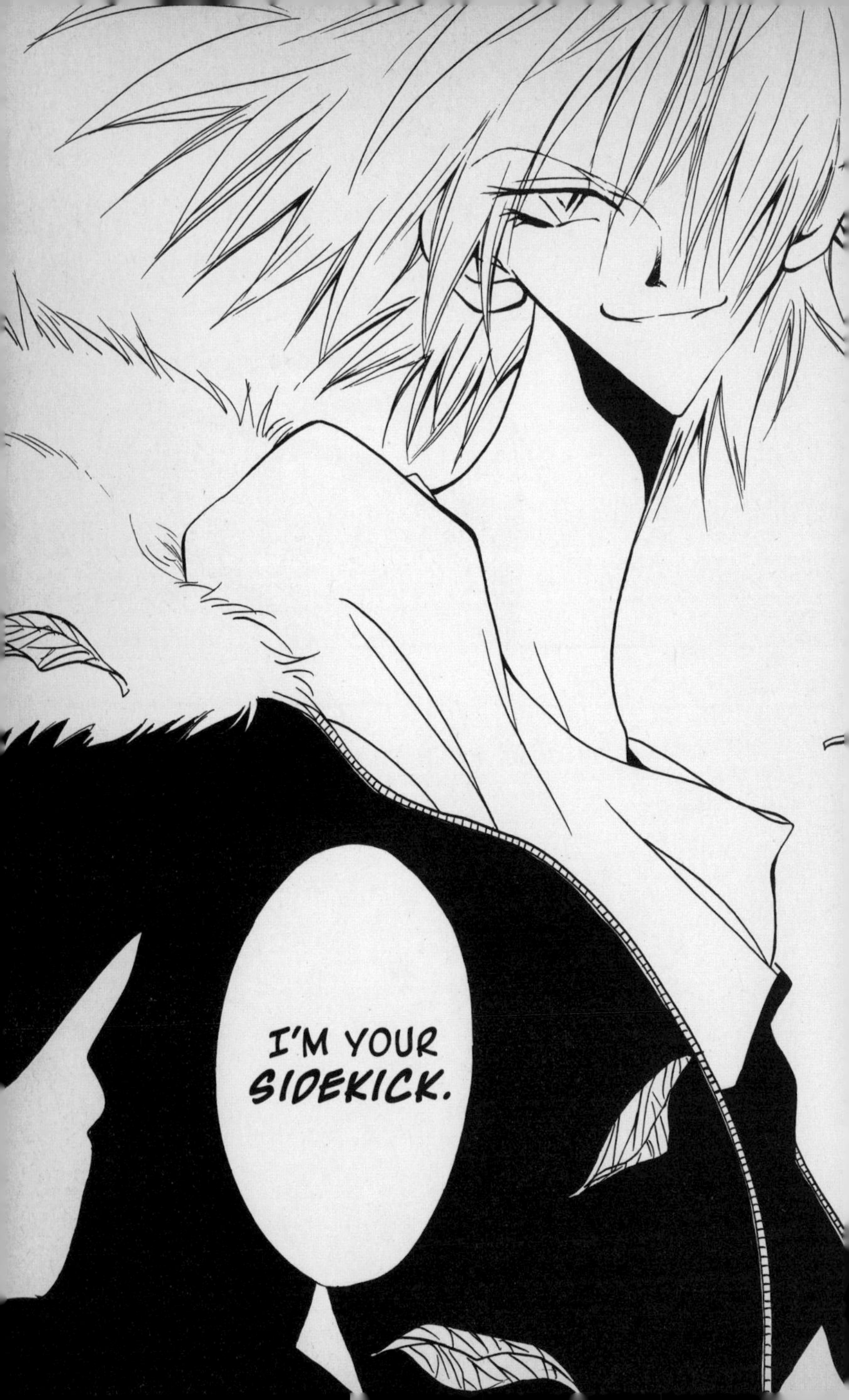
I'M YOUR SIDEKICK.

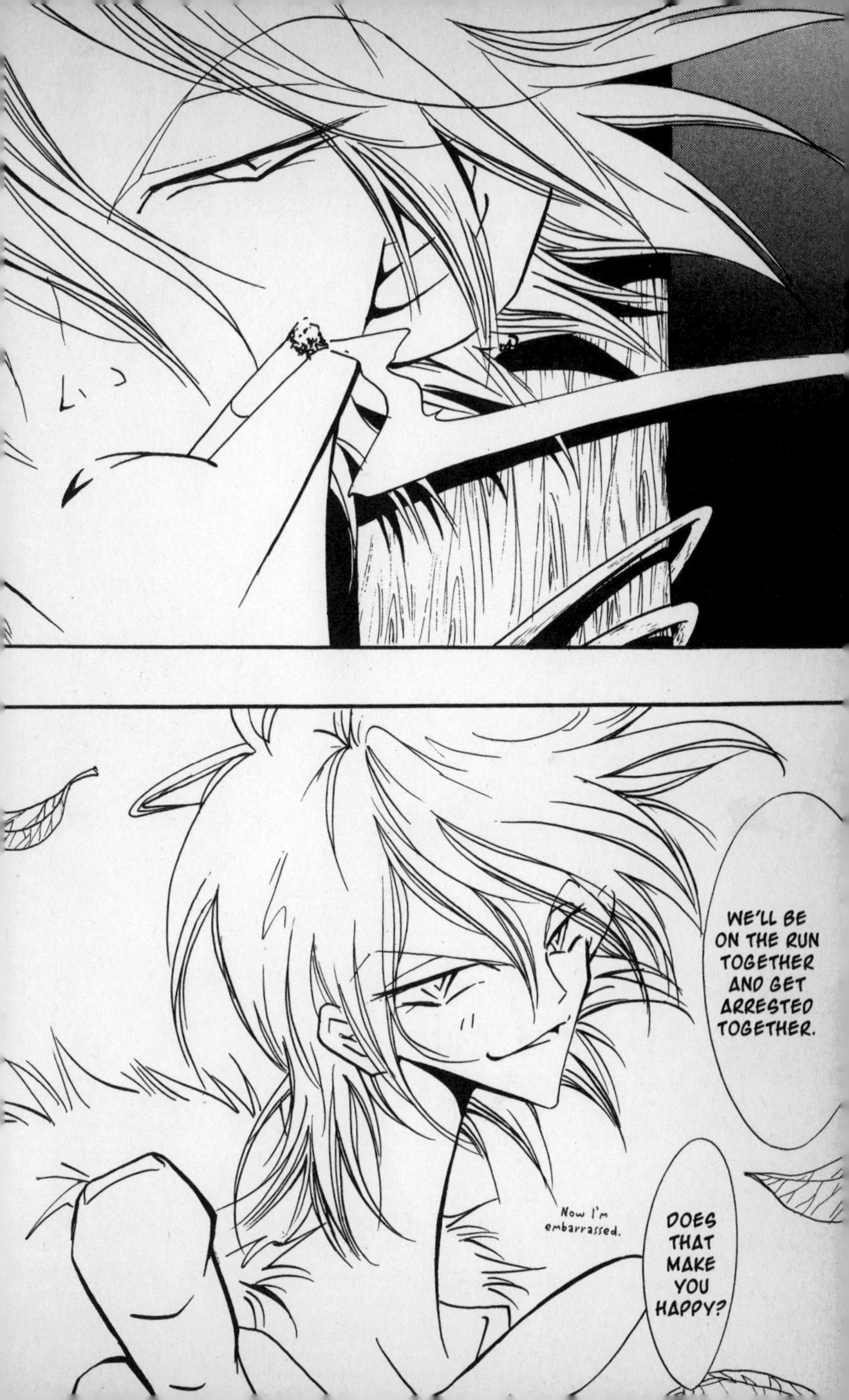
WE'LL BE ON THE RUN TOGETHER AND GET ARRESTED TOGETHER.
DOES THAT MAKE YOU HAPPY?
Now I'm embarrassed.

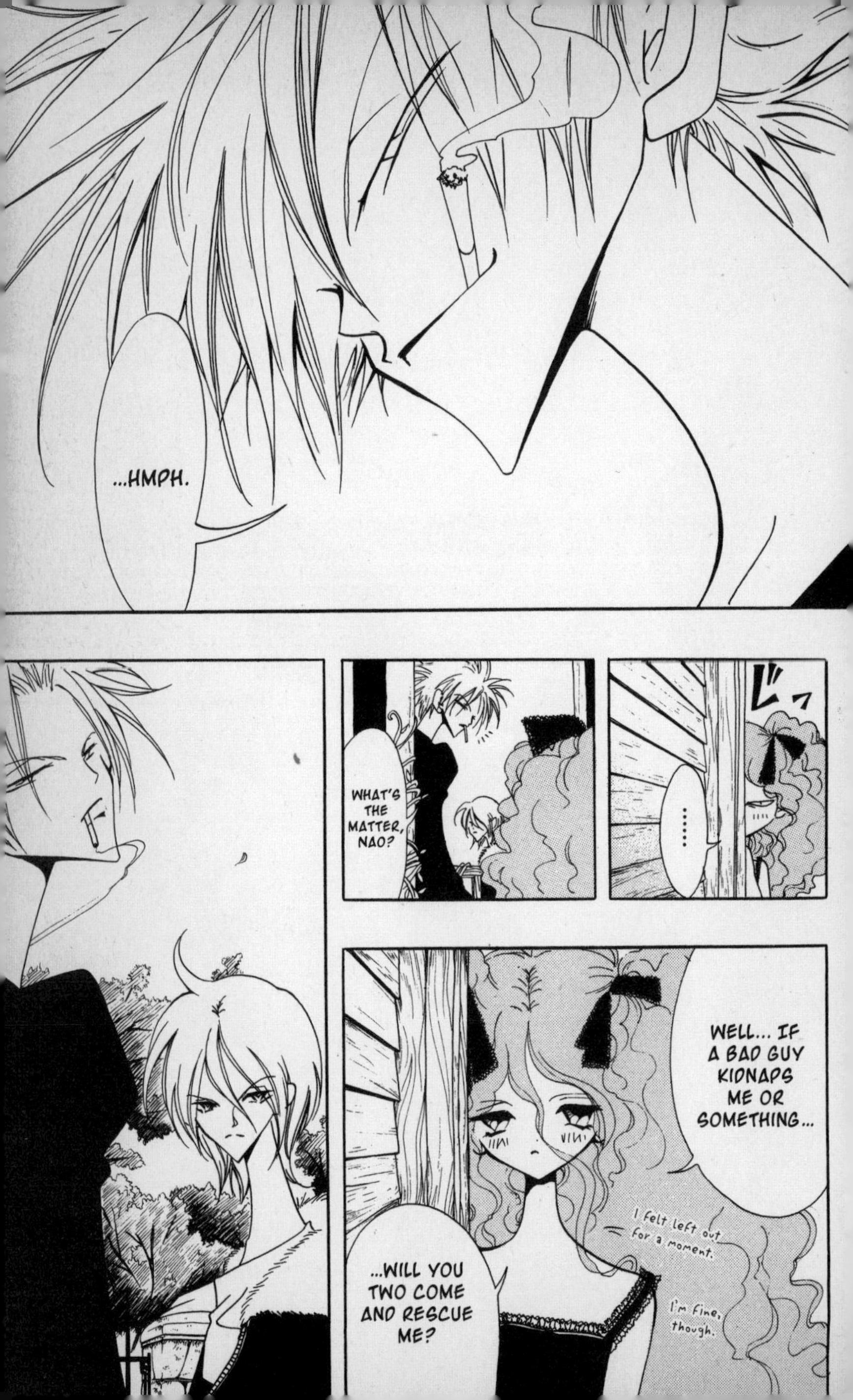

...HMPH.
ジッ
......
WHAT'S THE MATTER, NAO?
WELL... IF A BAD GUY KIDNAPS ME OR SOMETHING...
...WILL YOU TWO COME AND RESCUE ME?
I felt left out for a moment.
I'm fine, though.

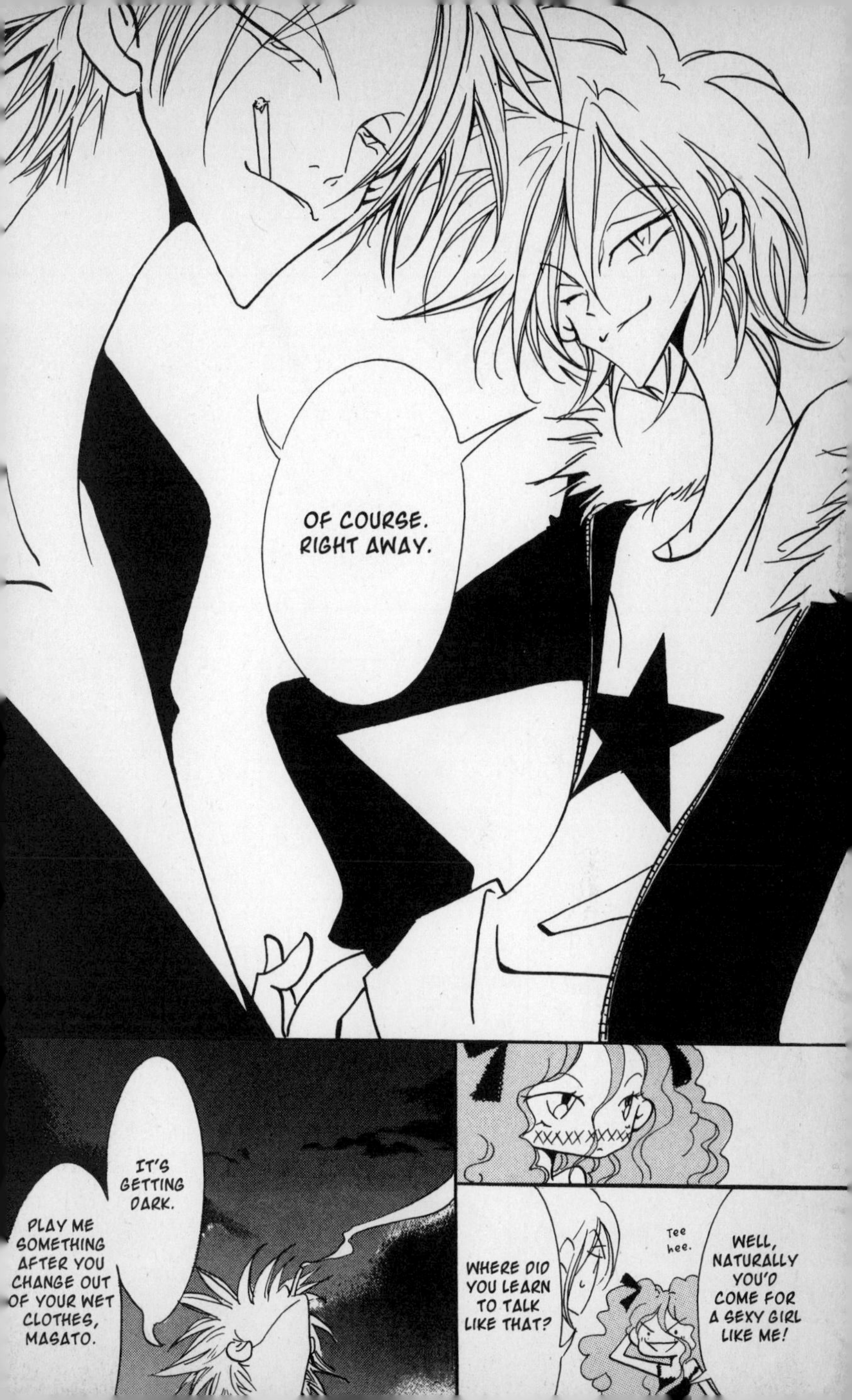
OF COURSE. RIGHT AWAY.
WELL, NATURALLY YOU'D COME FOR A SEXY GIRL LIKE ME!
Tee hee.
WHERE DID YOU LEARN TO TALK LIKE THAT?
IT'S GETTING DARK.
PLAY ME SOMETHING AFTER YOU CHANGE OUT OF YOUR WET CLOTHES, MASATO.

MY LIFE WITH USHITORA...

OKAY.

"I KNEW YOUR PARENTS AND TOOK YOU IN WHEN THEY DIED!"

THAT'S WHAT USHITORA TELLS ME.

FOR AS LONG AS I CAN REMEMBER, USHITORA HAS BEEN WITH ME AND OUR LIFE HAS BEEN LIKE THIS!

I DON'T REMEMBER ANYTHING BEFORE THAT.

...SINCE I WAS FOUR YEARS OLD.

THIS IS OUR LIFE...

AS FAR AS I KNOW, I HAVE BEEN LIVING WITH USHITORA FOR 11 YEARS...

IF YOU THINK I CAN'T GO TO SCHOOL WITH A LIFE LIKE THAT... YOU'RE RIGHT.

WE MOVE AROUND A LOT, SOMETIMES AFTER ONE MONTH, SOMETIMES LONGER LIKE SIX MONTHS...

WE MOVED INTO THIS HOUSE DEEP IN THE MOUNTAINS TWO MONTHS AGO, I THINK.

I'VE NEVER BEEN TO SCHOOL IN MY LIFE. USHITORA TAUGHT ME HOW TO WRITE AND THE THINGS I NEED TO SURVIVE.

...AS IF WE'RE ON THE RUN.

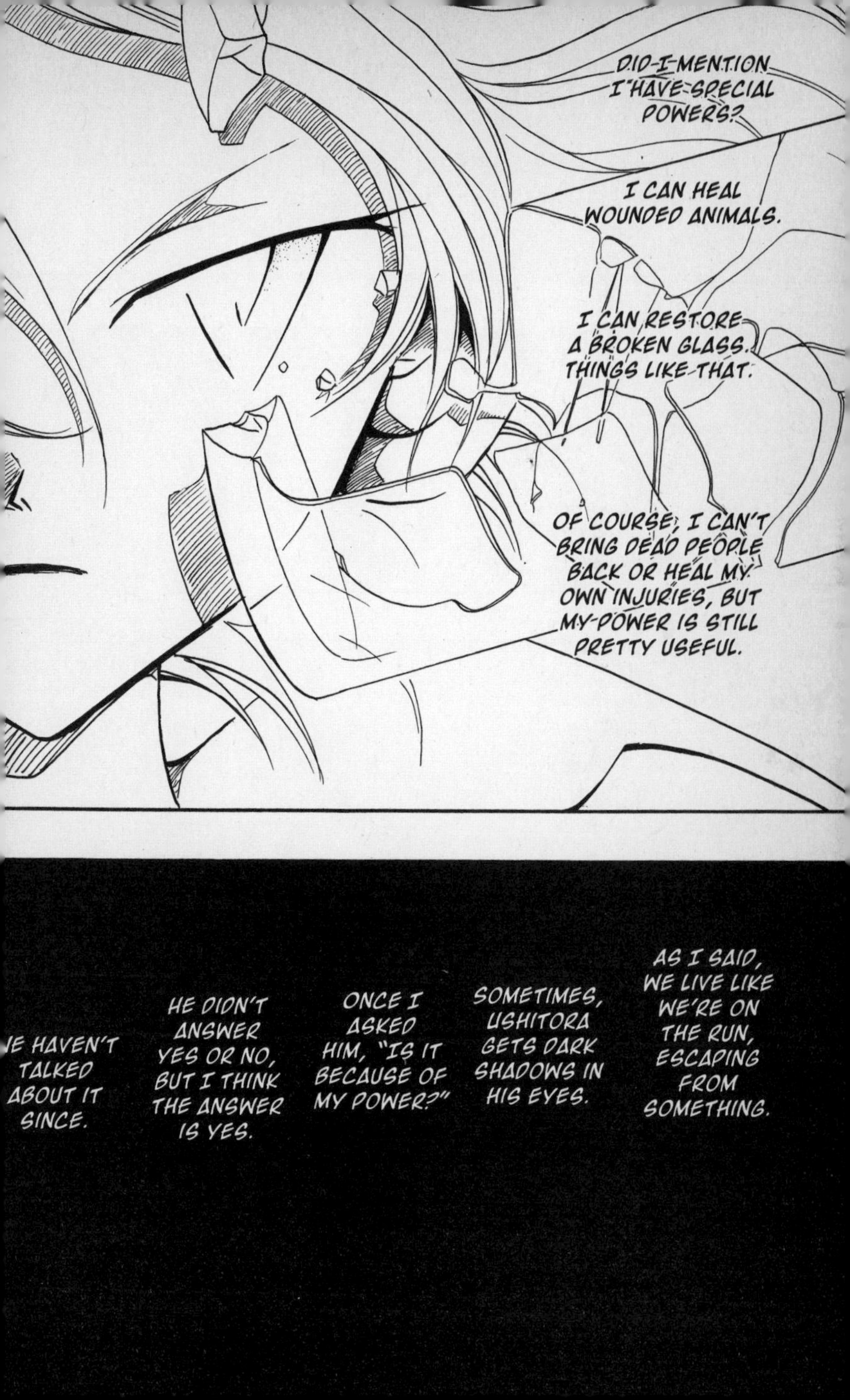

DID I MENTION I HAVE SPECIAL POWERS?
I CAN HEAL WOUNDED ANIMALS.
I CAN RESTORE A BROKEN GLASS. THINGS LIKE THAT.
OF COURSE, I CAN'T BRING DEAD PEOPLE BACK OR HEAL MY OWN INJURIES, BUT MY POWER IS STILL PRETTY USEFUL.
AS I SAID, WE LIVE LIKE WE'RE ON THE RUN, ESCAPING FROM SOMETHING.
SOMETIMES, USHITORA GETS DARK SHADOWS IN HIS EYES.
ONCE I ASKED HIM, "IS IT BECAUSE OF MY POWER?"
HE DIDN'T ANSWER YES OR NO, BUT I THINK THE ANSWER IS YES.
E HAVEN'T TALKED ABOUT IT SINCE.

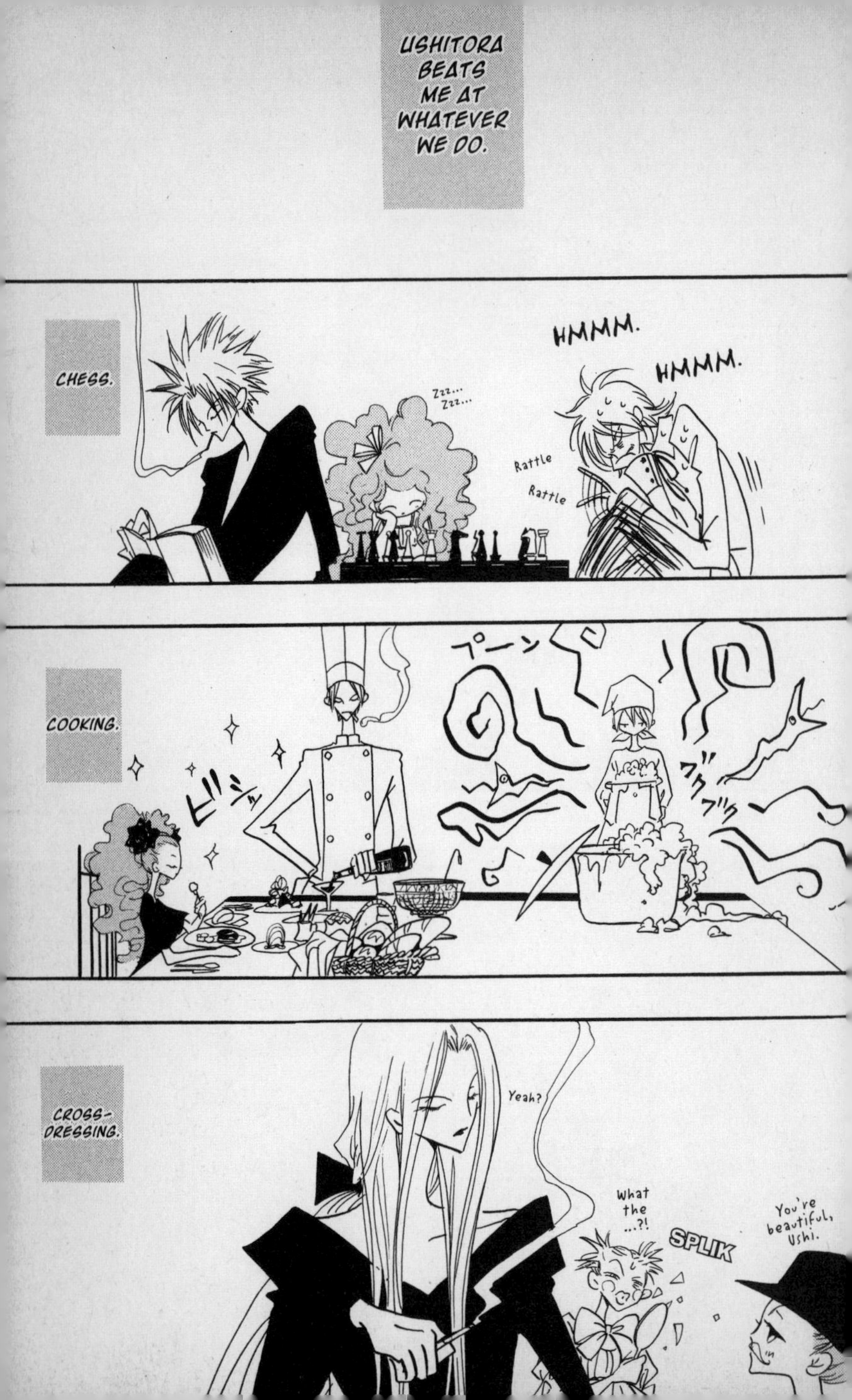
USHITORA BEATS ME AT WHATEVER WE DO.
HMMM.
HMMM.
Zzz... Zzz...
Rattle
Rattle
CHESS.
プーン
ブクブク
ビシッ
COOKING.
CROSS-DRESSING.
Yeah?
You're beautiful, Ushi.
SPLIK
What the ...?!

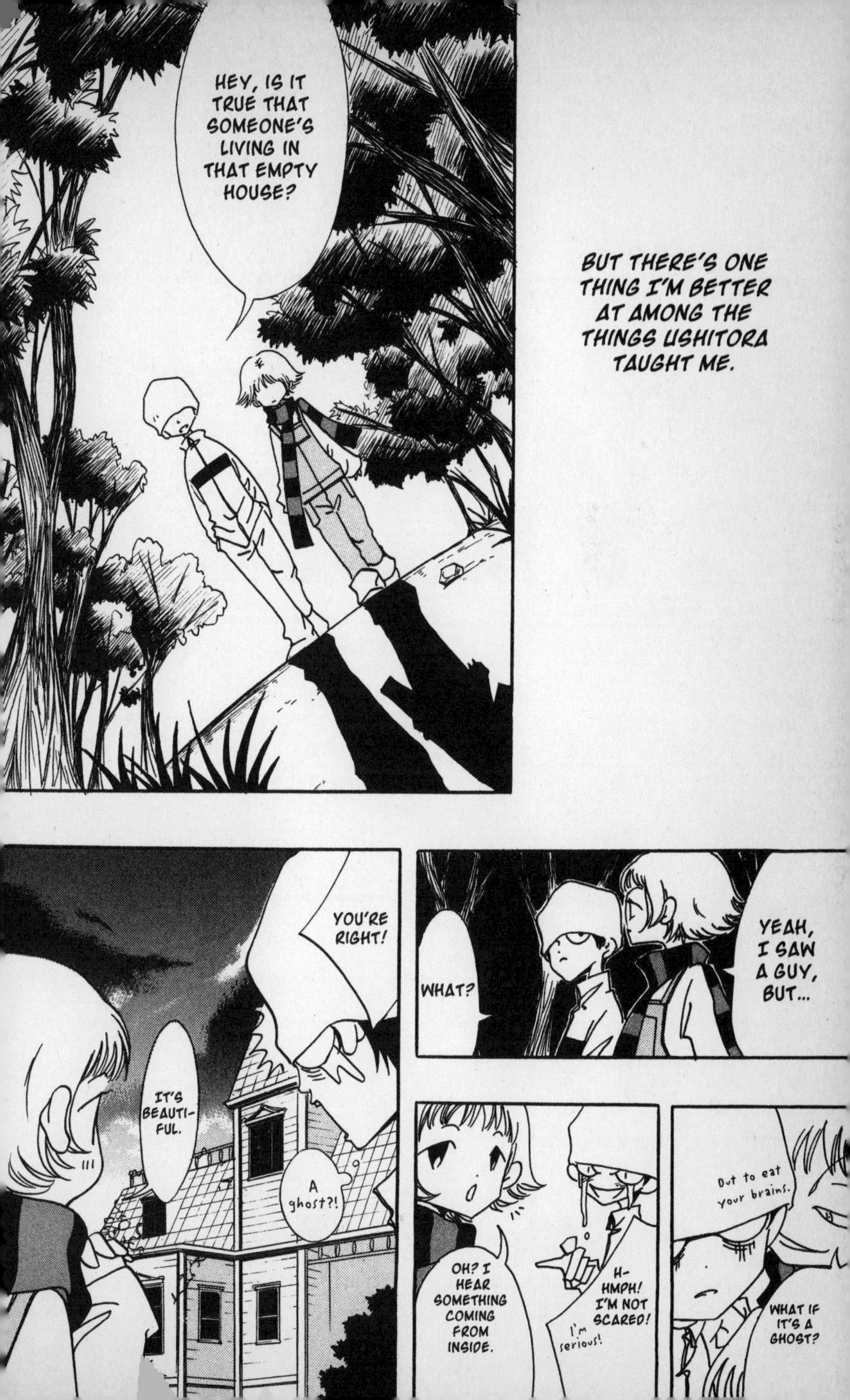
BUT THERE'S ONE THING I'M BETTER AT AMONG THE THINGS USHITORA TAUGHT ME.
HEY, IS IT TRUE THAT SOMEONE'S LIVING IN THAT EMPTY HOUSE?
YEAH, I SAW A GUY, BUT...
WHAT?
WHAT IF IT'S A GHOST?
Out to eat your brains.
H-HMPH! I'M NOT SCARED!
I'm serious!
OH? I HEAR SOMETHING COMING FROM INSIDE.
A ghost?!
YOU'RE RIGHT!
IT'S BEAUTI-FUL.

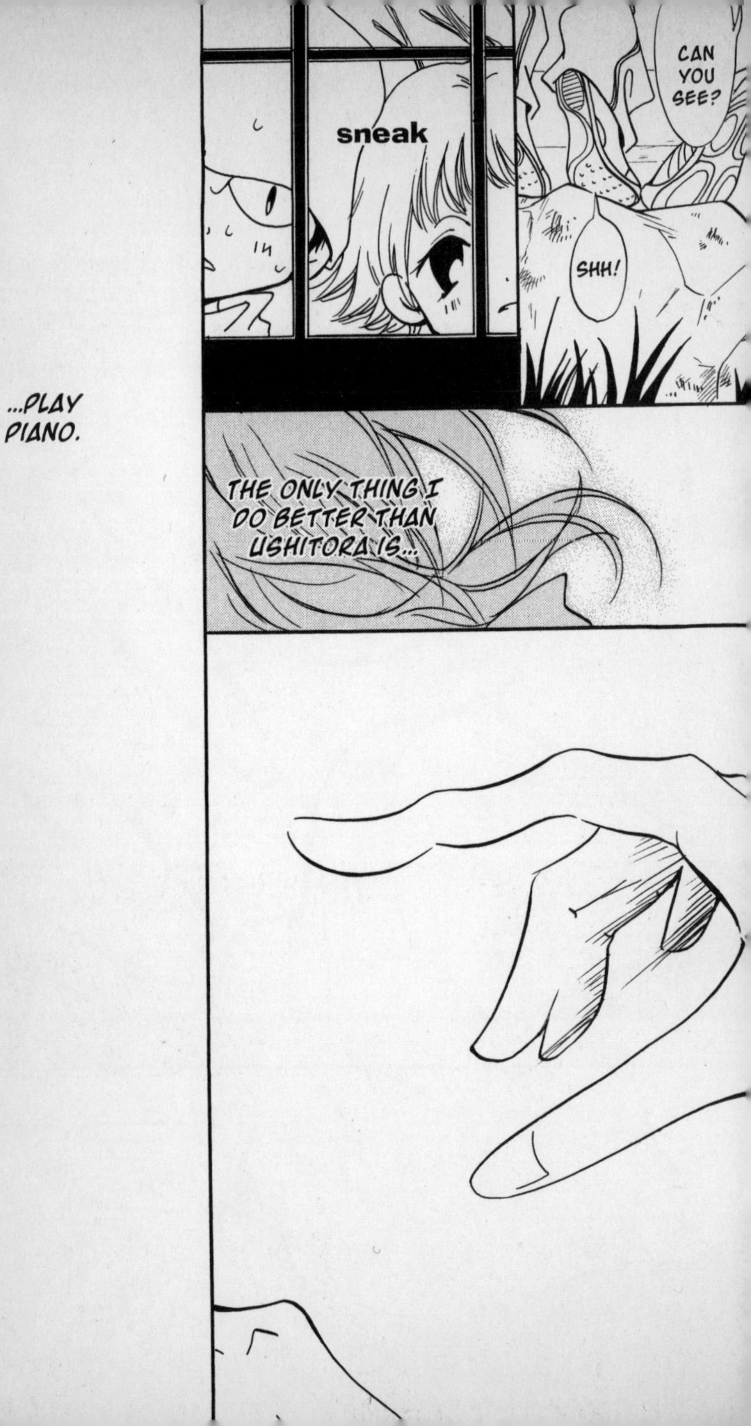
CAN YOU SEE?
SHH!
sneak
THE ONLY THING I DO BETTER THAN USHITORA IS...
...PLAY PIANO.

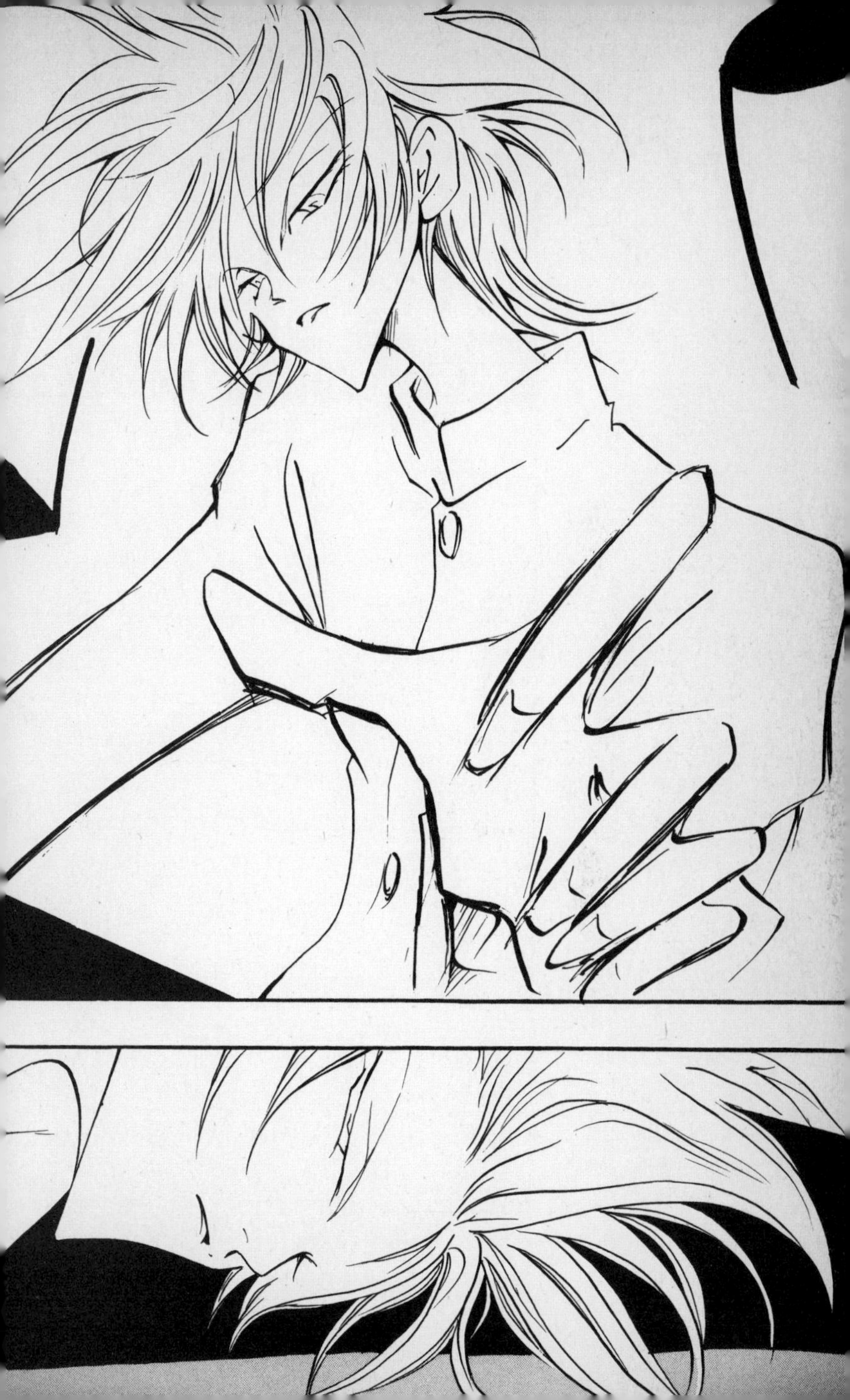

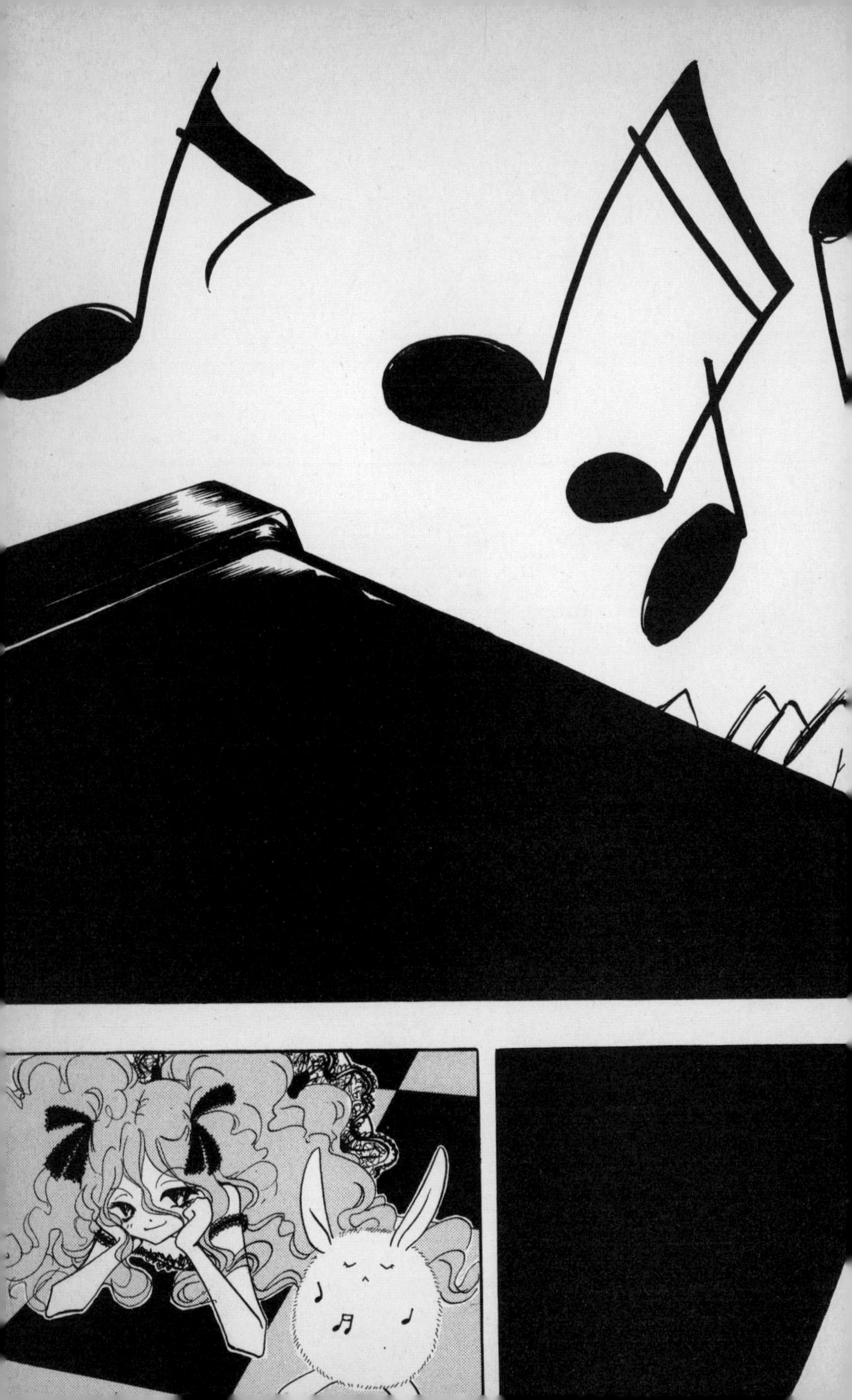

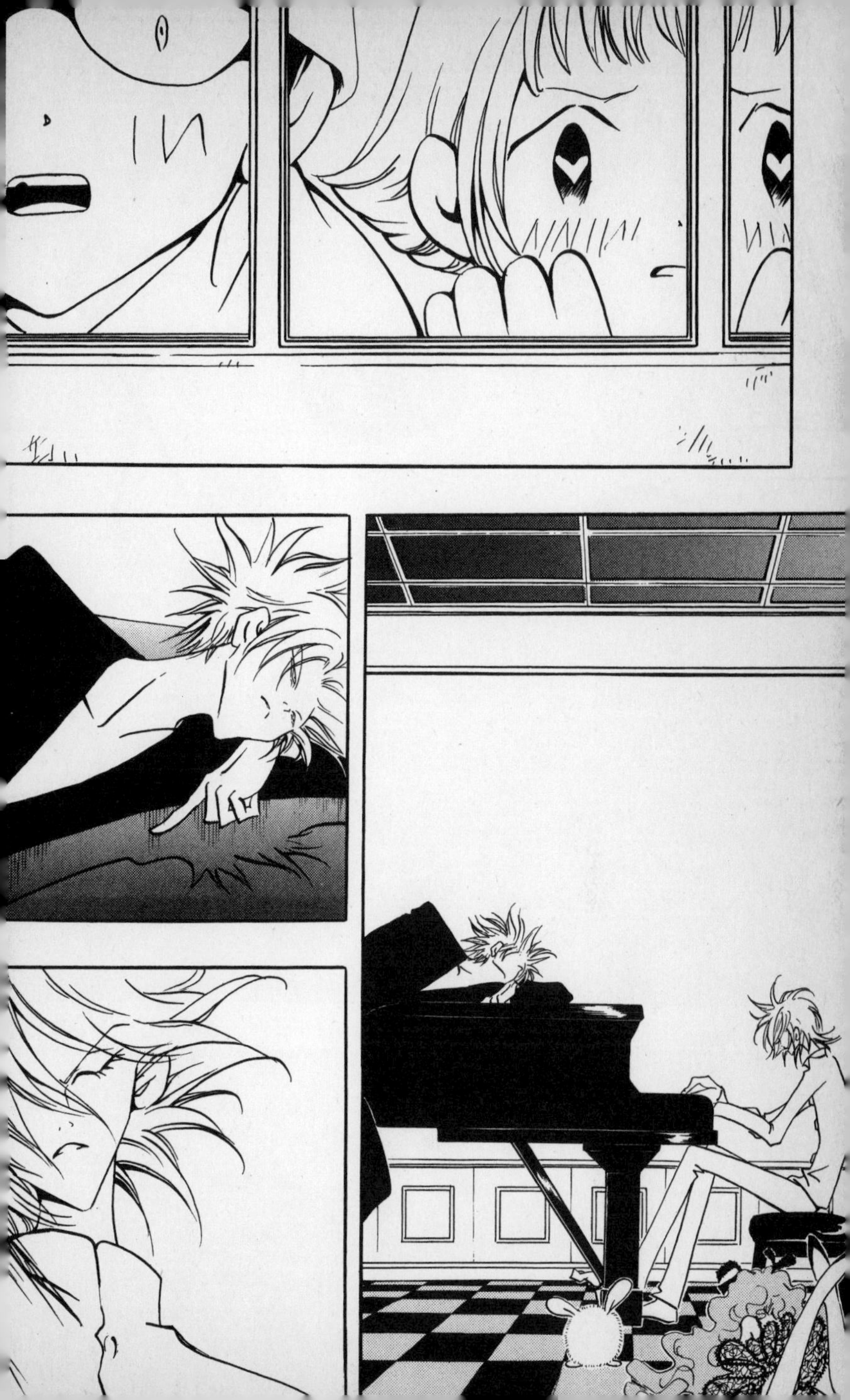

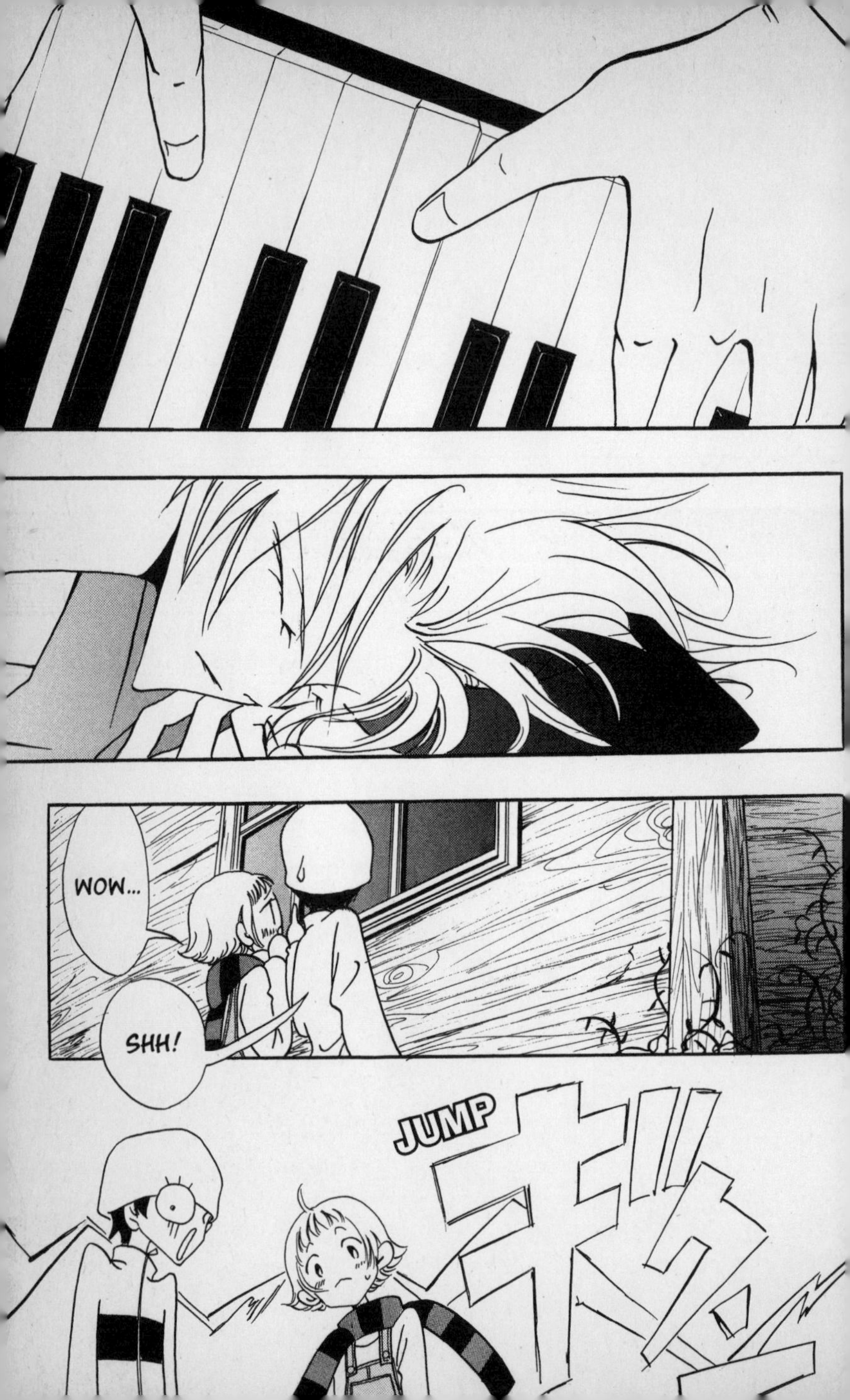

WOW...
SHH!
JUMP

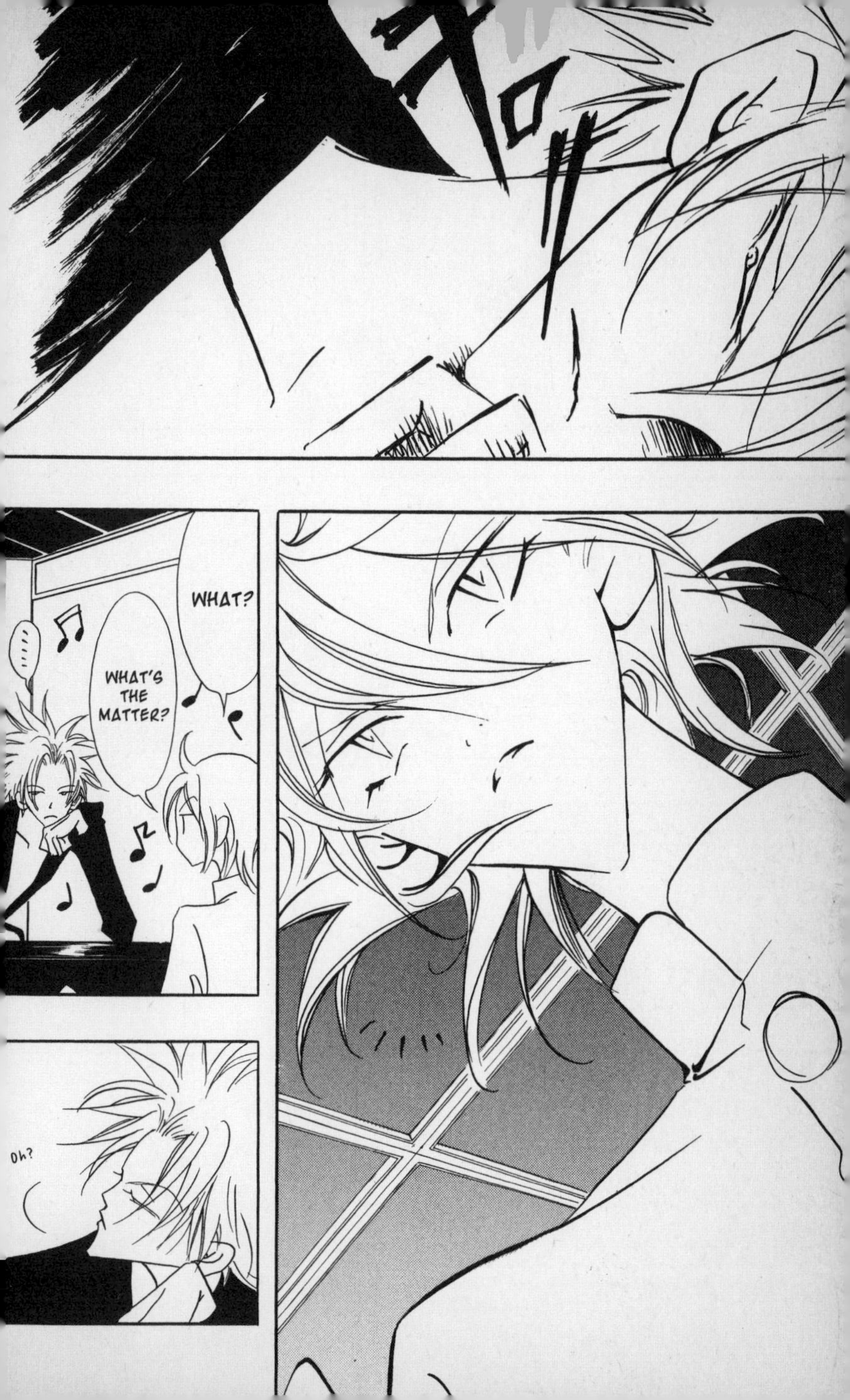
WHAT?
WHAT'S THE MATTER?
...
Oh?

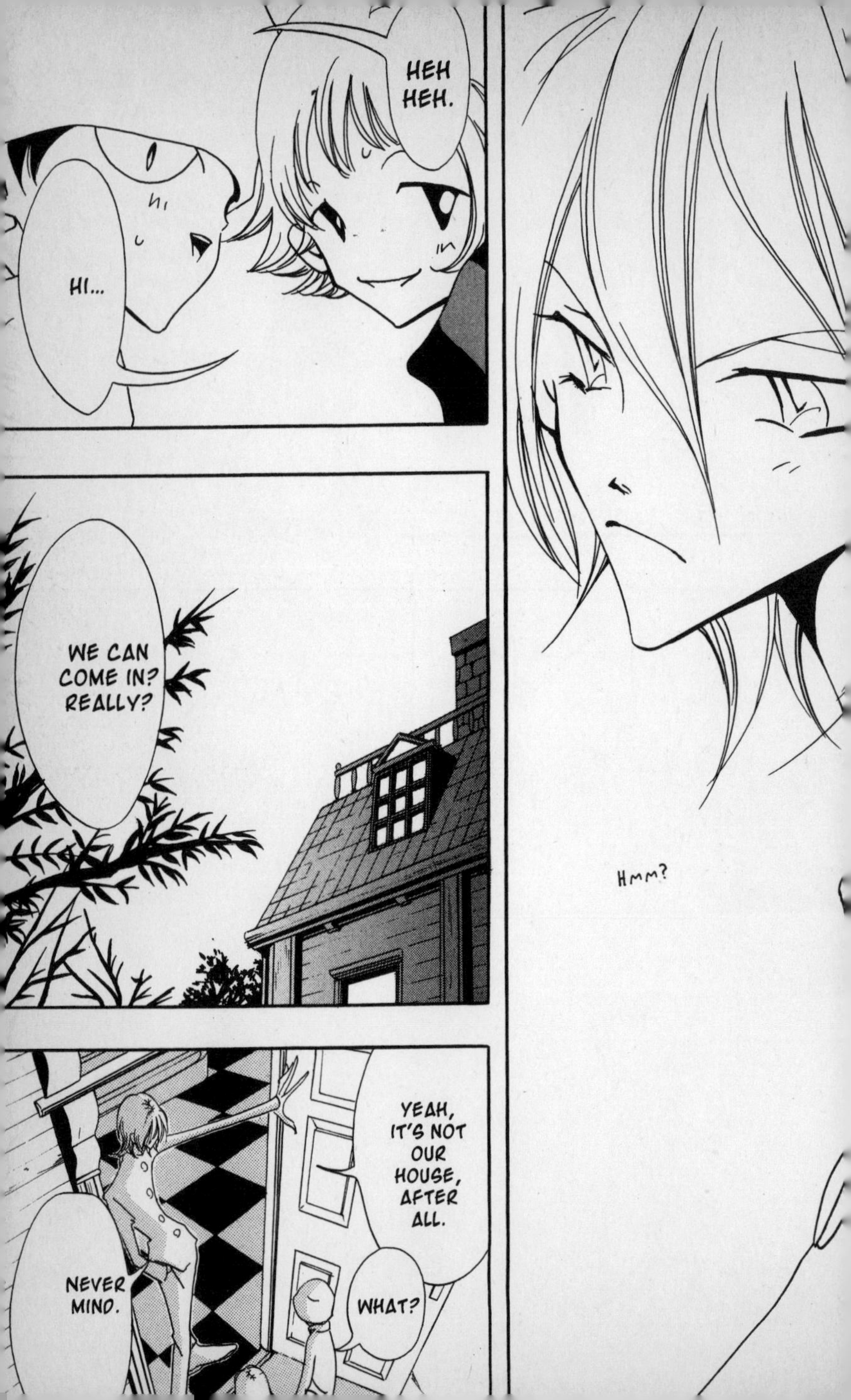
HMM?
HEH HEH.
HI...
WE CAN COME IN? REALLY?
YEAH, IT'S NOT OUR HOUSE, AFTER ALL.
WHAT?
NEVER MIND.

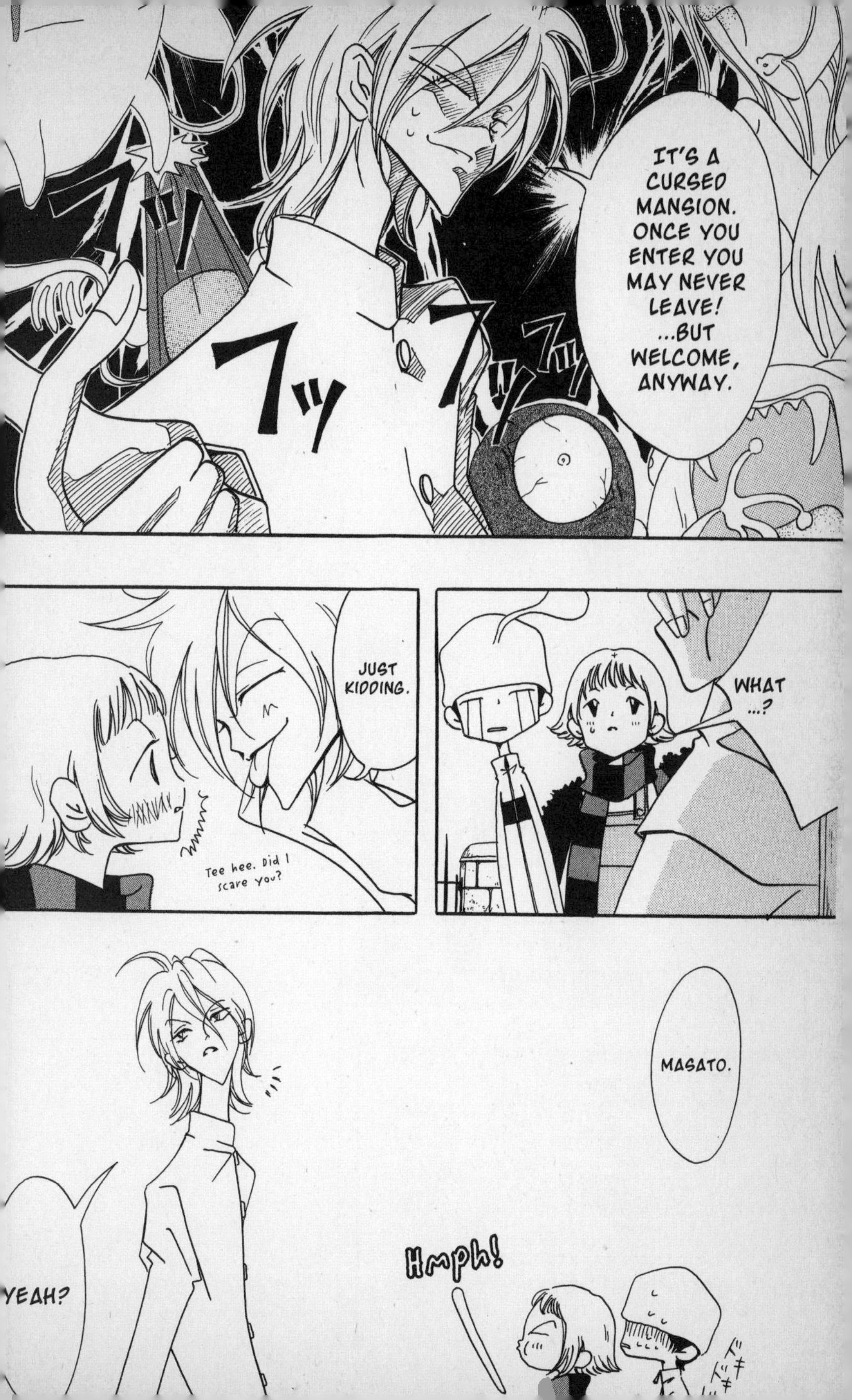
IT'S A CURSED MANSION. ONCE YOU ENTER YOU MAY NEVER LEAVE! ...BUT WELCOME, ANYWAY.
WHAT ...?
JUST KIDDING.
Tee hee. Did I scare you?
MASATO.
Hmph!
ドキドキ
YEAH?

I'M GOING UPSTAIRS TO READ.

HE SCARED ME WHEN HE LOOKED AT US...A LITTLE BIT.

HE LOOKS SCARY.

That girl is super cute.

IS HE YOUR BROTHER?

Aye, sir! Meow!

YEAH, HE DOES LOOK SCARY FROM THE OUTSIDE.

I can't wait to tell him that later!

SCARY? HA HA.

NOPE.

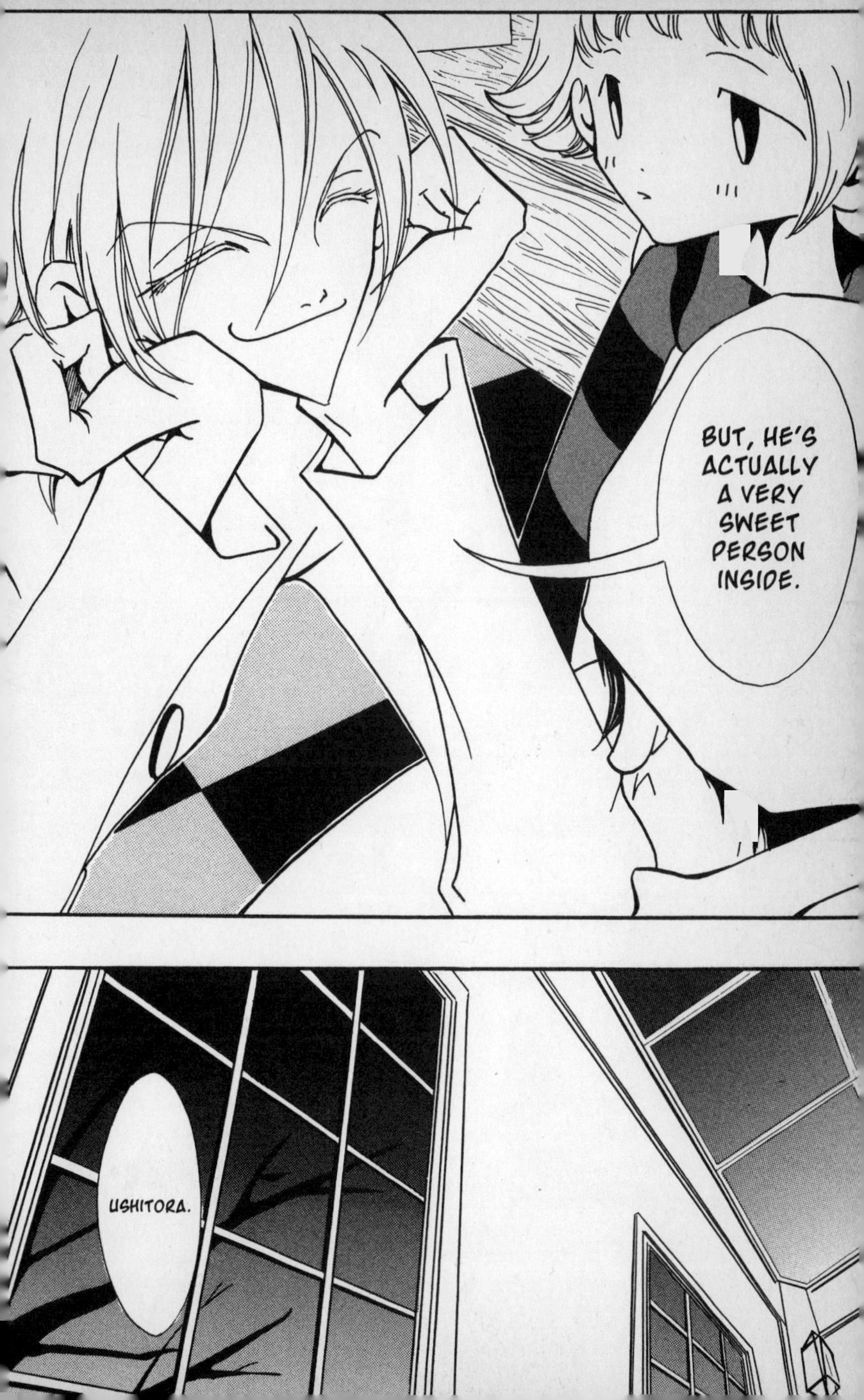
BUT, HE'S ACTUALLY A VERY SWEET PERSON INSIDE.
USHITORA.

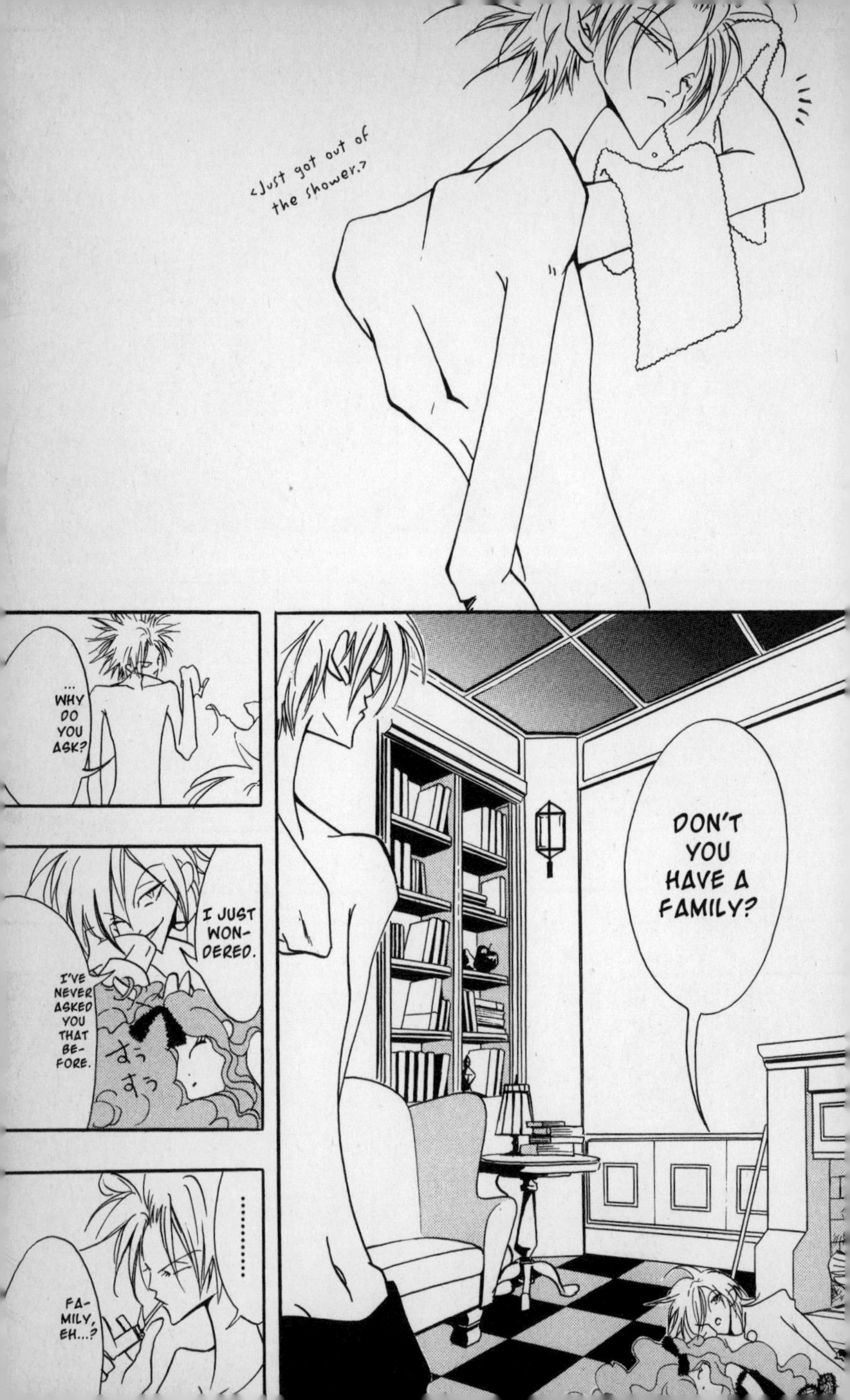
<Just got out of the shower.>
DON'T YOU HAVE A FAMILY?
...WHY DO YOU ASK?
I JUST WON-DERED.
I'VE NEVER ASKED YOU THAT BE-FORE.
すぅ すぅ
....
FA-MILY, EH...?

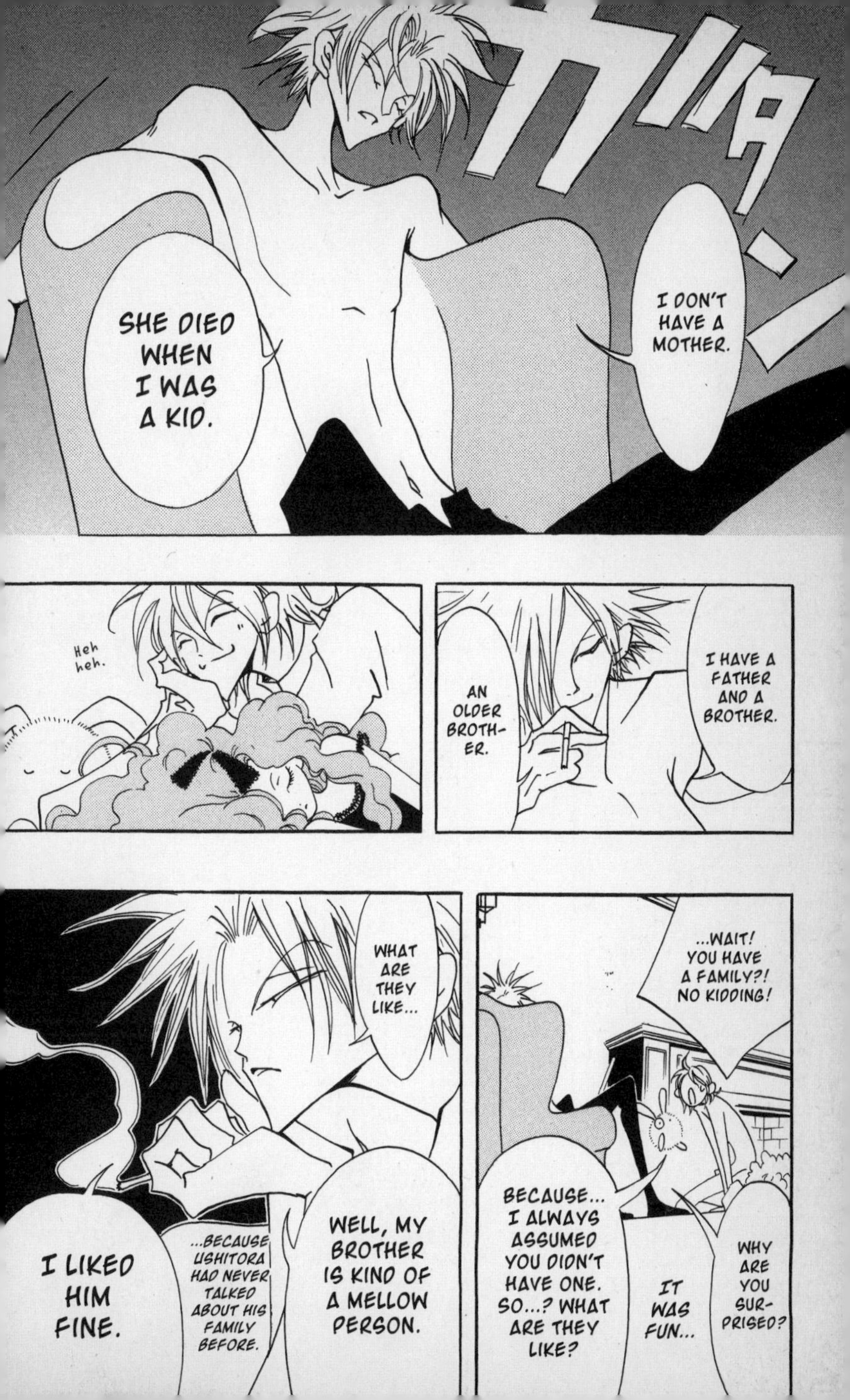
I DON'T HAVE A MOTHER.
SHE DIED WHEN I WAS A KID.
I HAVE A FATHER AND A BROTHER.
AN OLDER BROTH-ER.
Heh heh.
...WAIT! YOU HAVE A FAMILY?! NO KIDDING!
WHY ARE YOU SUR-PRISED?
IT WAS FUN...
BECAUSE... I ALWAYS ASSUMED YOU DIDN'T HAVE ONE. SO...? WHAT ARE THEY LIKE?
WHAT ARE THEY LIKE...
WELL, MY BROTHER IS KIND OF A MELLOW PERSON.
...BECAUSE USHITORA HAD NEVER TALKED ABOUT HIS FAMILY BEFORE.
I LIKED HIM FINE.

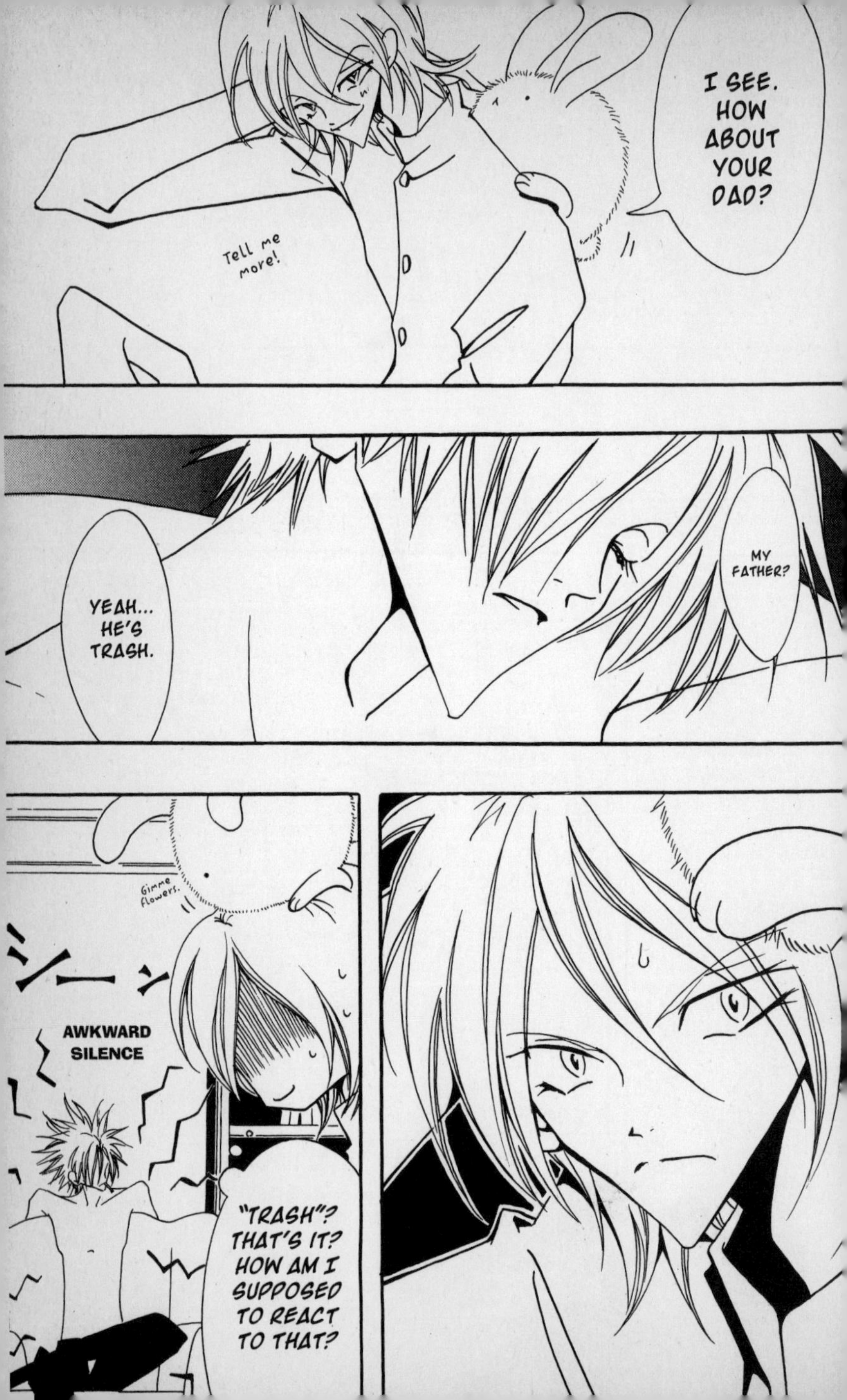
I SEE. HOW ABOUT YOUR DAD?
Tell me more!
MY FATHER?
YEAH... HE'S TRASH.
Gimme flowers.
AWKWARD SILENCE
"TRASH"? THAT'S IT? HOW AM I SUPPOSED TO REACT TO THAT?

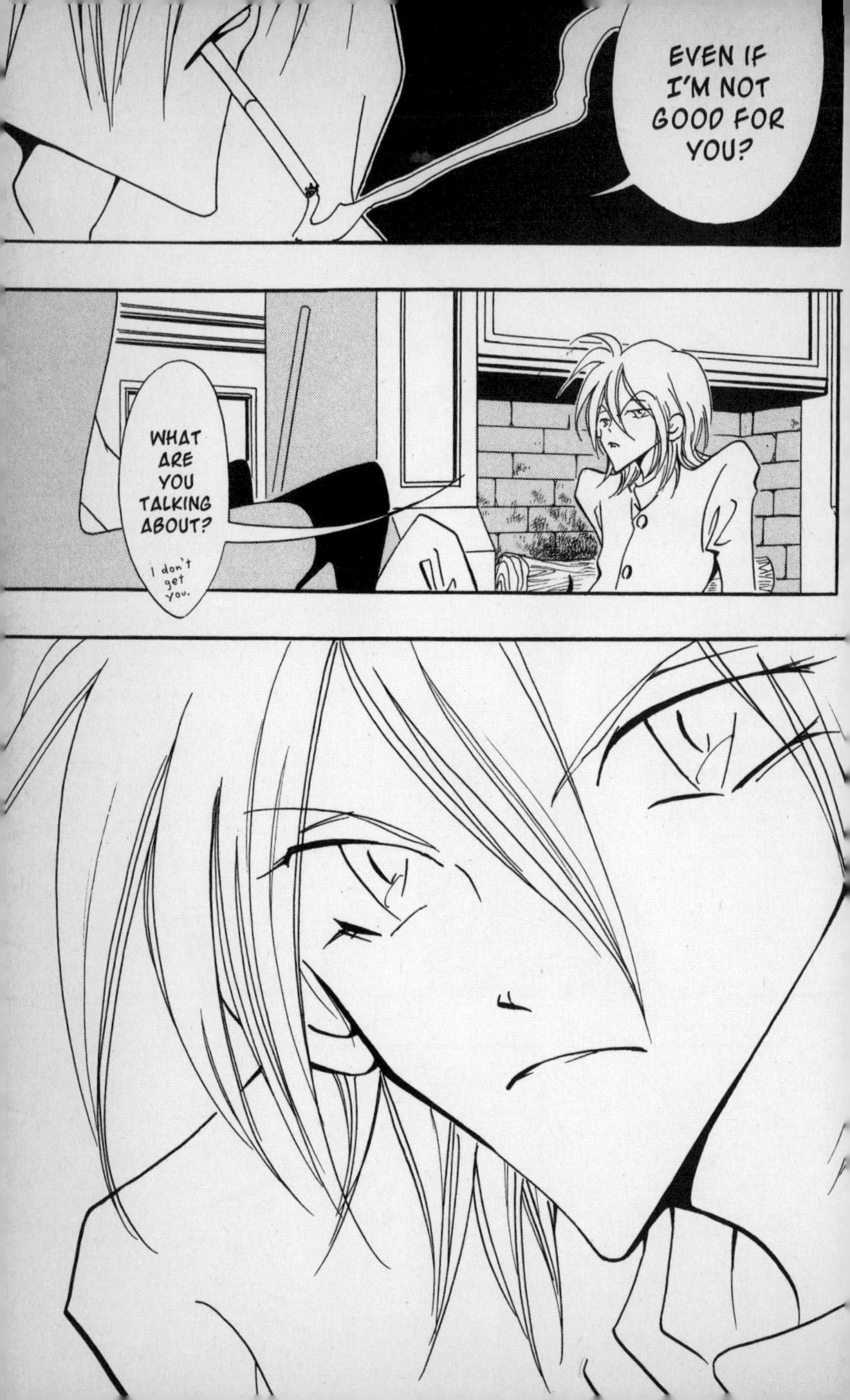
EVEN IF I'M NOT GOOD FOR YOU?
WHAT ARE YOU TALKING ABOUT?
I don't get you.

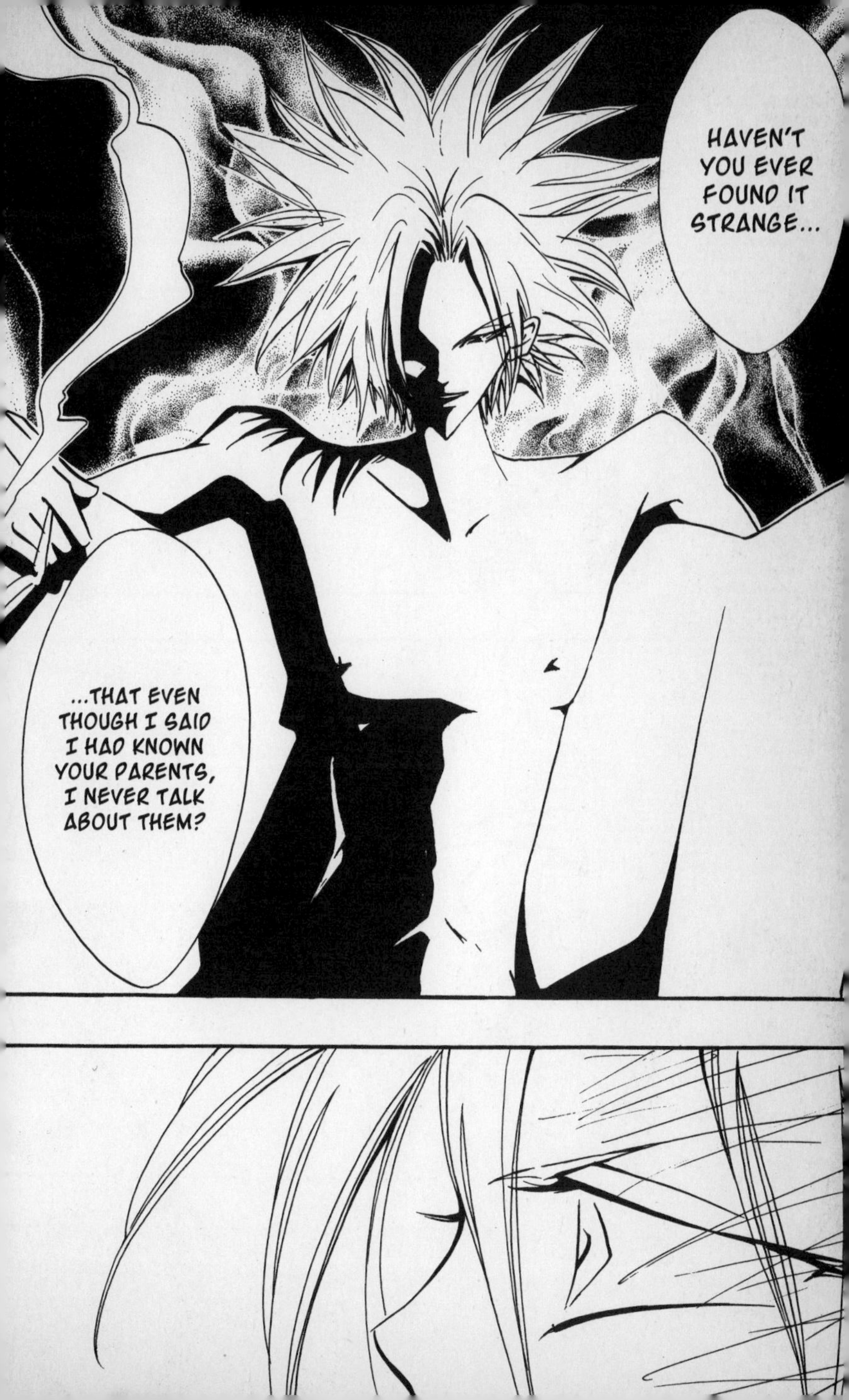
HAVEN'T YOU EVER FOUND IT STRANGE...
...THAT EVEN THOUGH I SAID I HAD KNOWN YOUR PARENTS, I NEVER TALK ABOUT THEM?

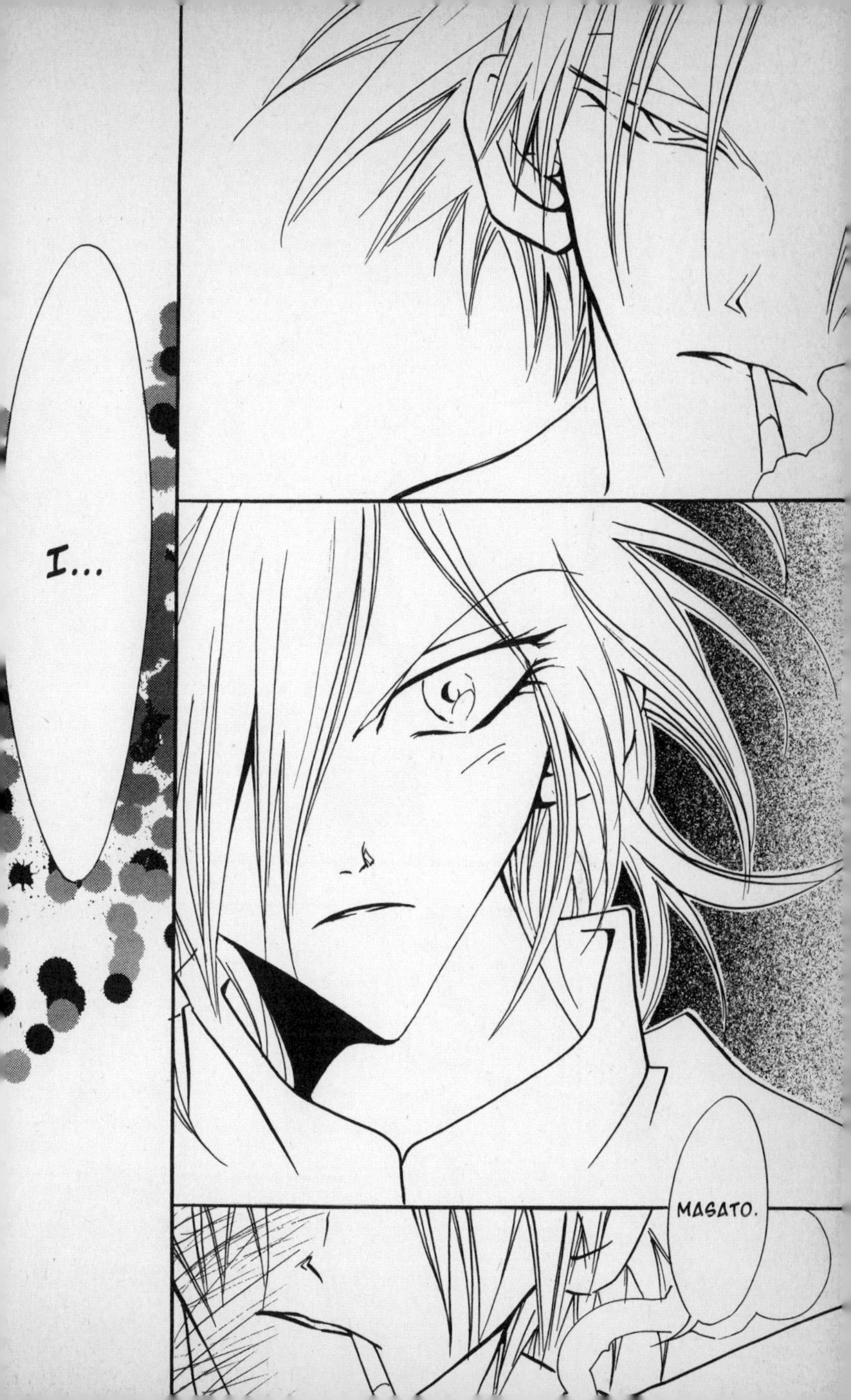
MASATO.
I...

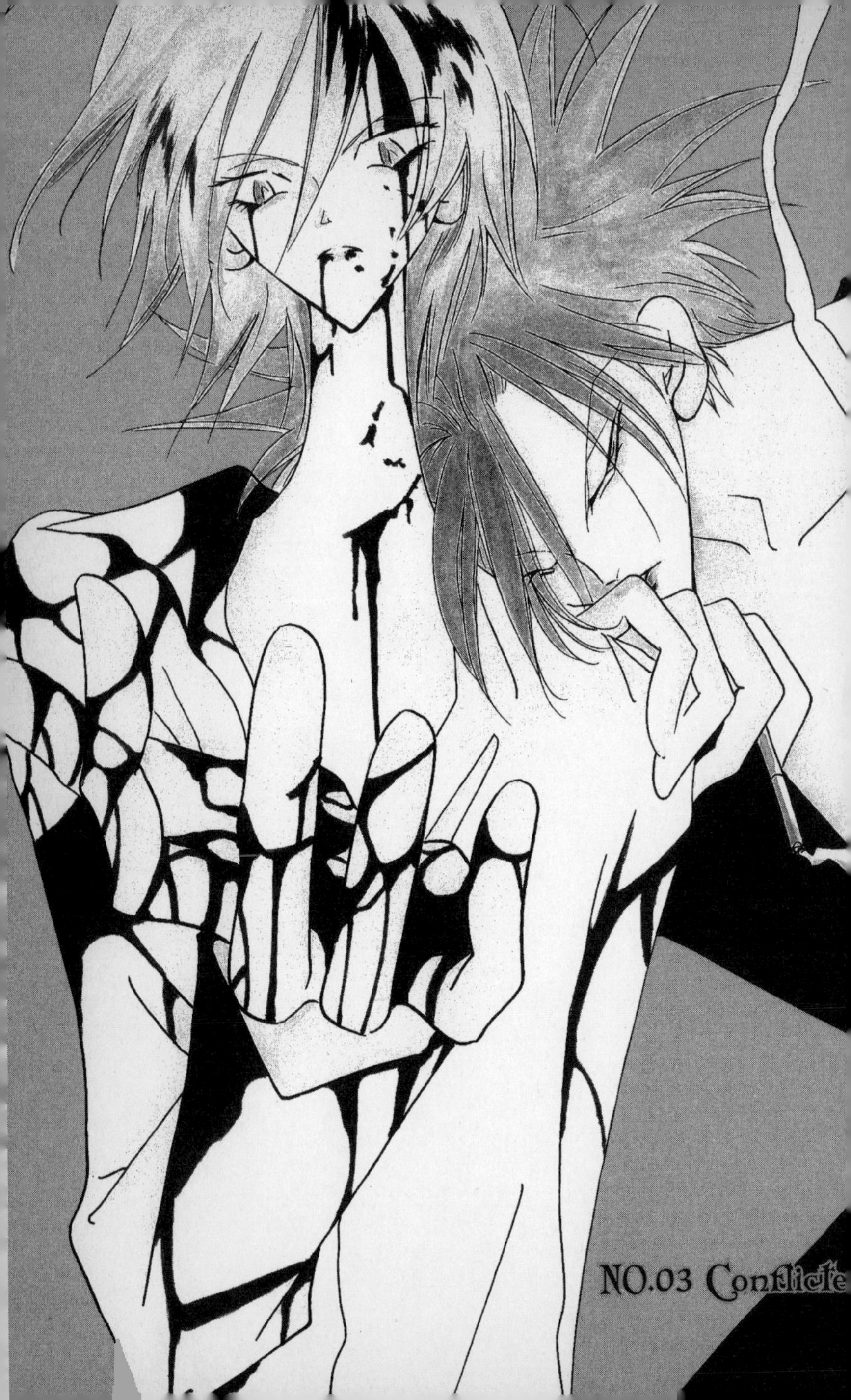
NO.03 Conflicte

NO.03

Conflicted

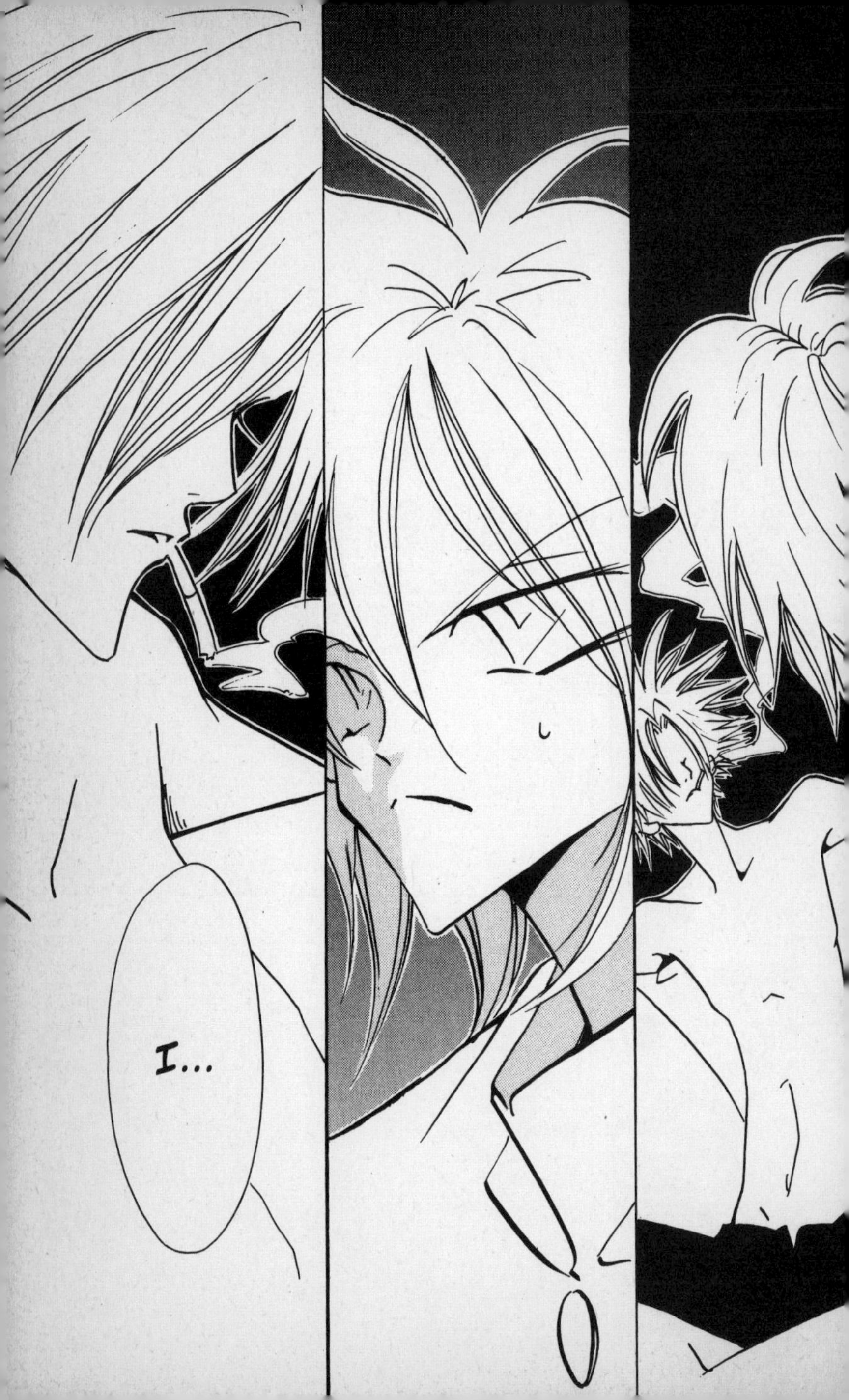
I...

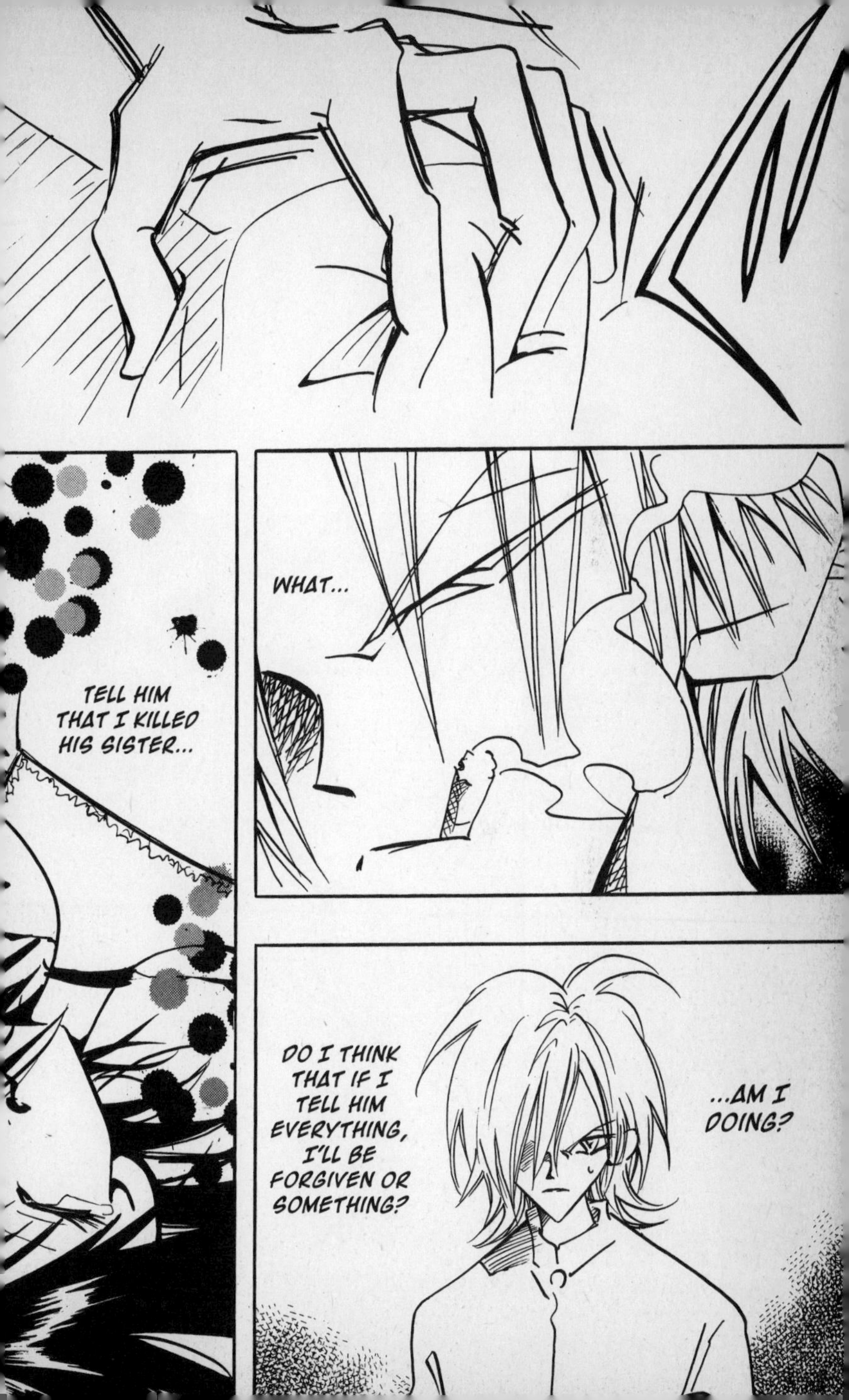
WHAT...
...AM I DOING?
DO I THINK THAT IF I TELL HIM EVERYTHING, I'LL BE FORGIVEN OR SOMETHING?
TELL HIM THAT I KILLED HIS SISTER...

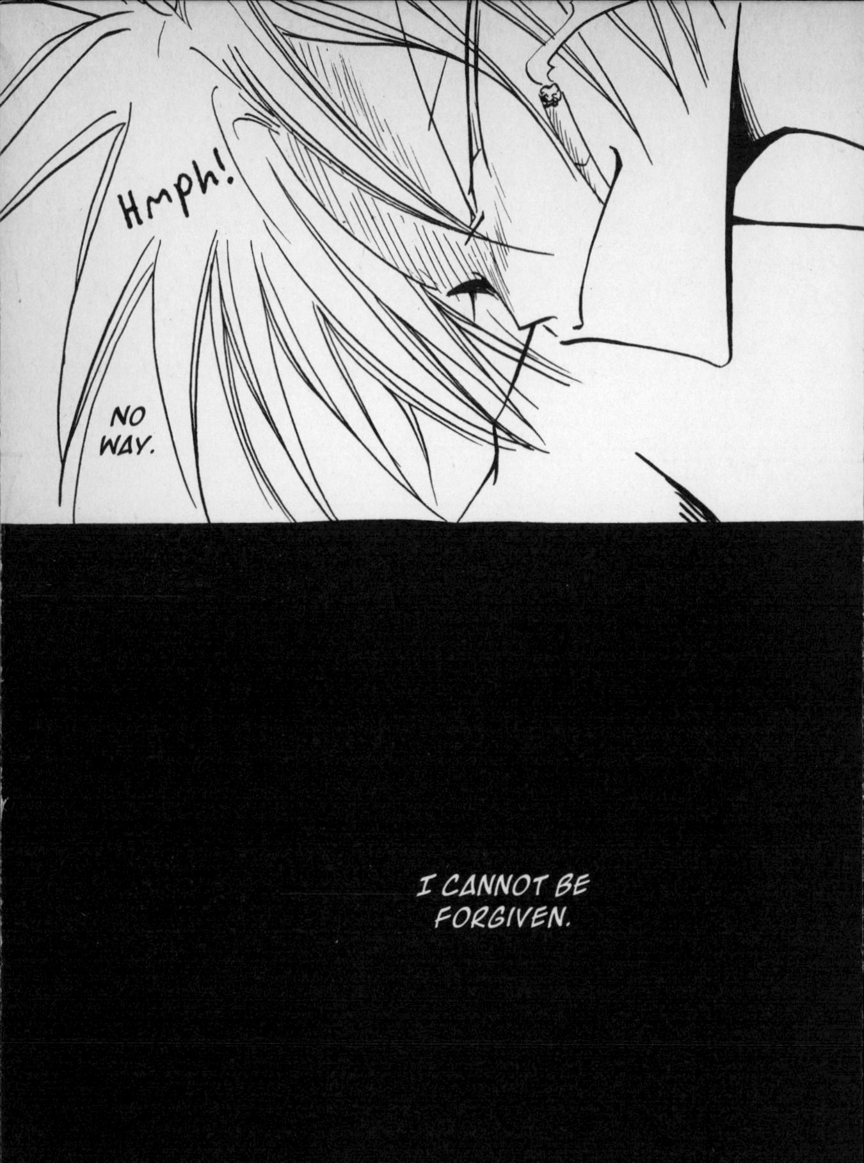
Hmph!
NO WAY.
I CANNOT BE FORGIVEN.

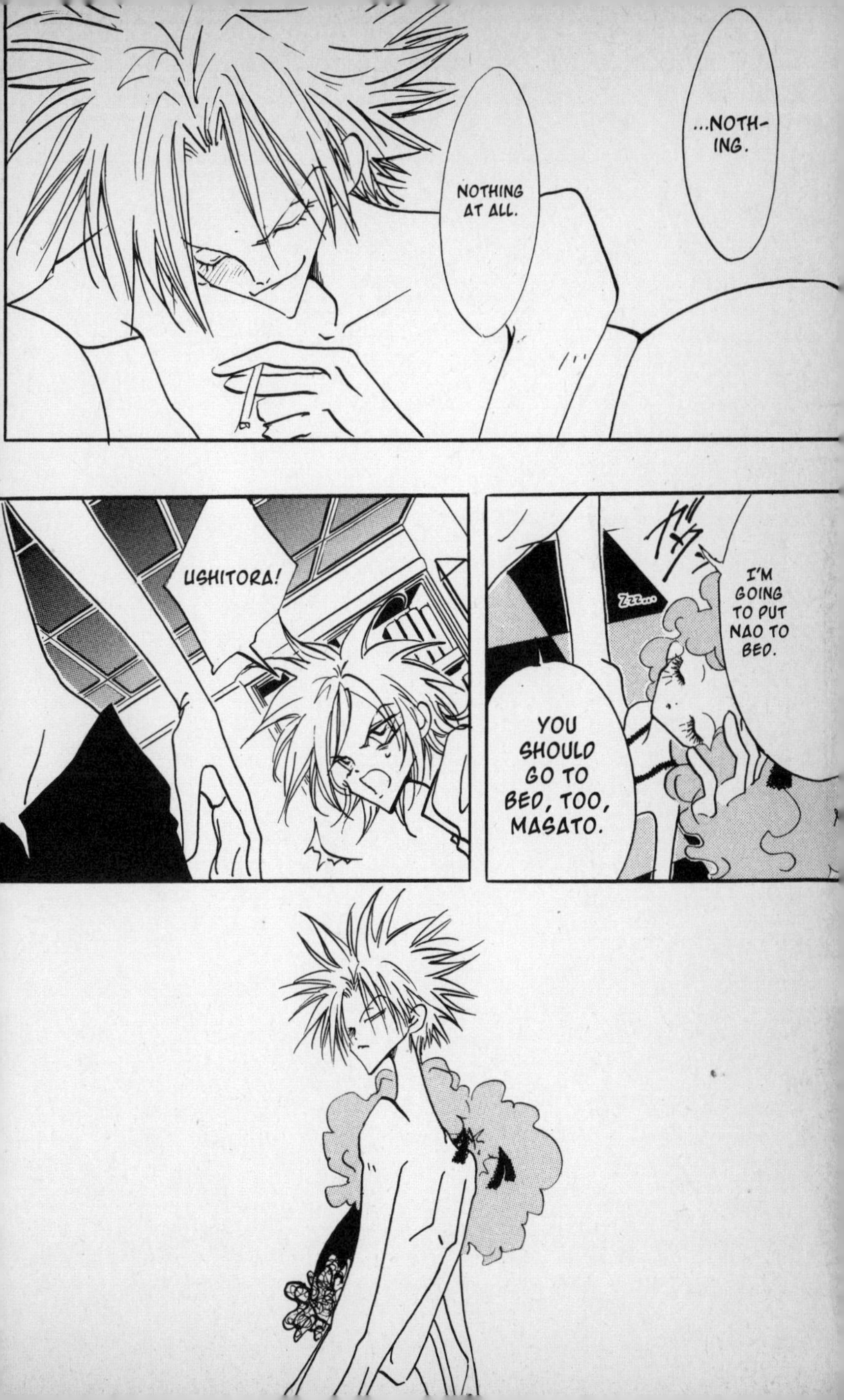
...NOTH-ING.
NOTHING AT ALL.
Zzz...
I'M GOING TO PUT NAO TO BED.
YOU SHOULD GO TO BED, TOO, MASATO.
USHITORA!

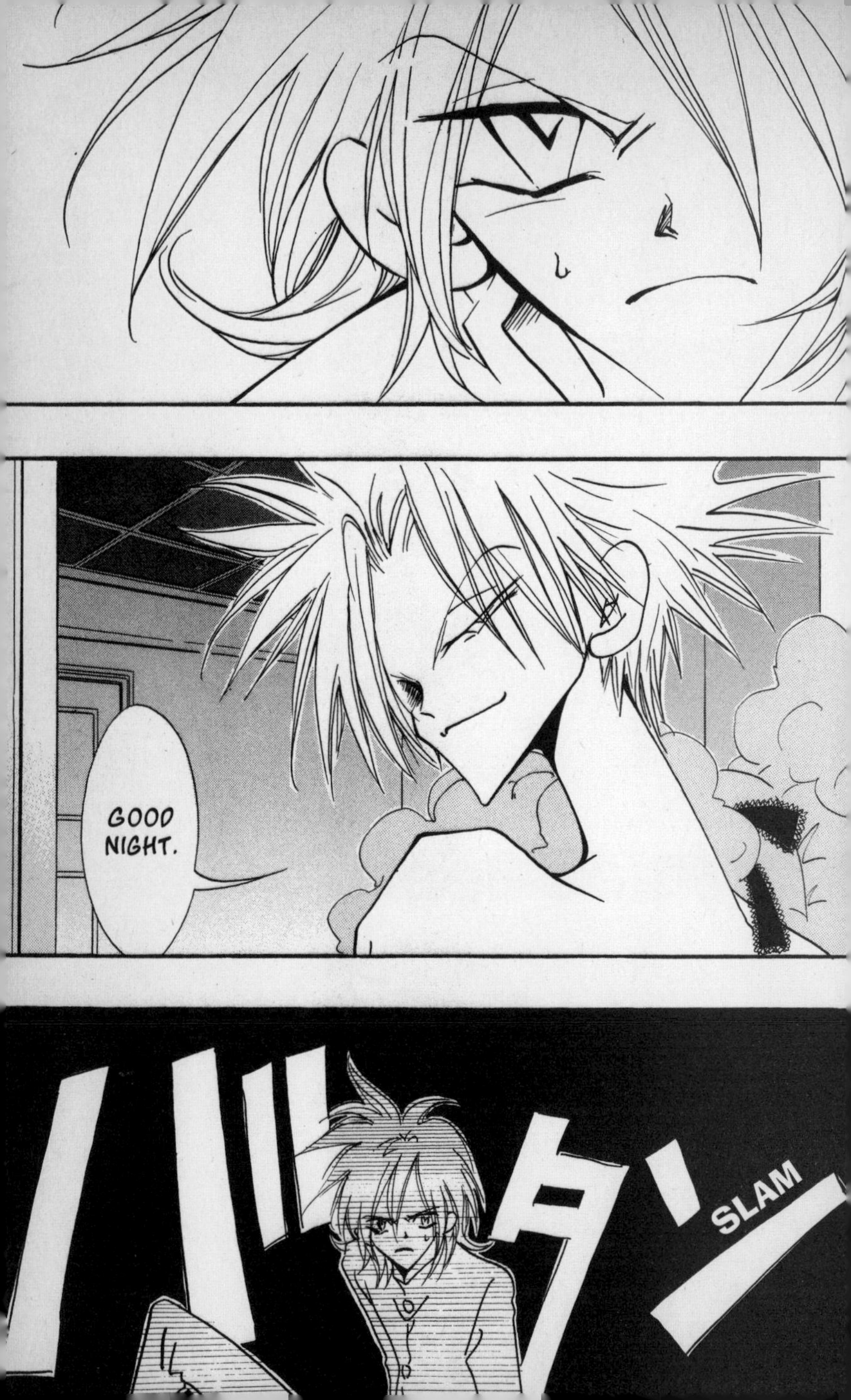
GOOD NIGHT.
SLAM

SIS?

ARE YOU ASLEEP?

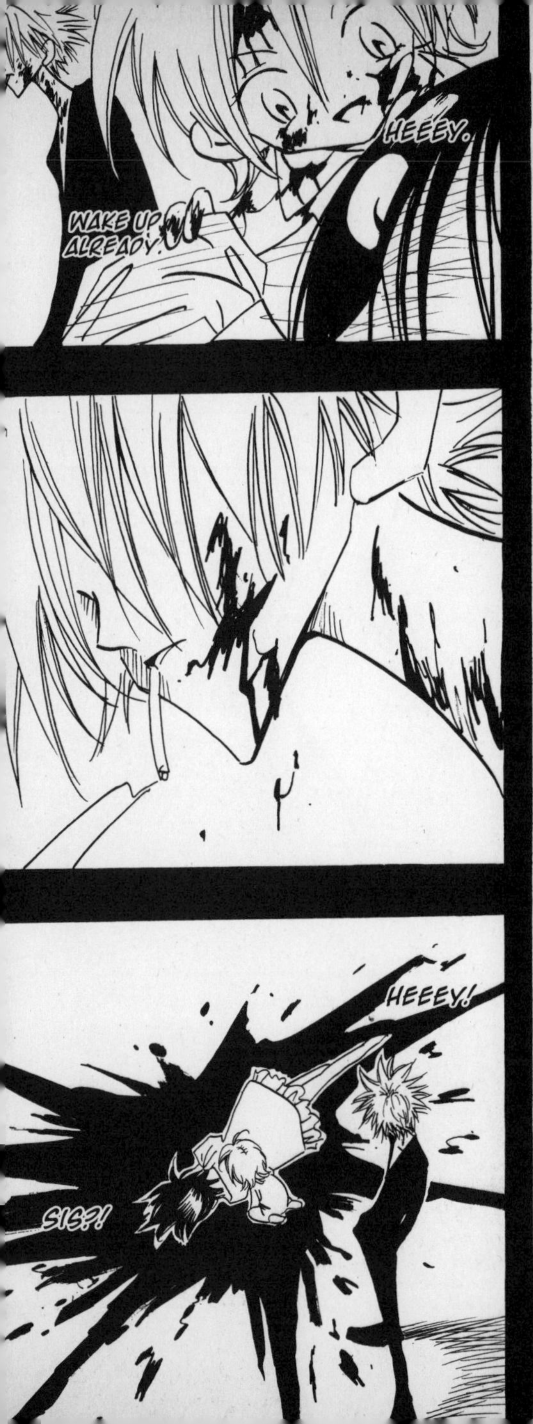
HEEEY.
WAKE UP ALREADY.
HEEEY!
SIS?!

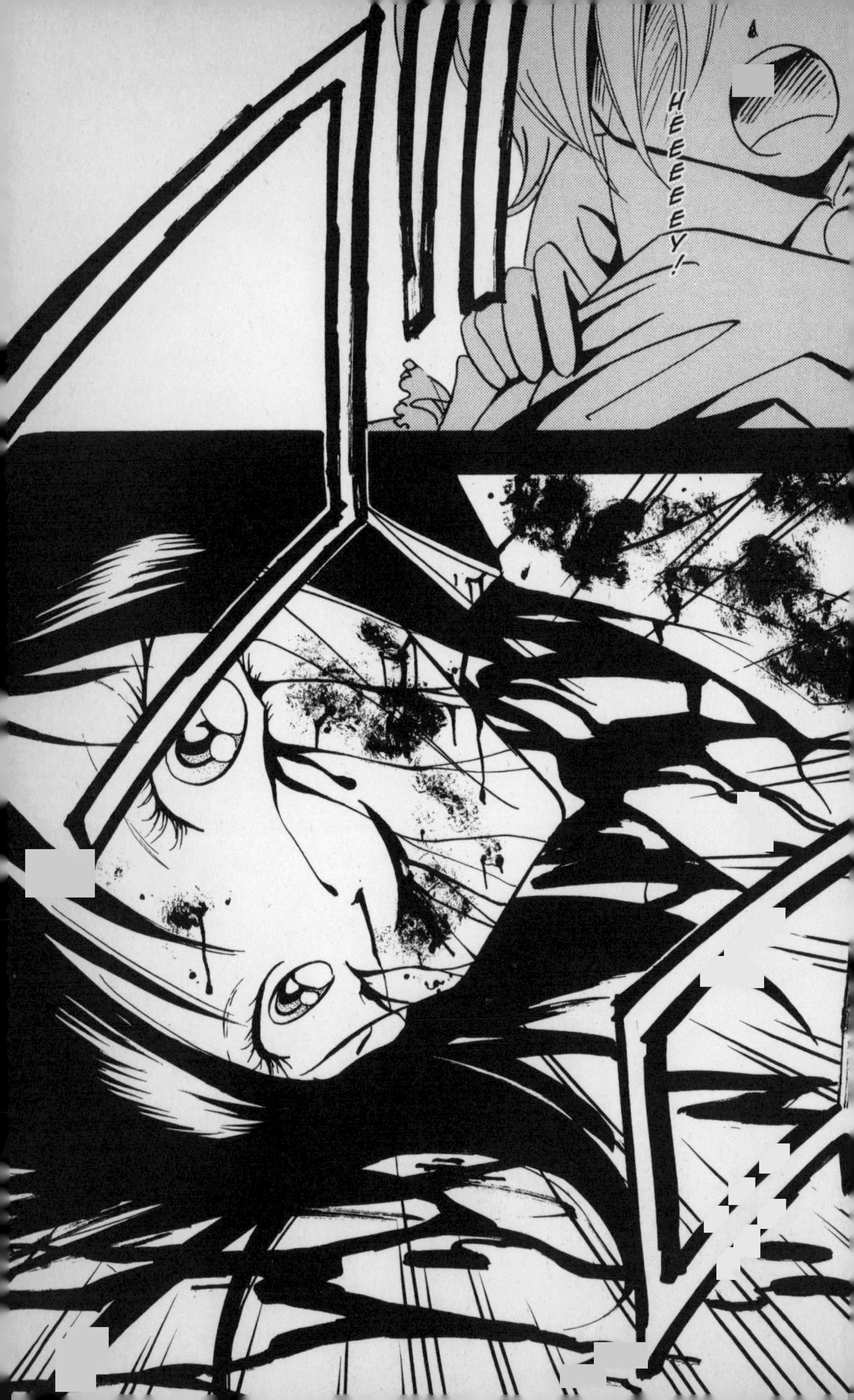
HEEEEEY!

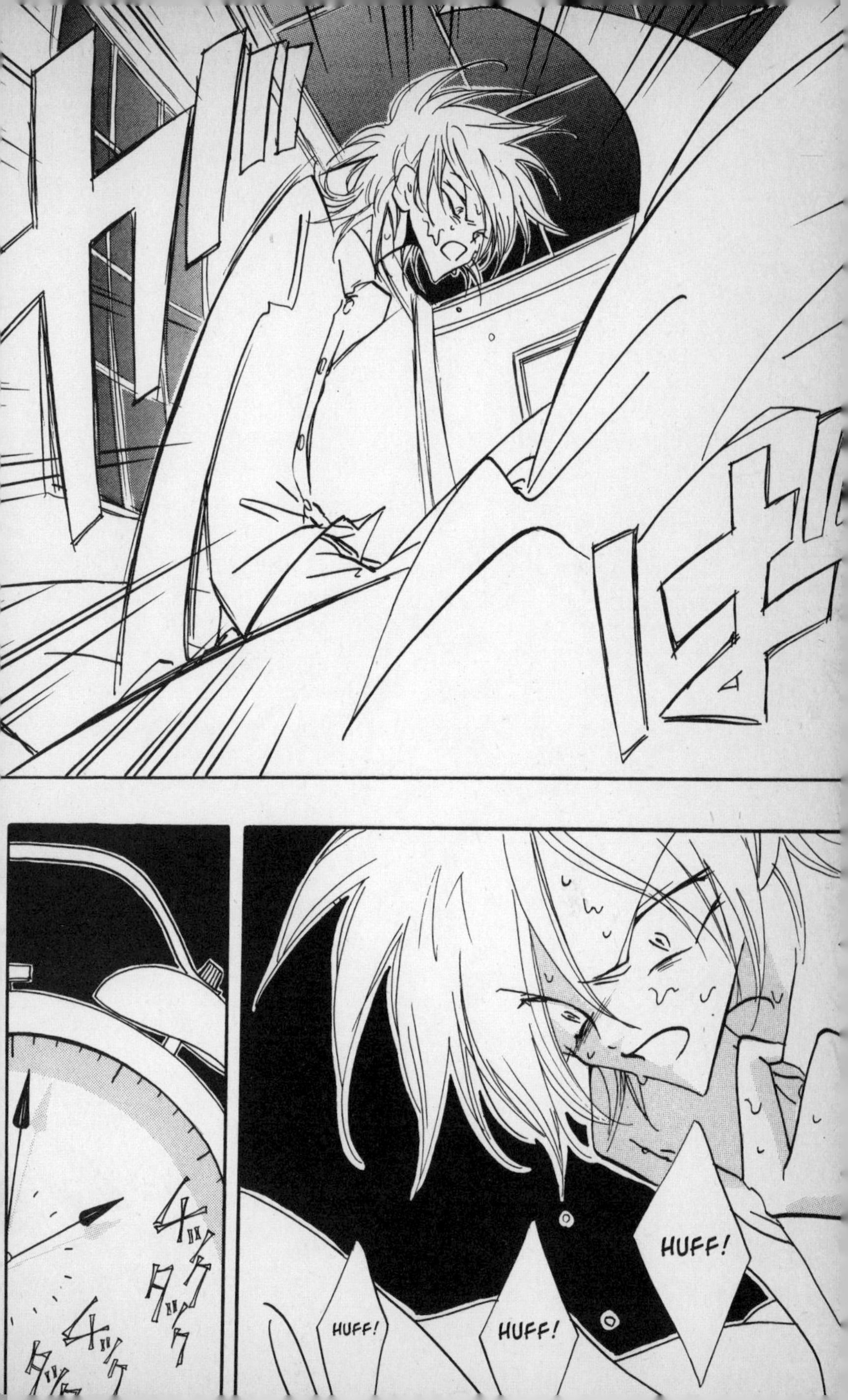
HUFF!
HUFF!
HUFF!

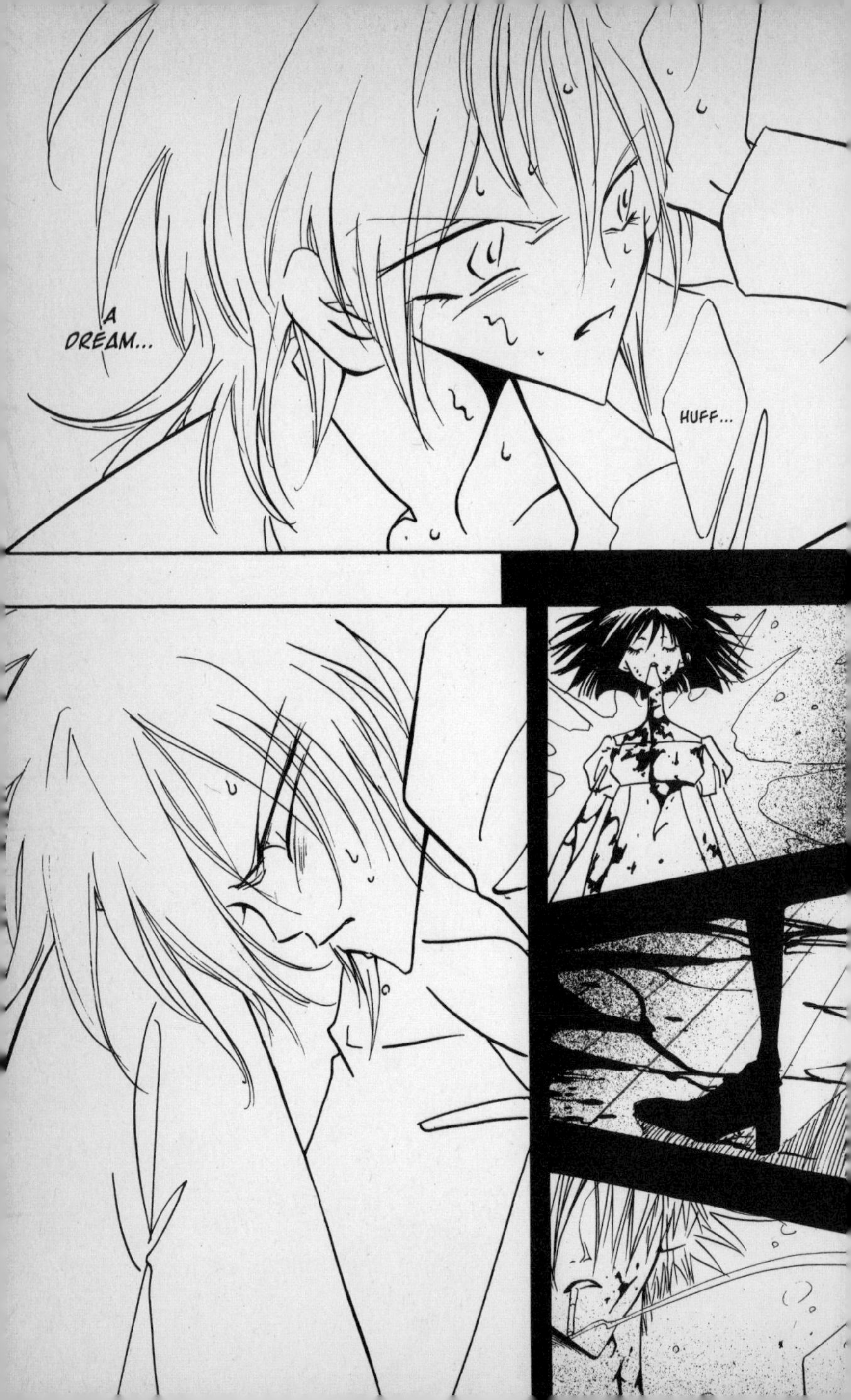
HUFF...
A DREAM...

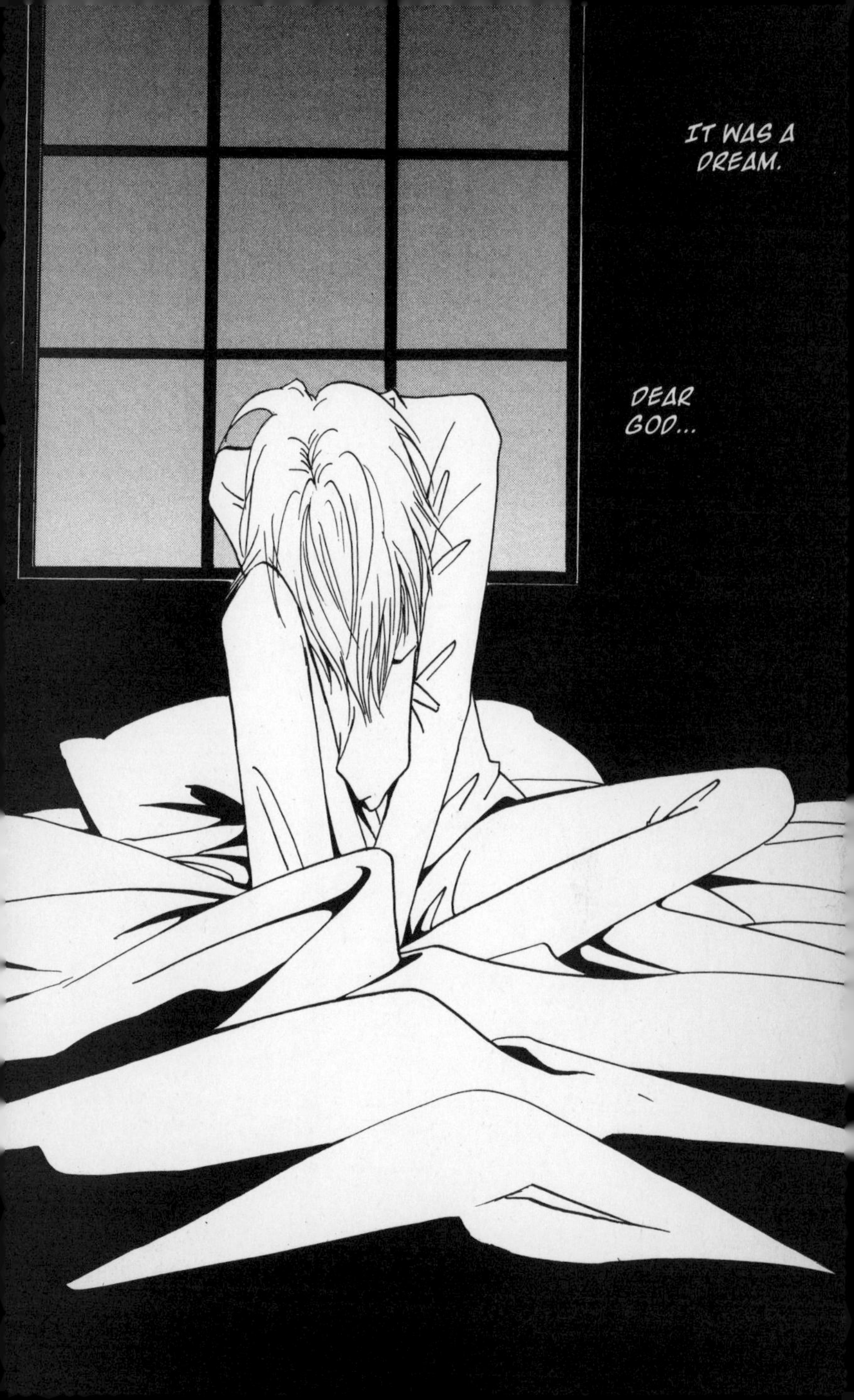
IT WAS A DREAM.
DEAR GOD...

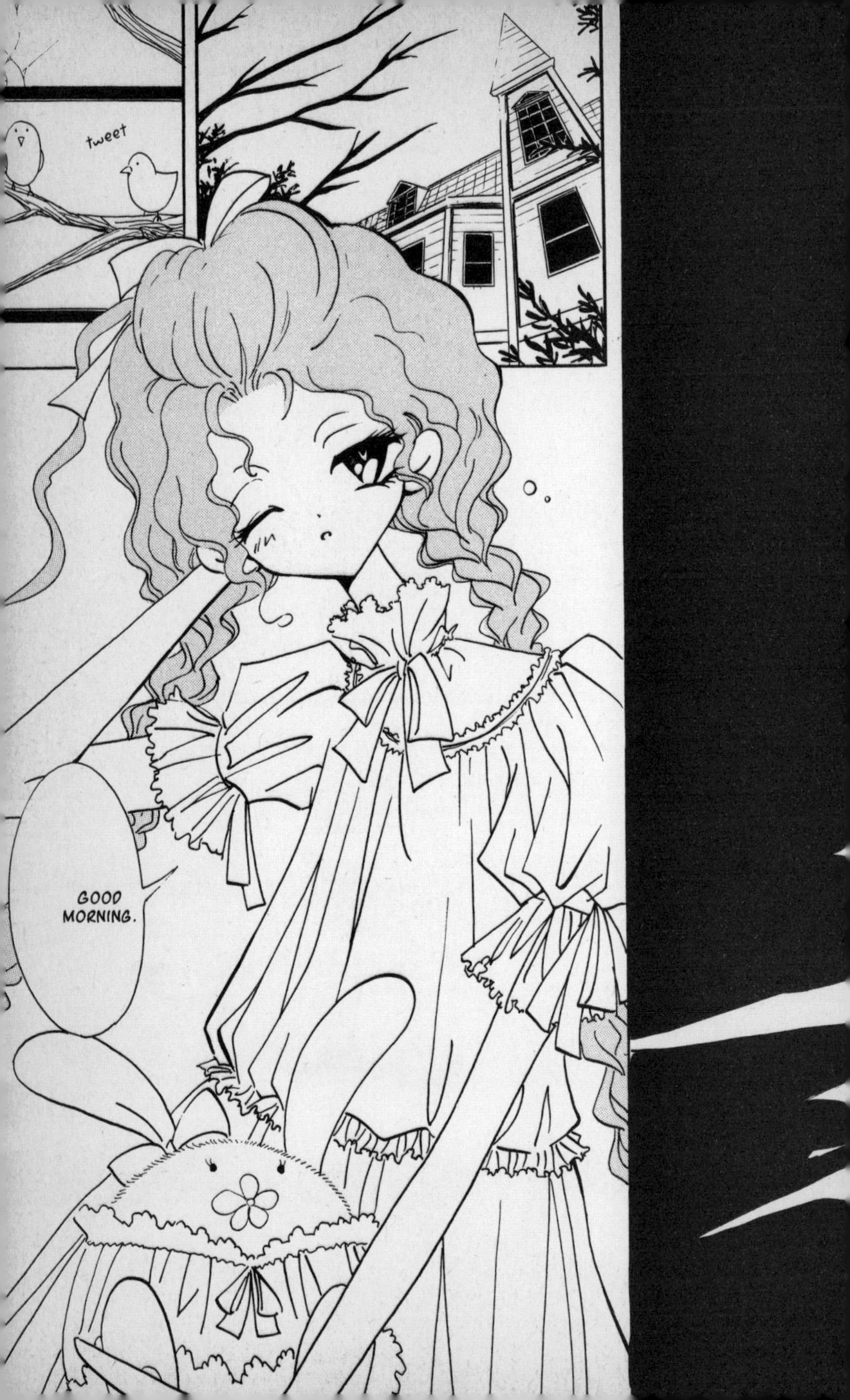
tweet
GOOD MORNING.

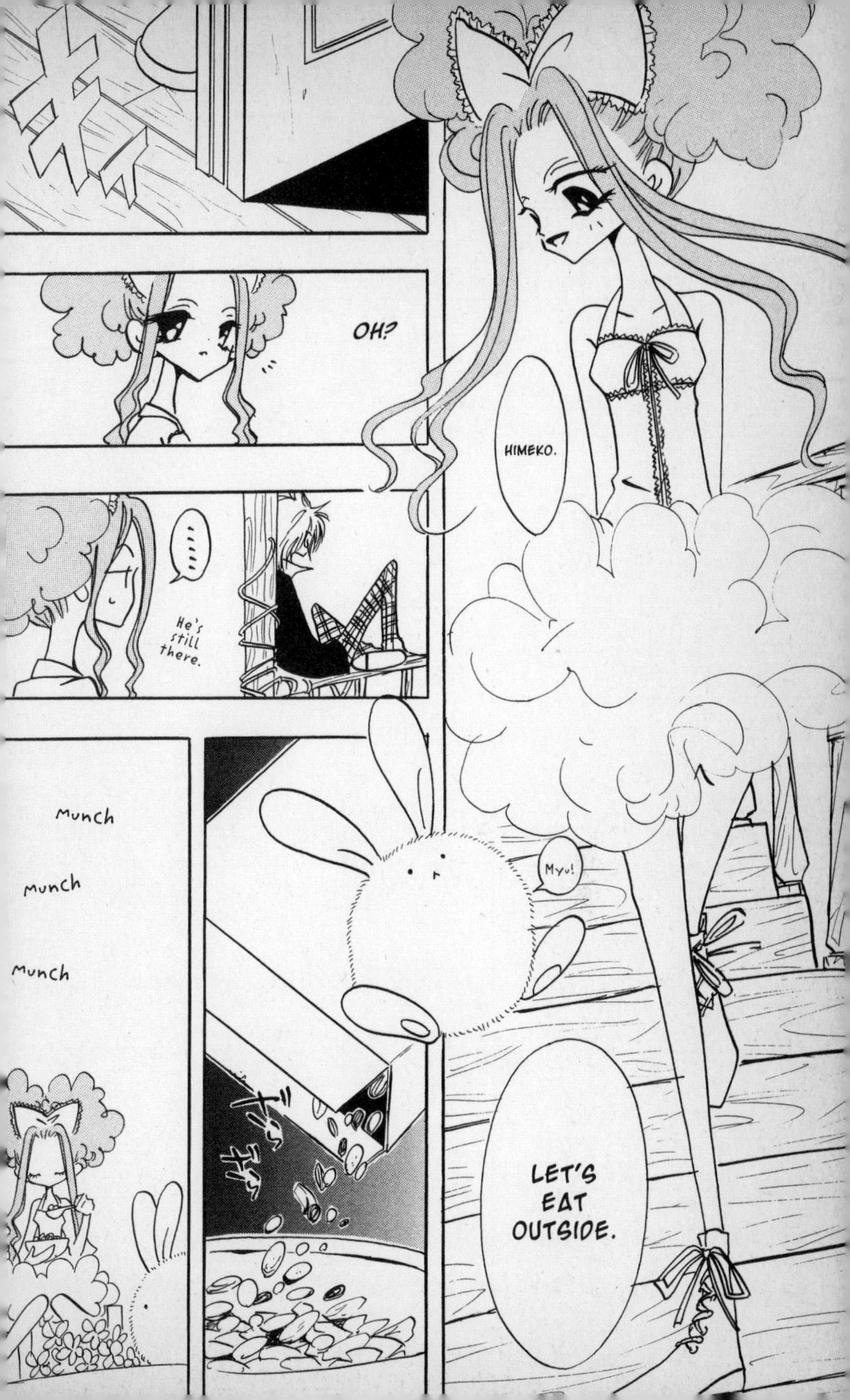
HIMEKO.
Myu!
LET'S EAT OUTSIDE.
OH?
......
He's still there.
Munch
Munch
Munch

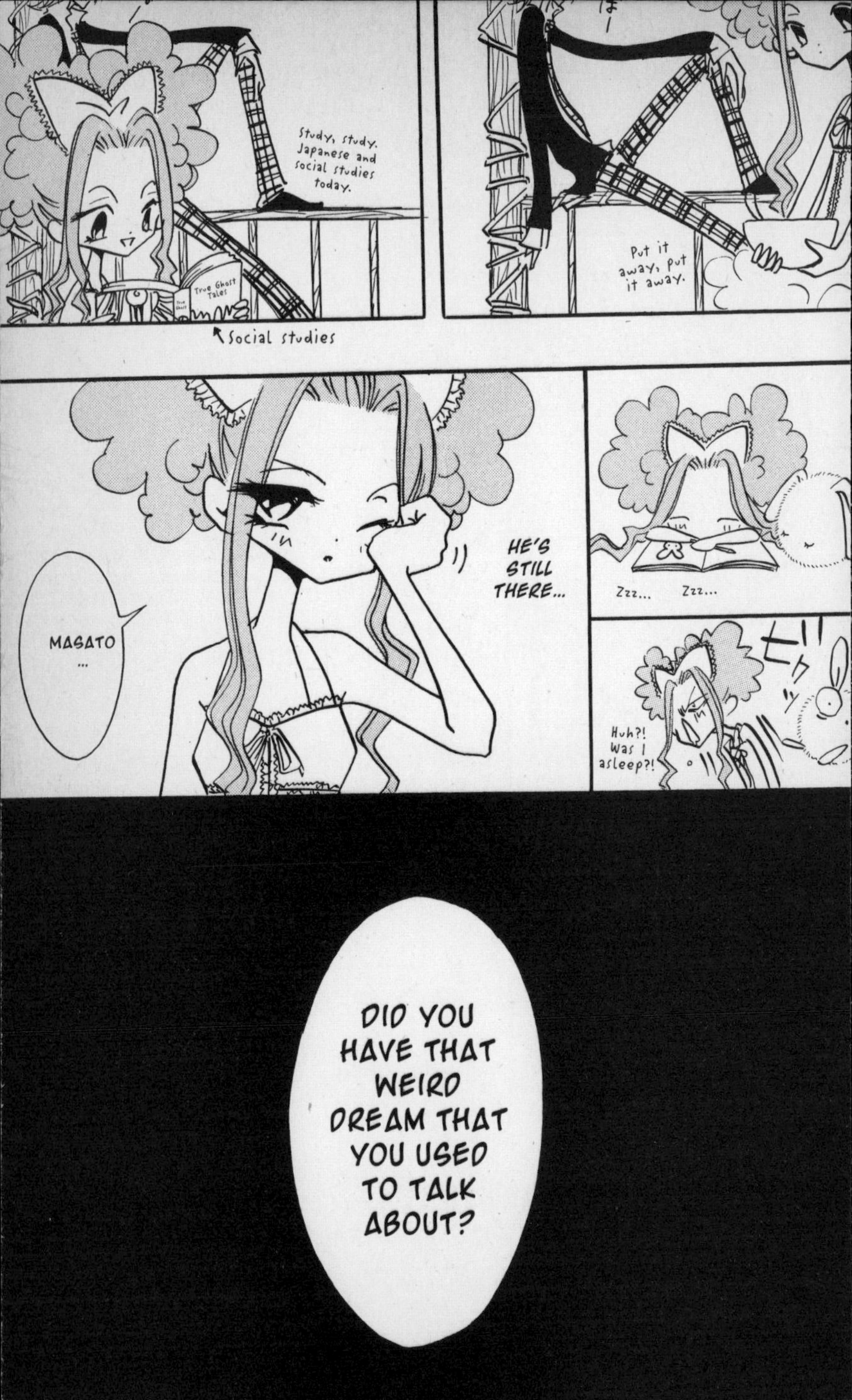
Put it away, put it away.
Study, study. Japanese and social studies today.
True Ghost Tales
↖Social studies
Zzz... Zzz...
ビクッ
Huh?! Was I asleep?!
HE'S STILL THERE...
MASATO ...
DID YOU HAVE THAT WEIRD DREAM THAT YOU USED TO TALK ABOUT?

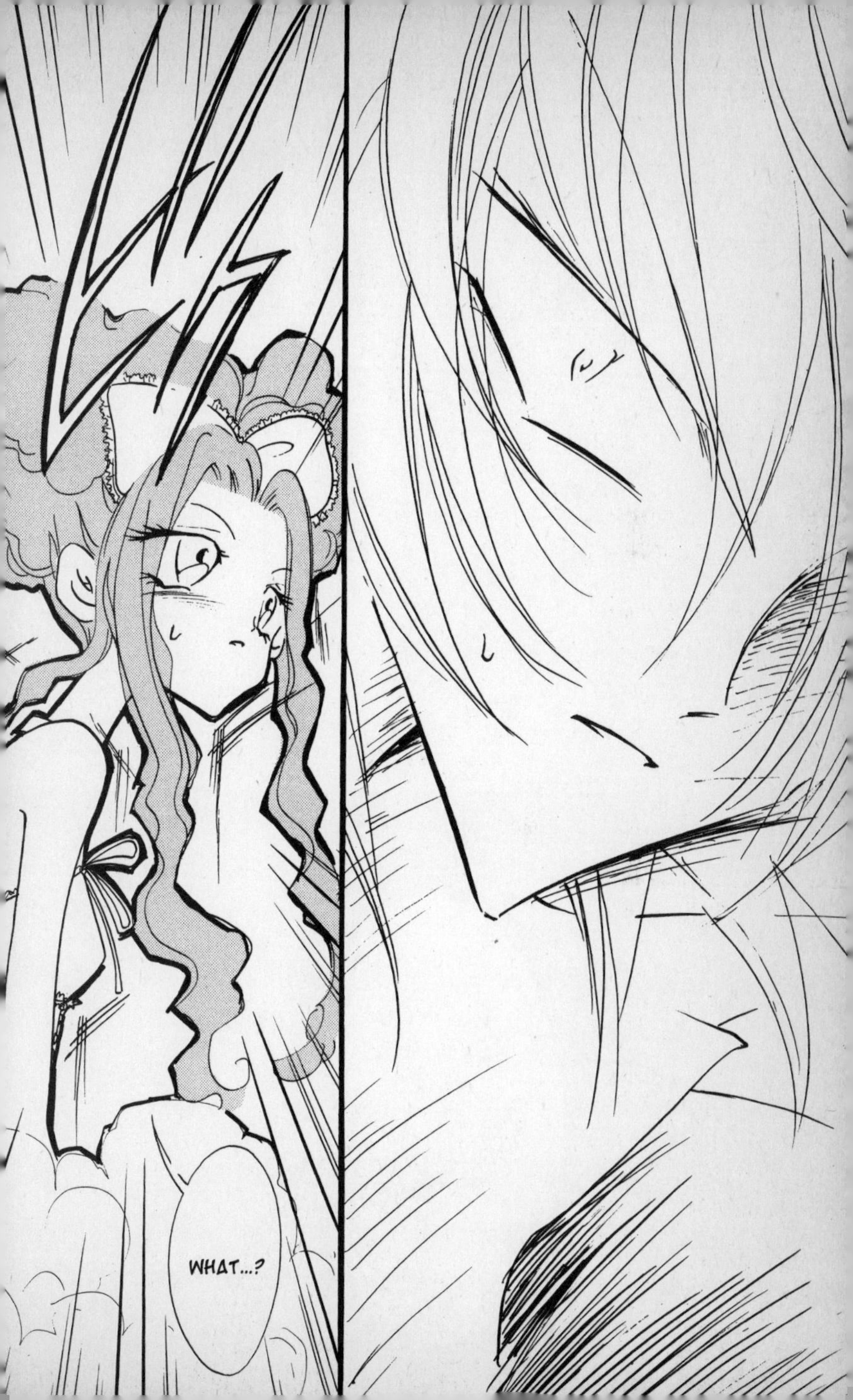
WHAT...?

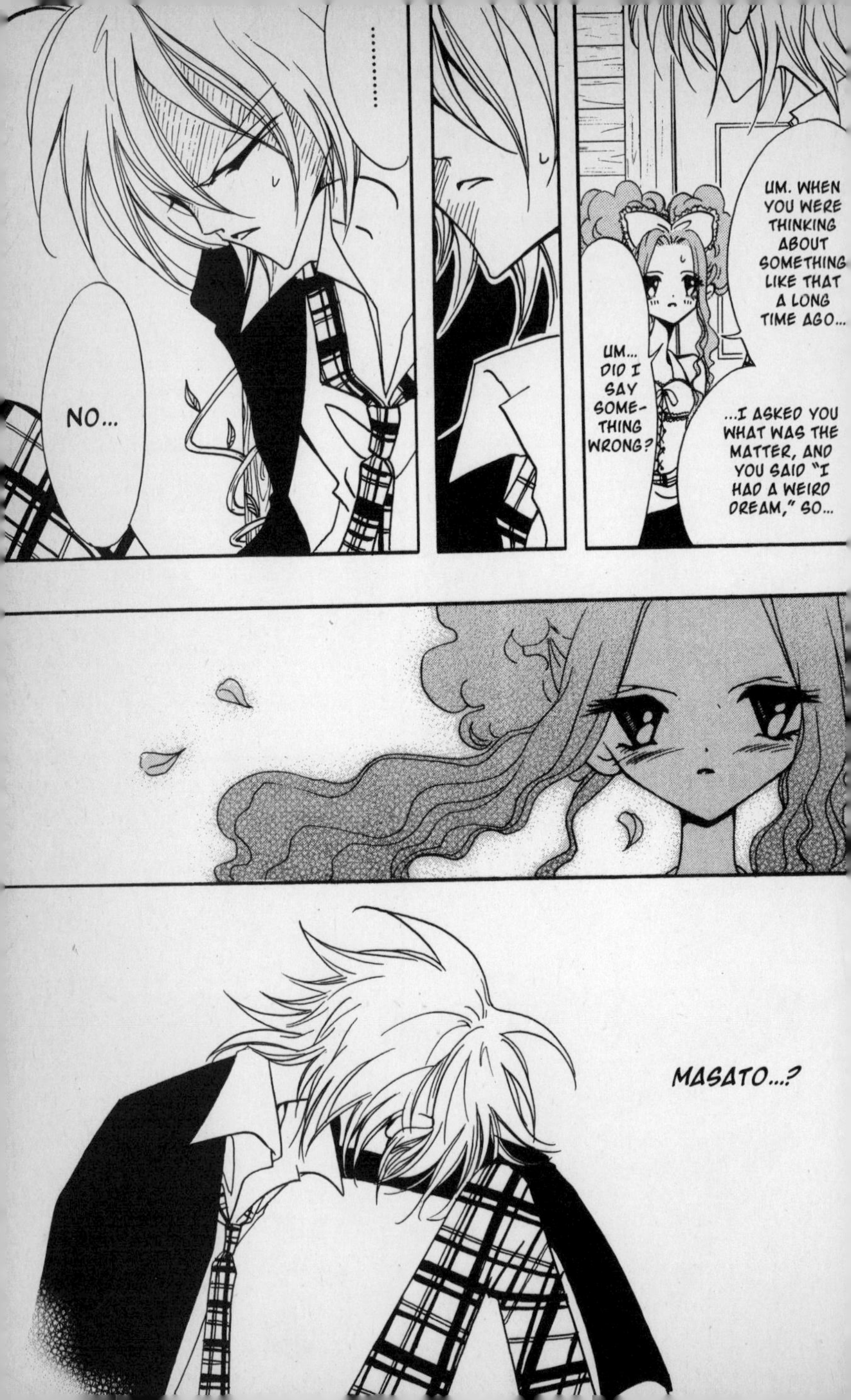
UM. WHEN YOU WERE THINKING ABOUT SOMETHING LIKE THAT A LONG TIME AGO...
...I ASKED YOU WHAT WAS THE MATTER, AND YOU SAID "I HAD A WEIRD DREAM," SO...
UM... DID I SAY SOME-THING WRONG?
......
NO...
MASATO...?

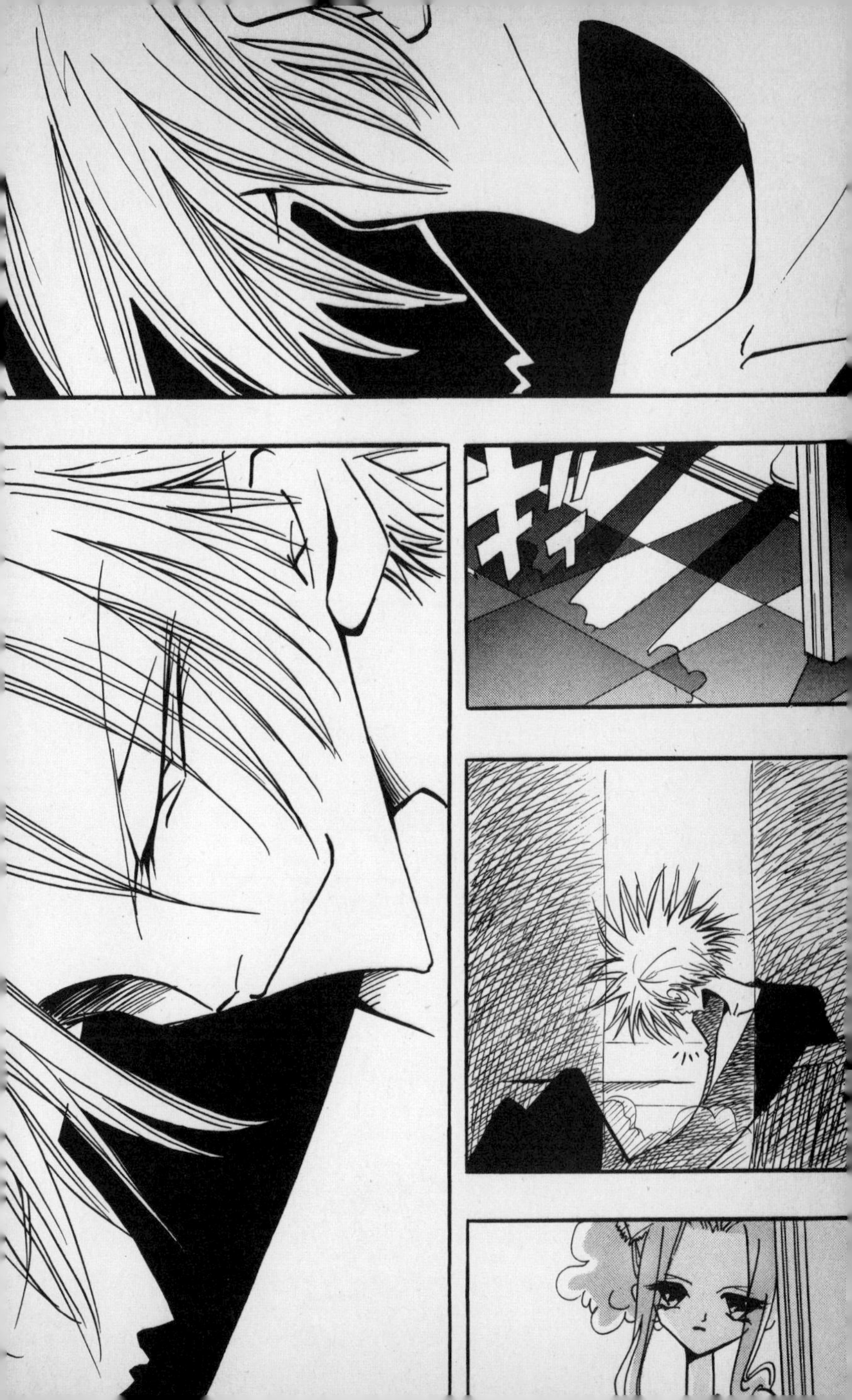
ギィ

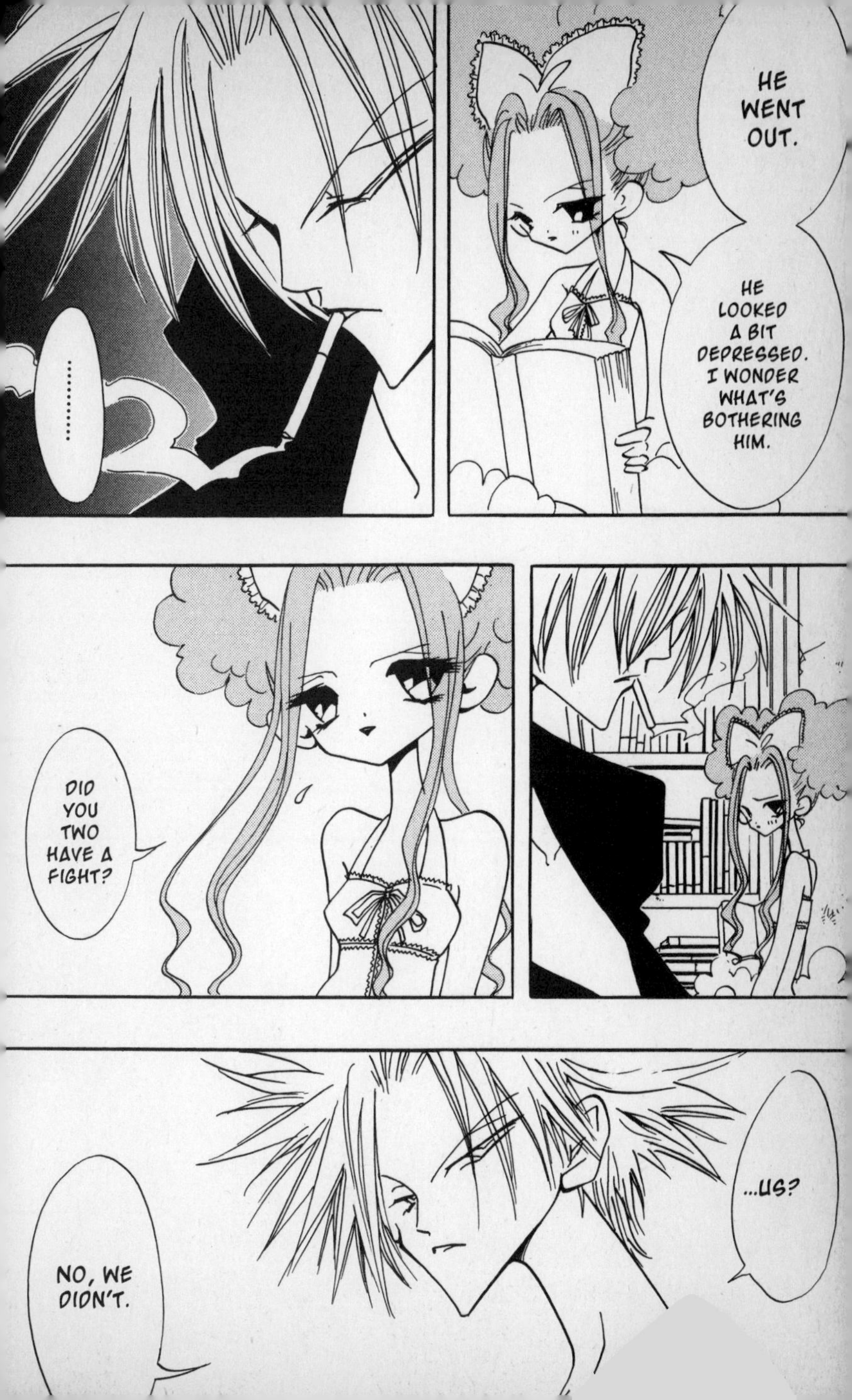
HE WENT OUT.
HE LOOKED A BIT DEPRESSED. I WONDER WHAT'S BOTHERING HIM.
....
DID YOU TWO HAVE A FIGHT?
...US?
NO, WE DIDN'T.

THAT'S GOOD, USHITORA! YOU'RE MUCH STRONGER, SO DON'T BULLY MASATO, GOT IT?

UNDERSTAND, USHITORA-KUN?

Heh Heh Heh.

...UH HUH.

I UNDERSTAND, MA'AM.

Heh

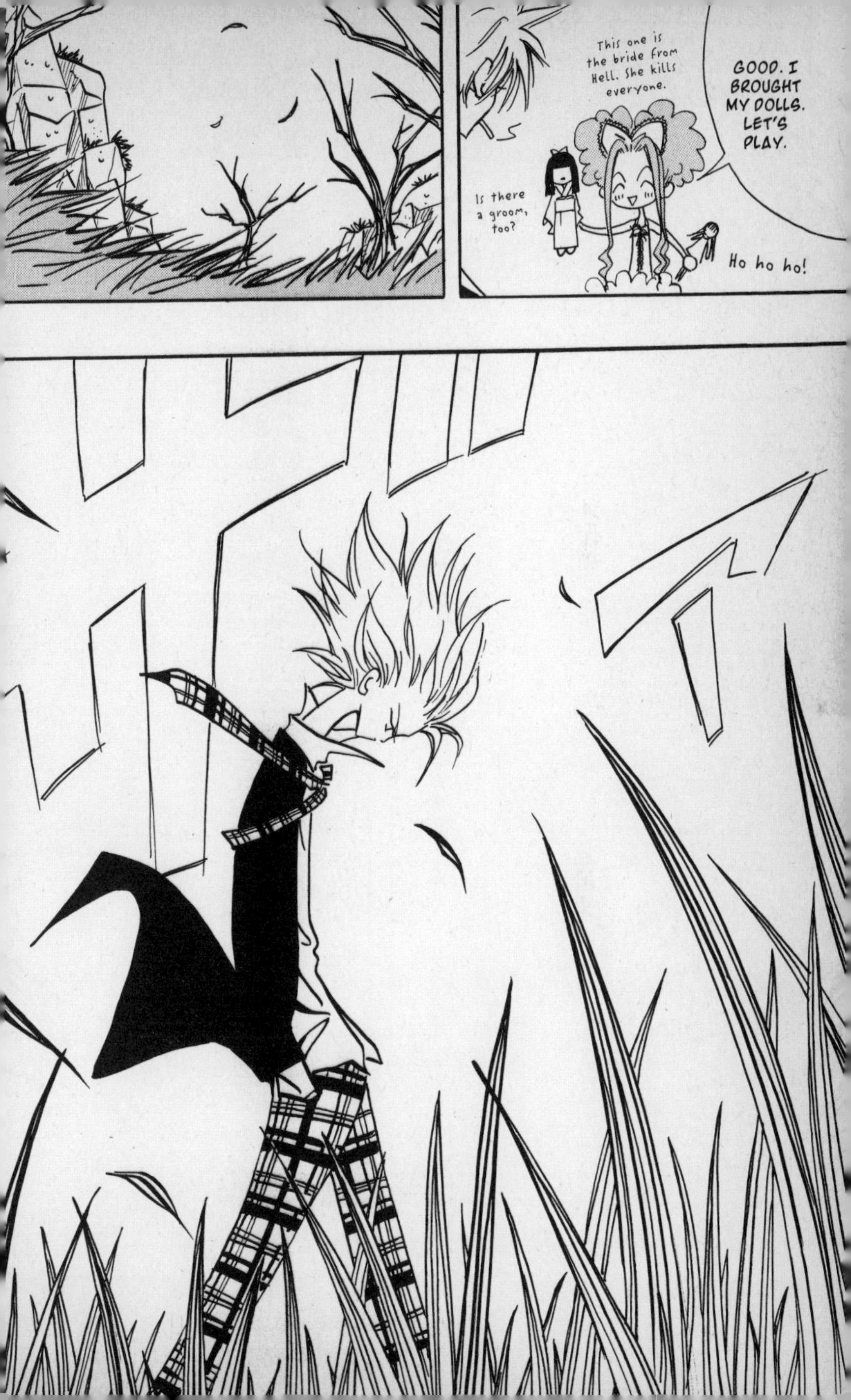
GOOD. I BROUGHT MY DOLLS. LET'S PLAY.
Ho ho ho!
This one is the bride from Hell. She kills everyone.
Is there a groom, too?

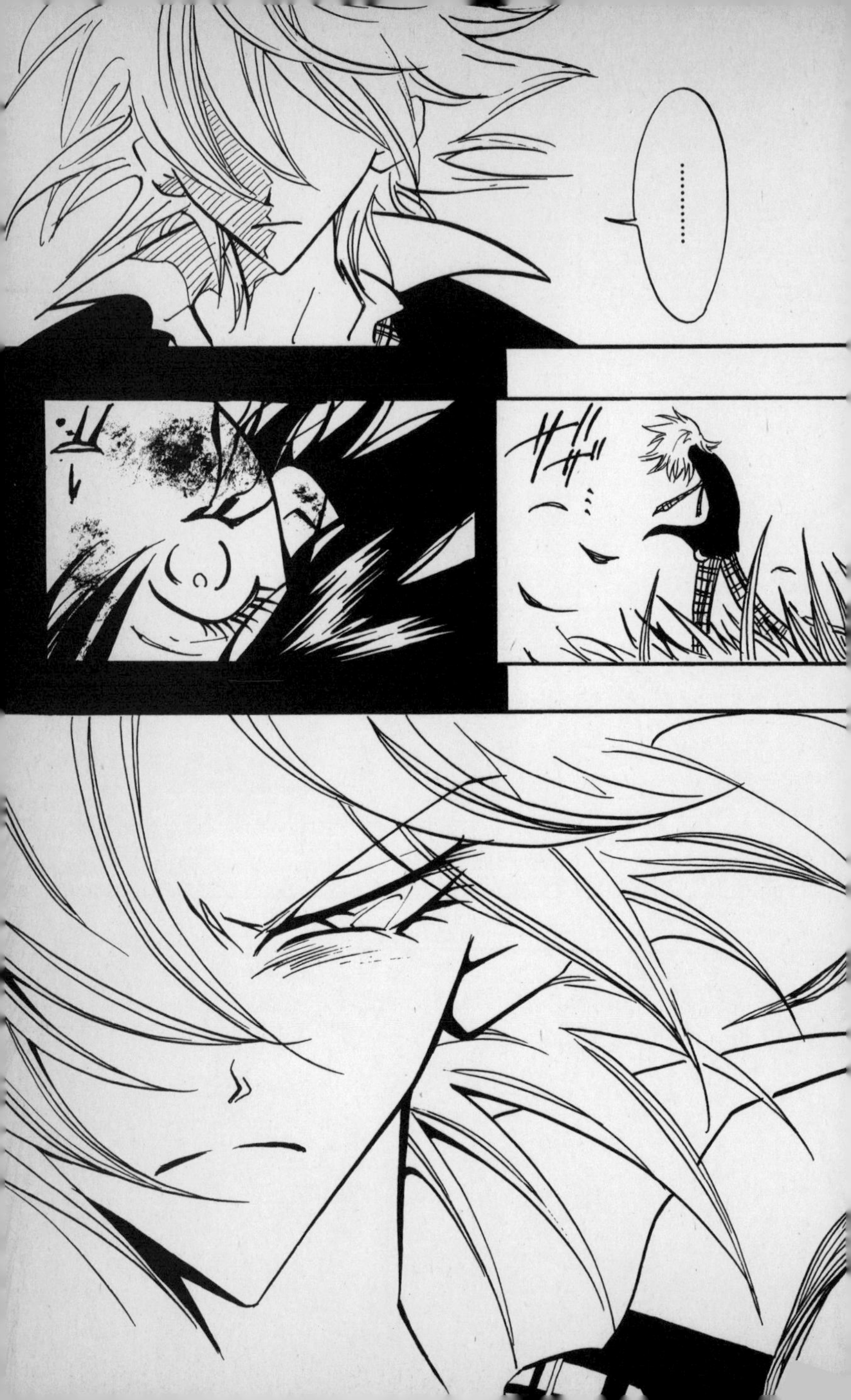
……
ザザ

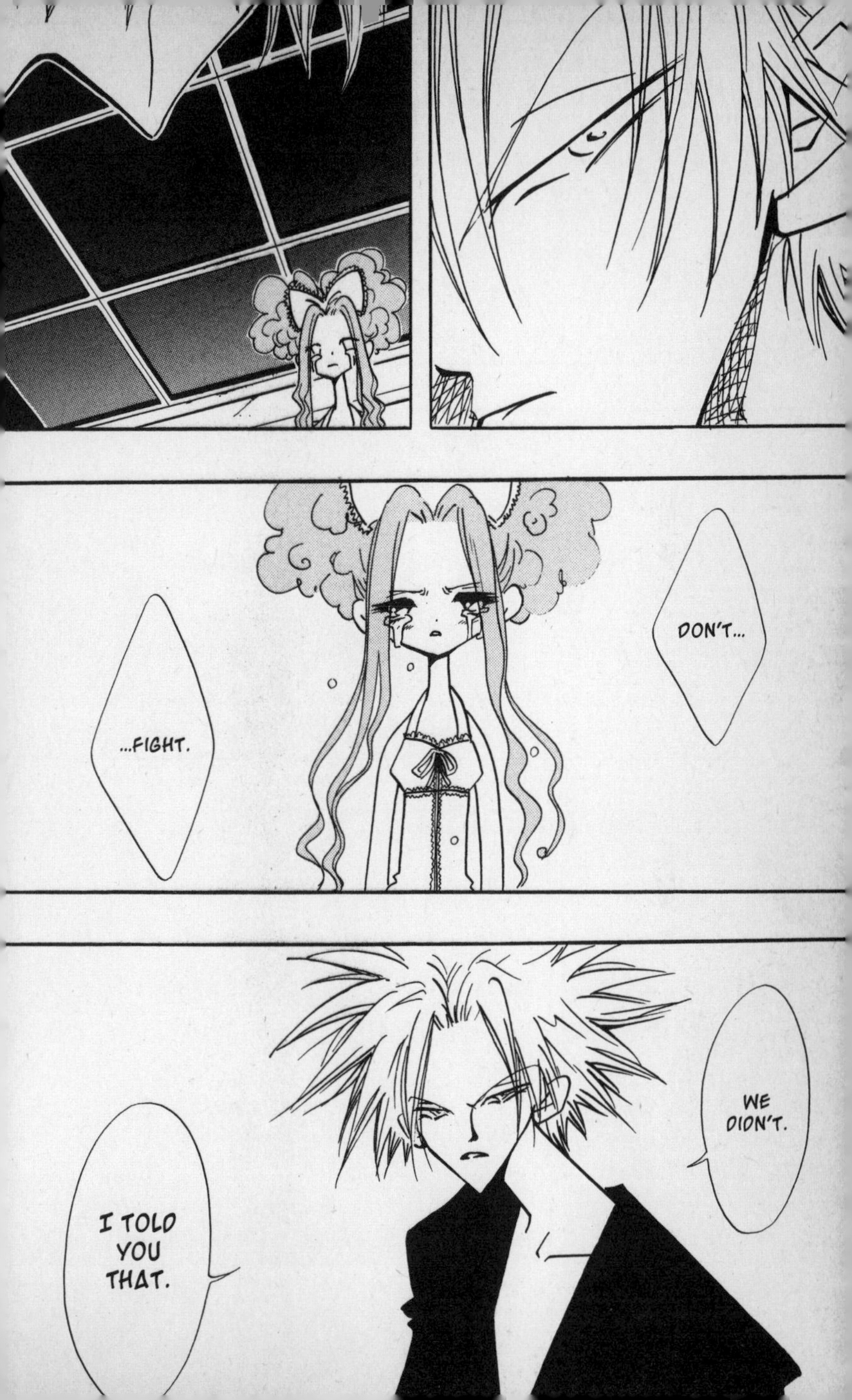
DON'T...
...FIGHT.
WE DIDN'T.
I TOLD YOU THAT.

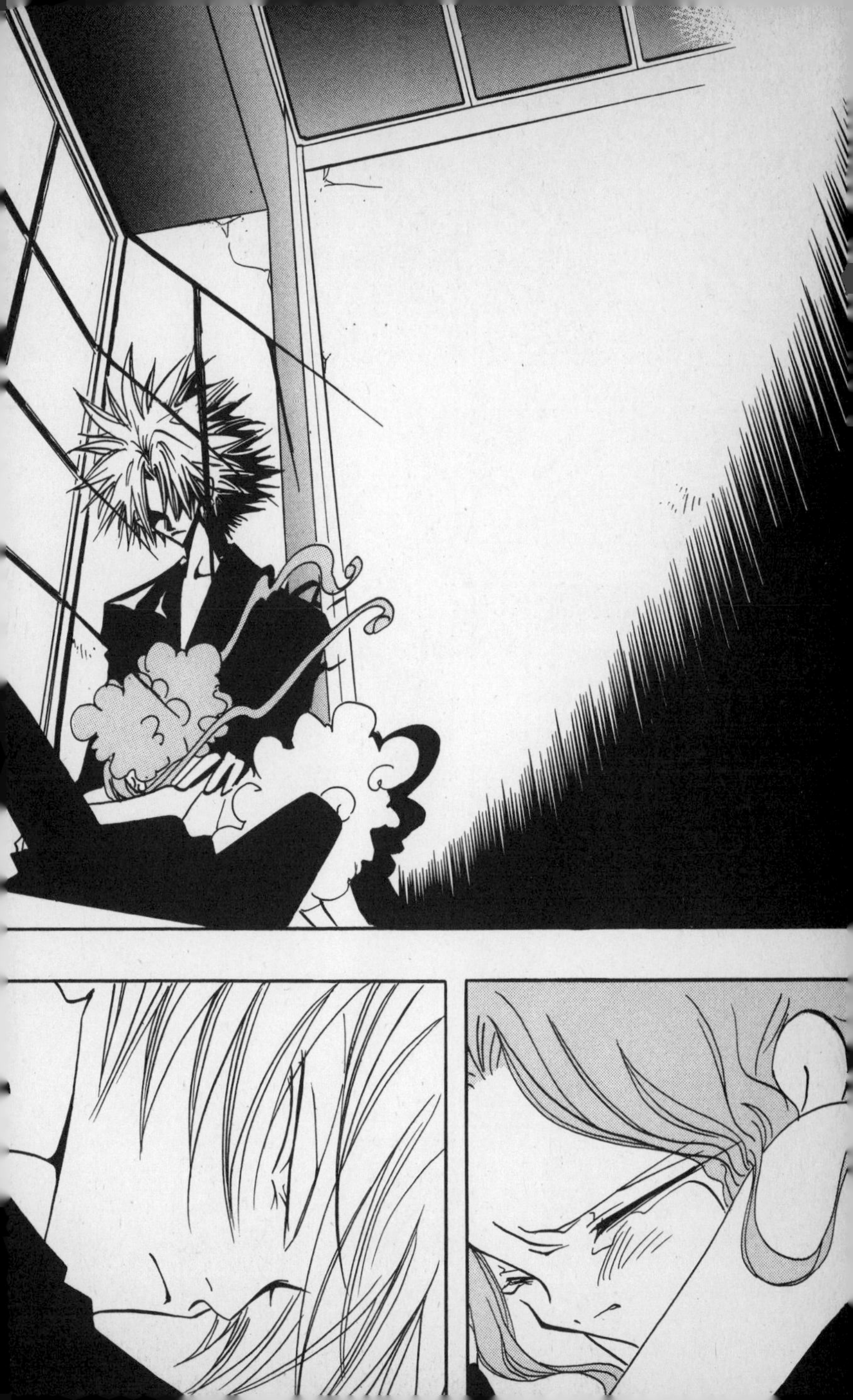

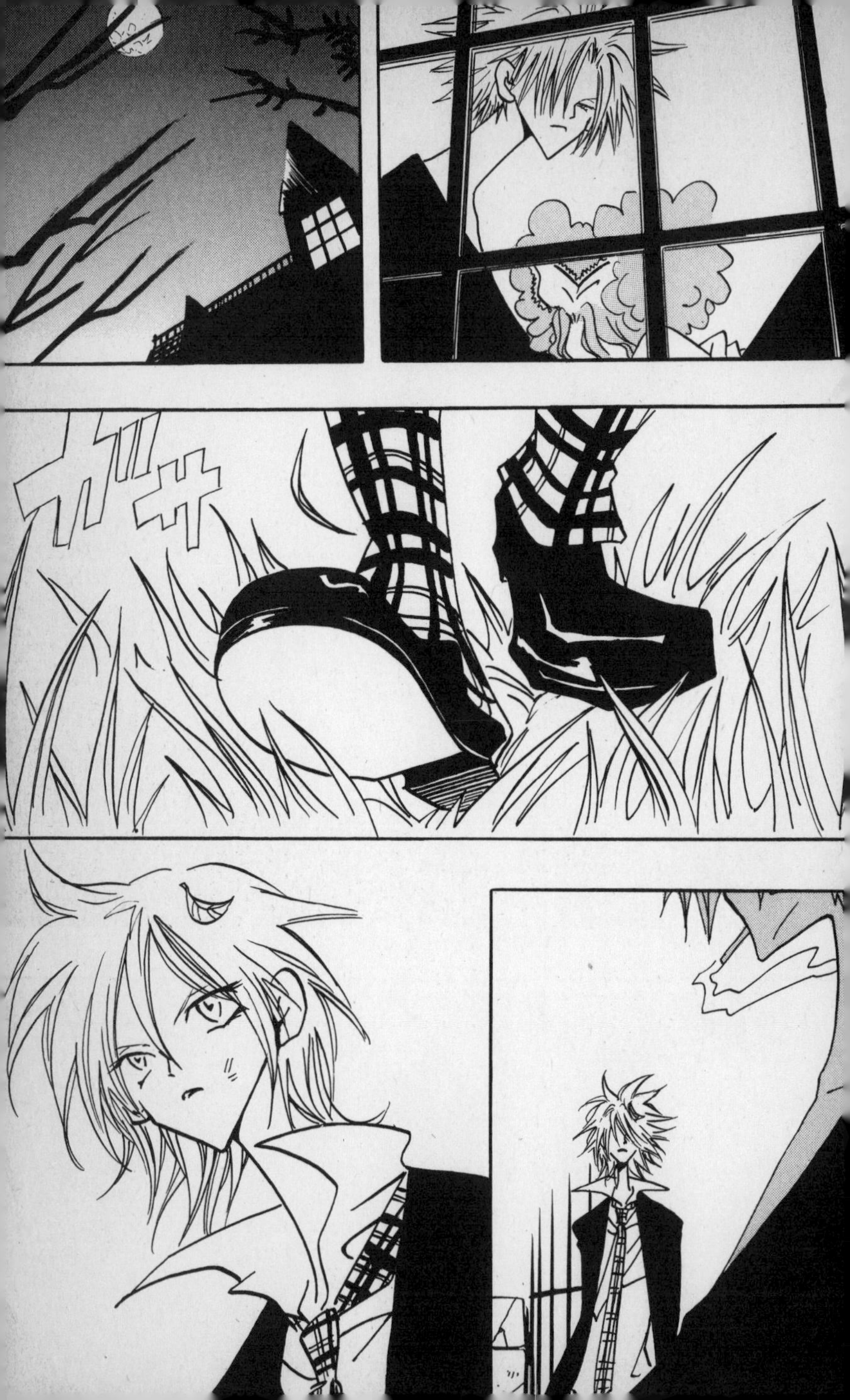
ガサ

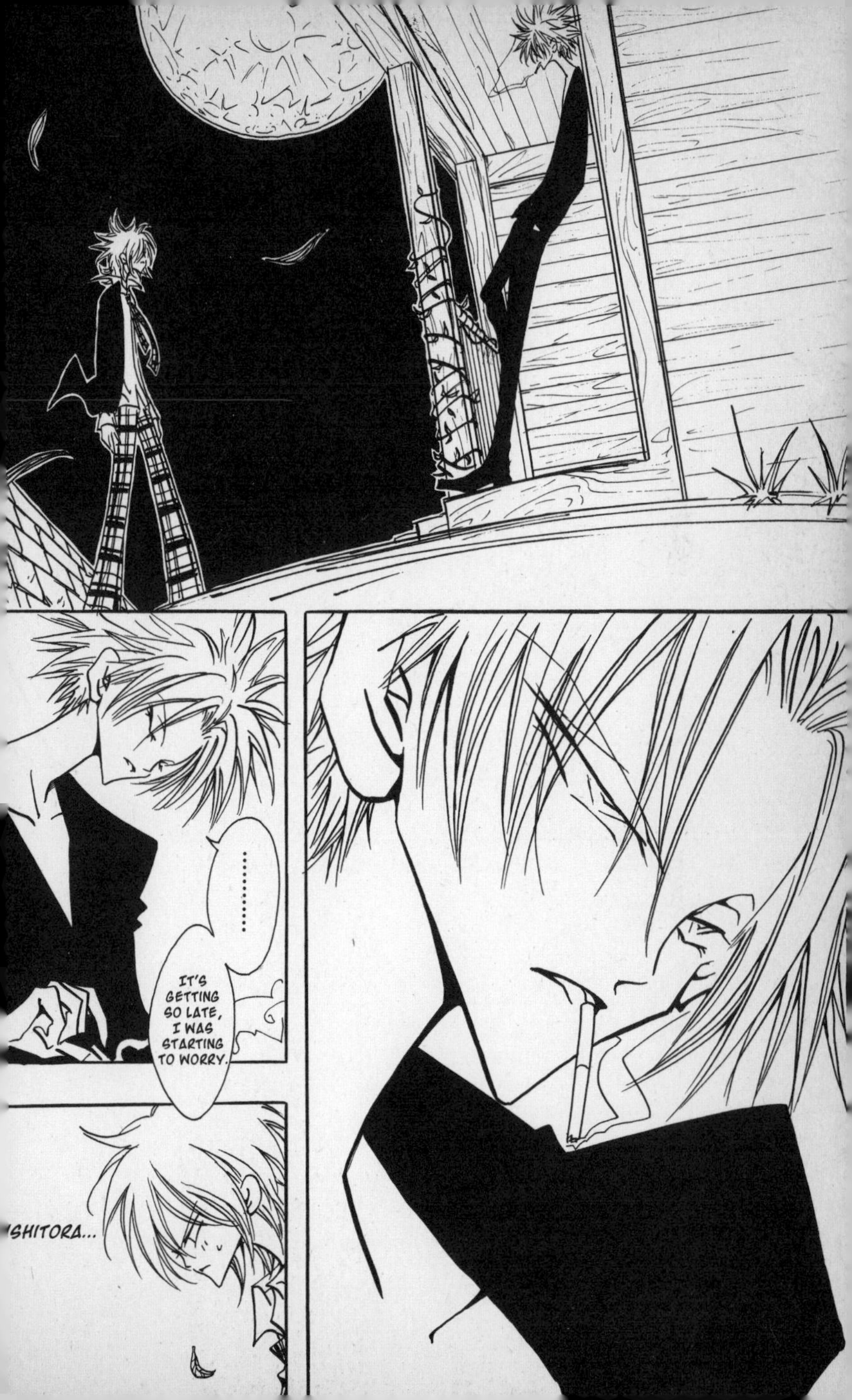
......
IT'S GETTING SO LATE, I WAS STARTING TO WORRY.
ISHITORA...

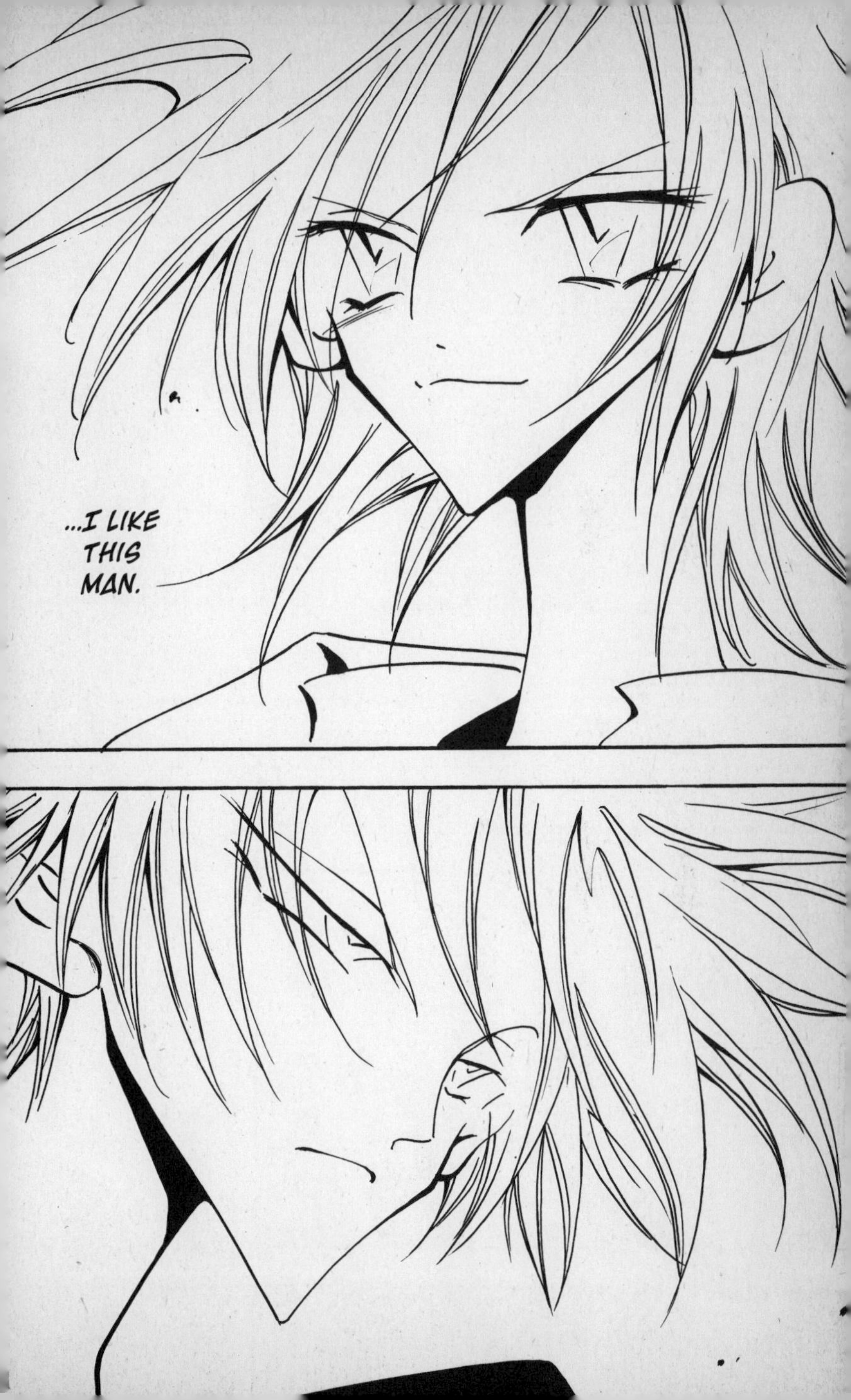
...I LIKE THIS MAN.

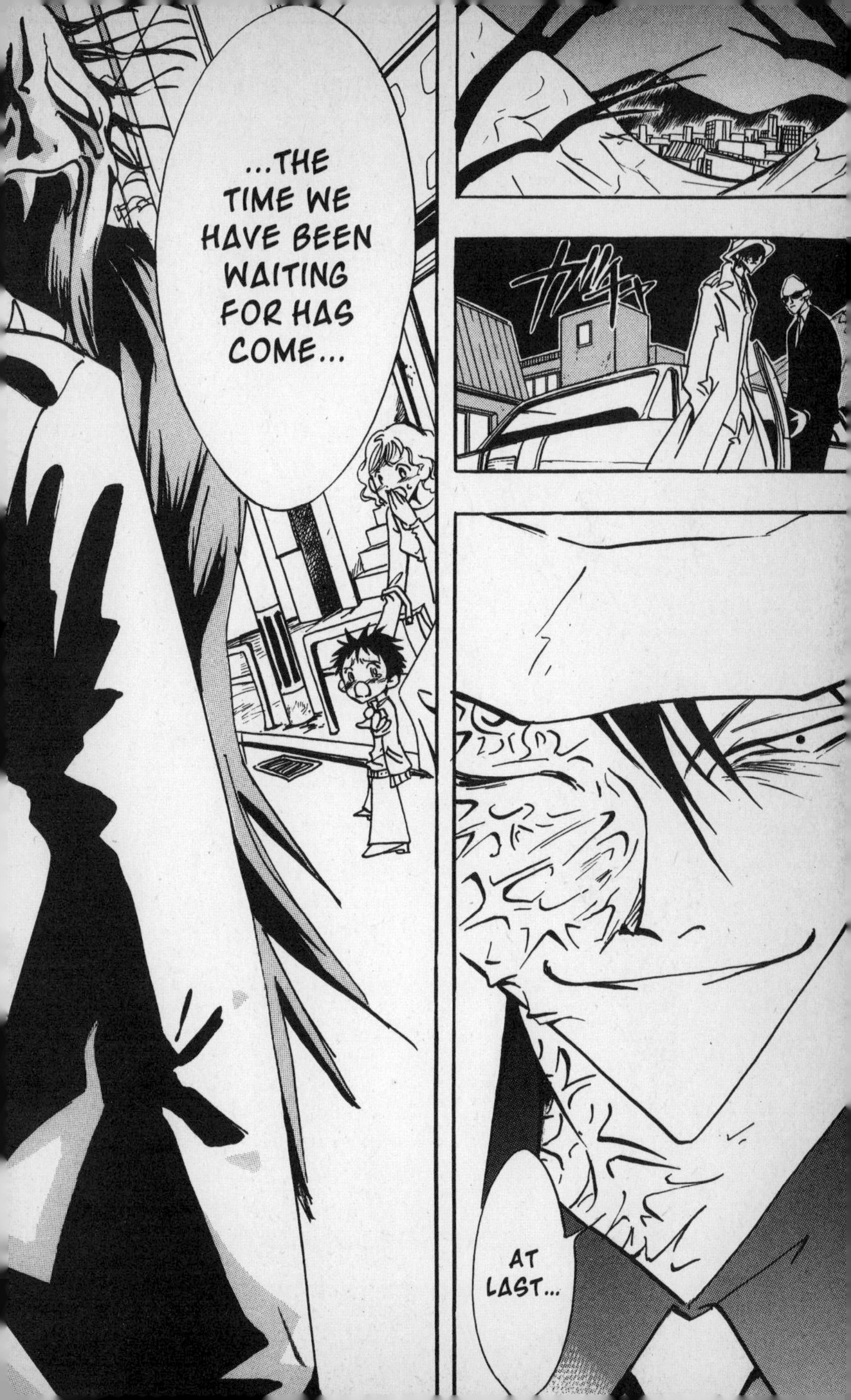
AT LAST...
...THE TIME WE HAVE BEEN WAITING FOR HAS COME...

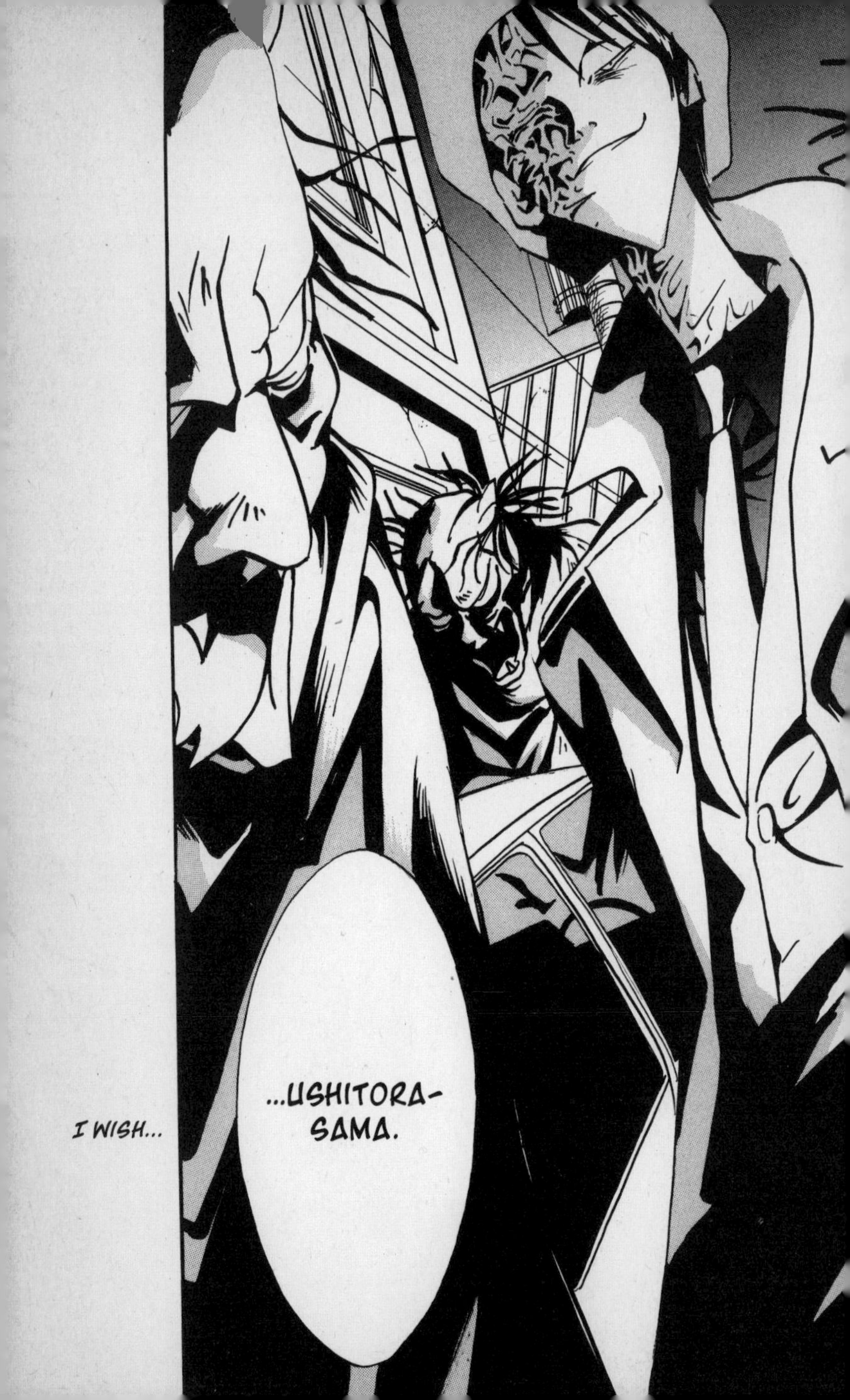
...USHITORA-SAMA.
I WISH...

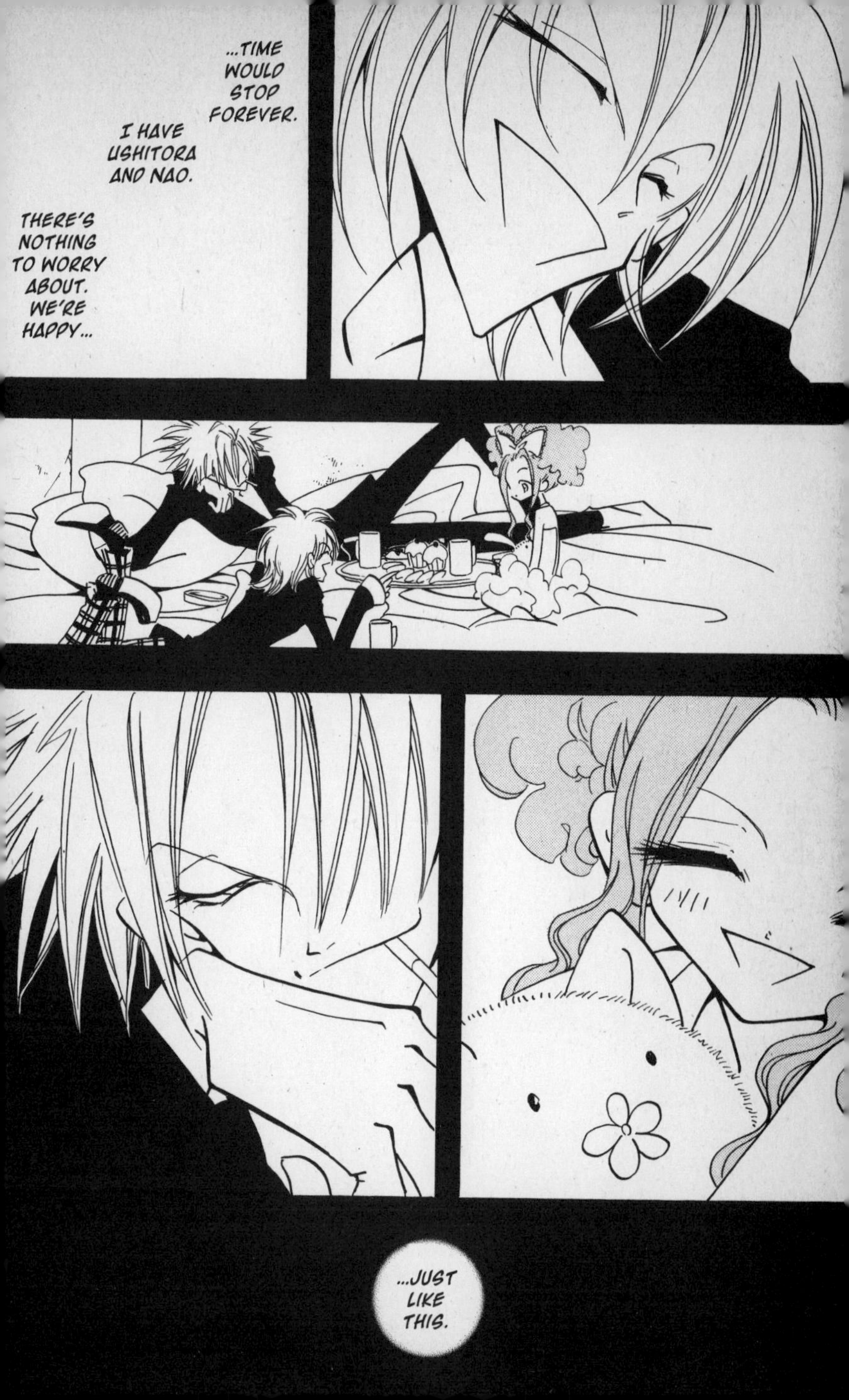
...TIME WOULD STOP FOREVER.
I HAVE USHITORA AND NAO.
THERE'S NOTHING TO WORRY ABOUT. WE'RE HAPPY...
...JUST LIKE THIS.

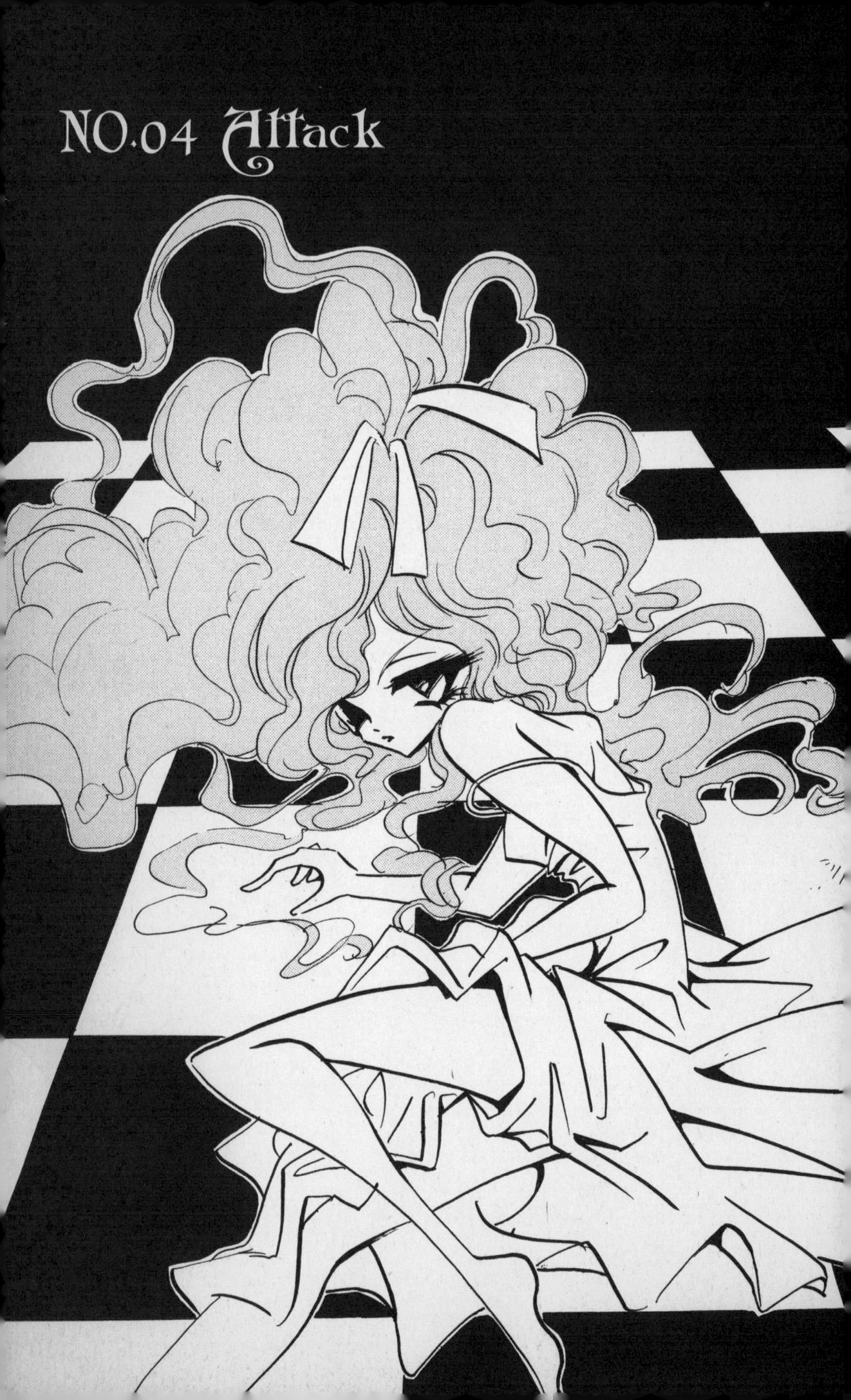
NO.04 Attack

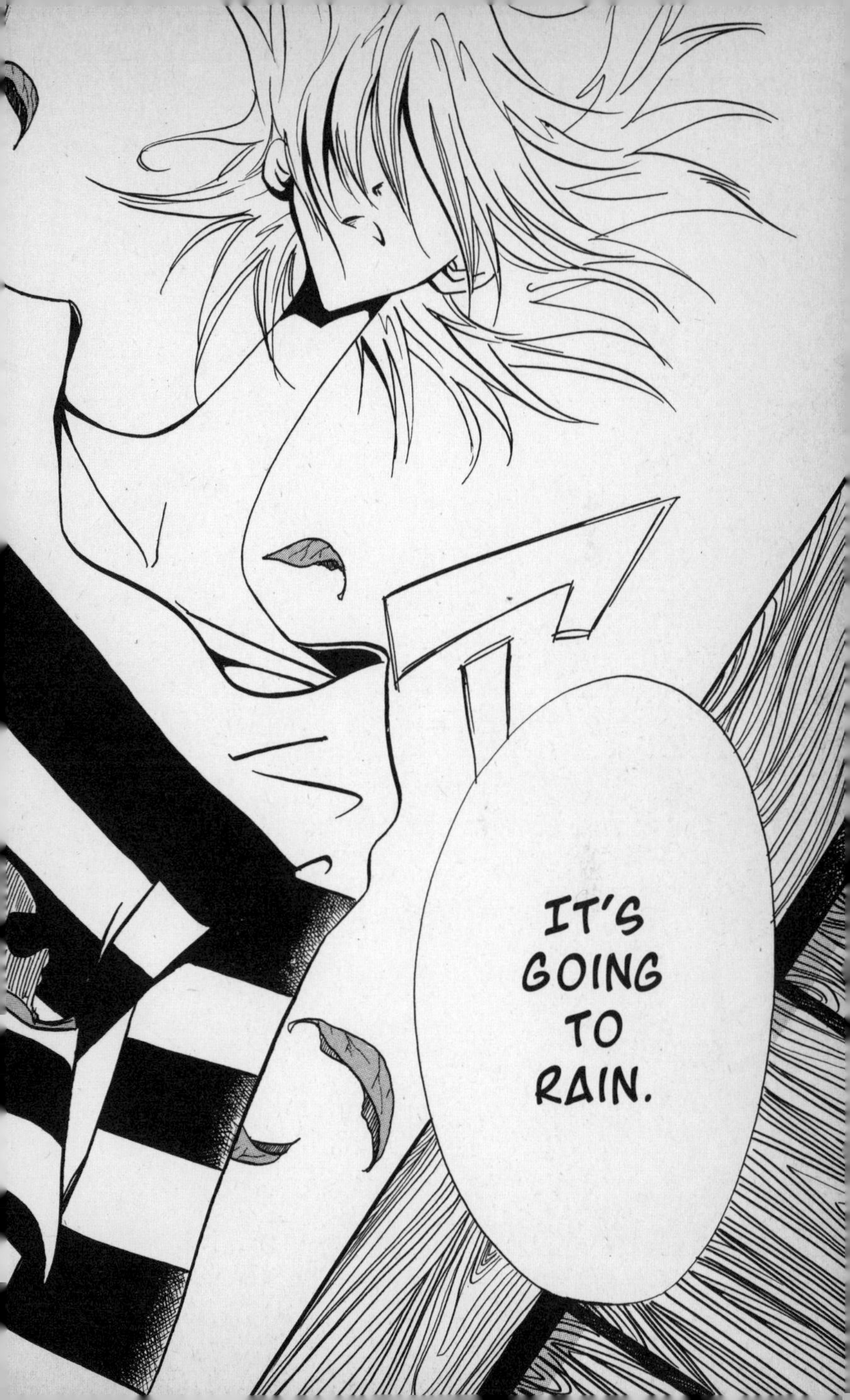
IT'S GOING TO RAIN.

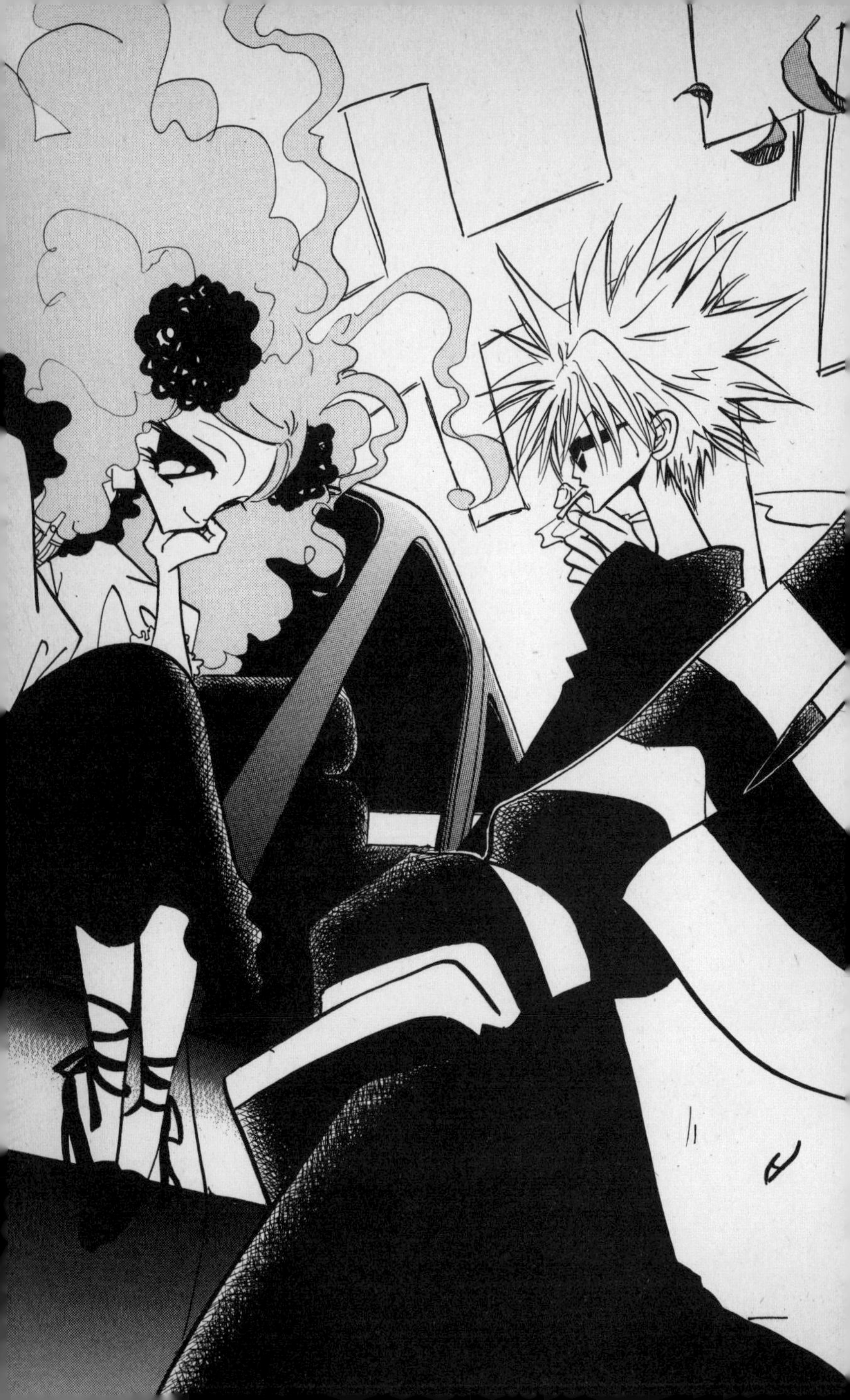

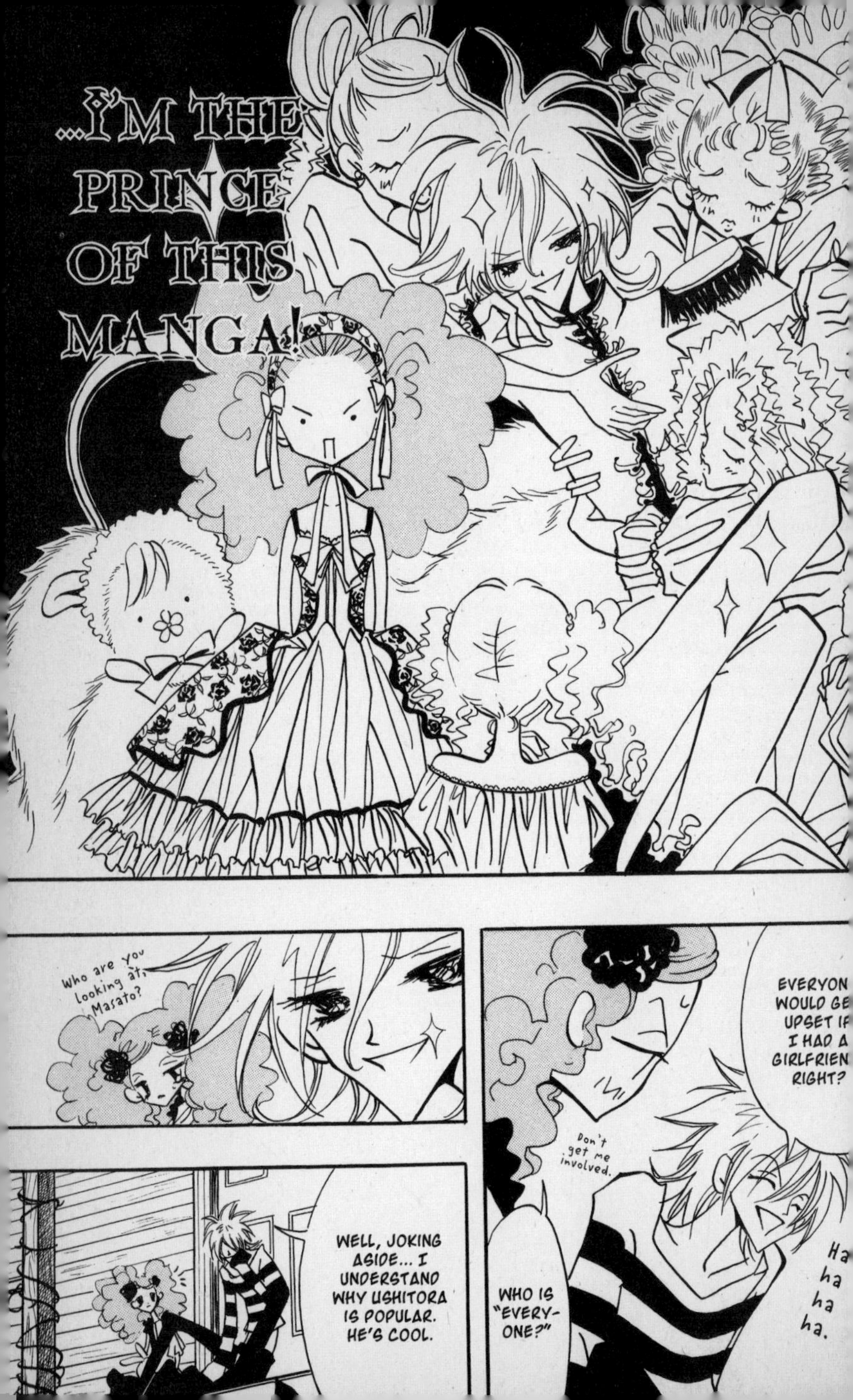
...I'M THE PRINCE OF THIS MANGA!
EVERYON WOULD GE UPSET IF I HAD A GIRLFRIEN RIGHT?
Don't get me involved.
Ha ha ha ha.
WHO IS "EVERY-ONE?"
Who are you looking at, Masato?
WELL, JOKING ASIDE... I UNDERSTAND WHY USHITORA IS POPULAR. HE'S COOL.

YOU SAY YOU'RE ORDINARY, BUT...

RIGHT?

...I THINK YOU'RE VERY COOL TO BE ABLE TO SAY, "I ALWAYS HAVE TO DO MY BEST TO LIVE."

MASATO...

Tee hee.

AND I DEPEND ON YOU AND USHITORA ALL THE TIME.

I don't do any housework.

I HAVE TO BE STRONG, TOO.

WHEN I'M UPSET, YOU'RE ALWAYS SO SWEET TO ME.

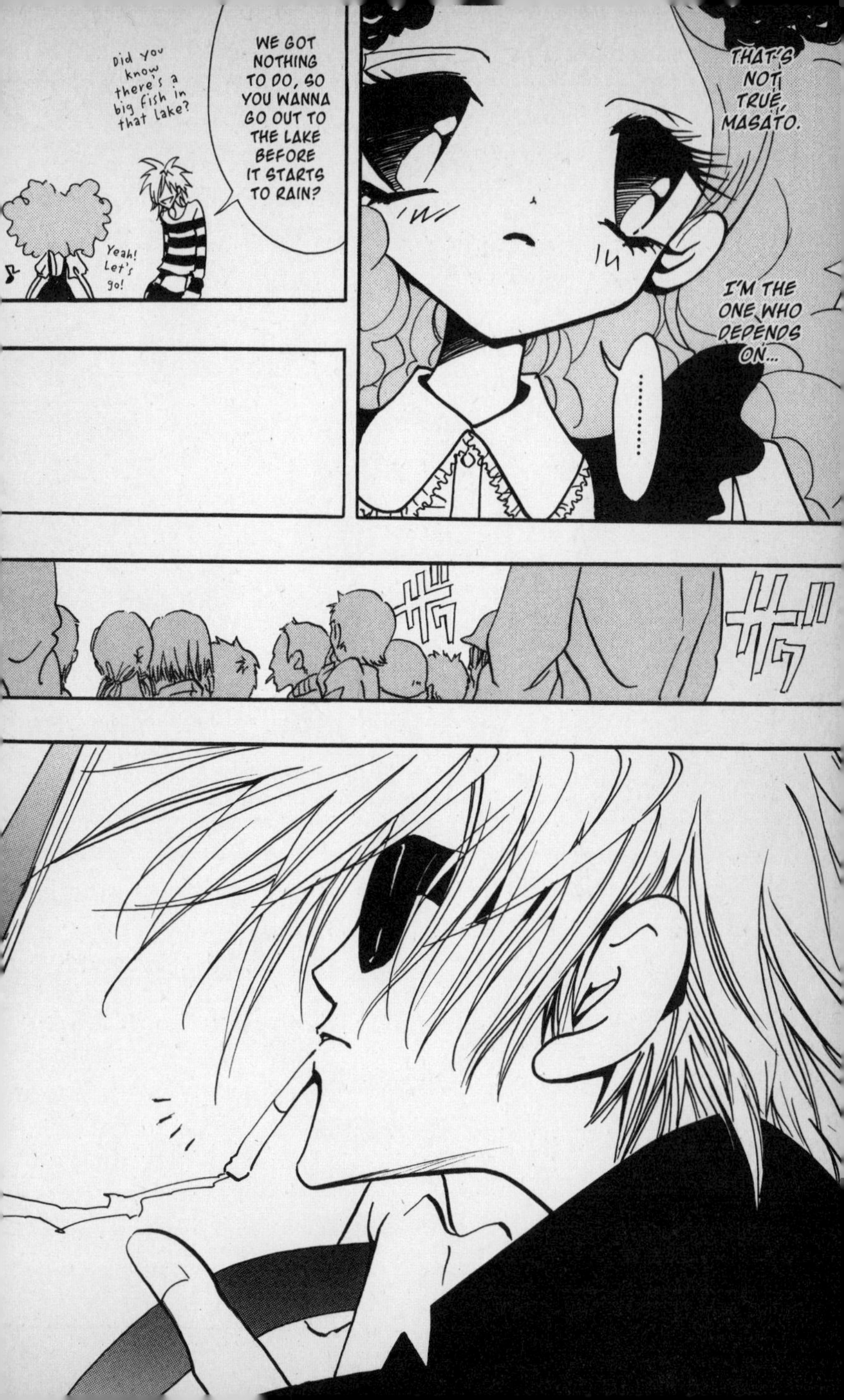
THAT'S NOT TRUE, MASATO.
I'M THE ONE WHO DEPENDS ON...
......
WE GOT NOTHING TO DO, SO YOU WANNA GO OUT TO THE LAKE BEFORE IT STARTS TO RAIN?
Did you know there's a big fish in that lake?
Yeah! Let's go!
ザワ
ザワ

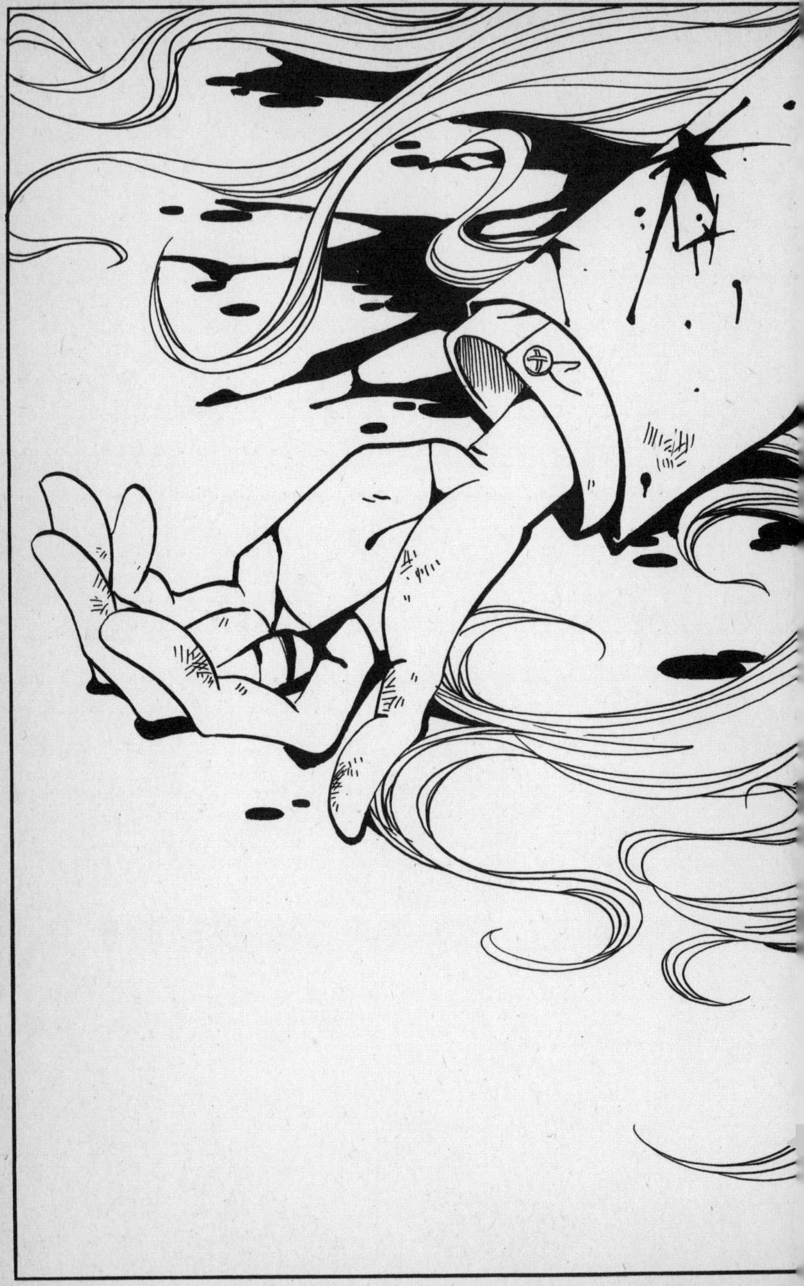

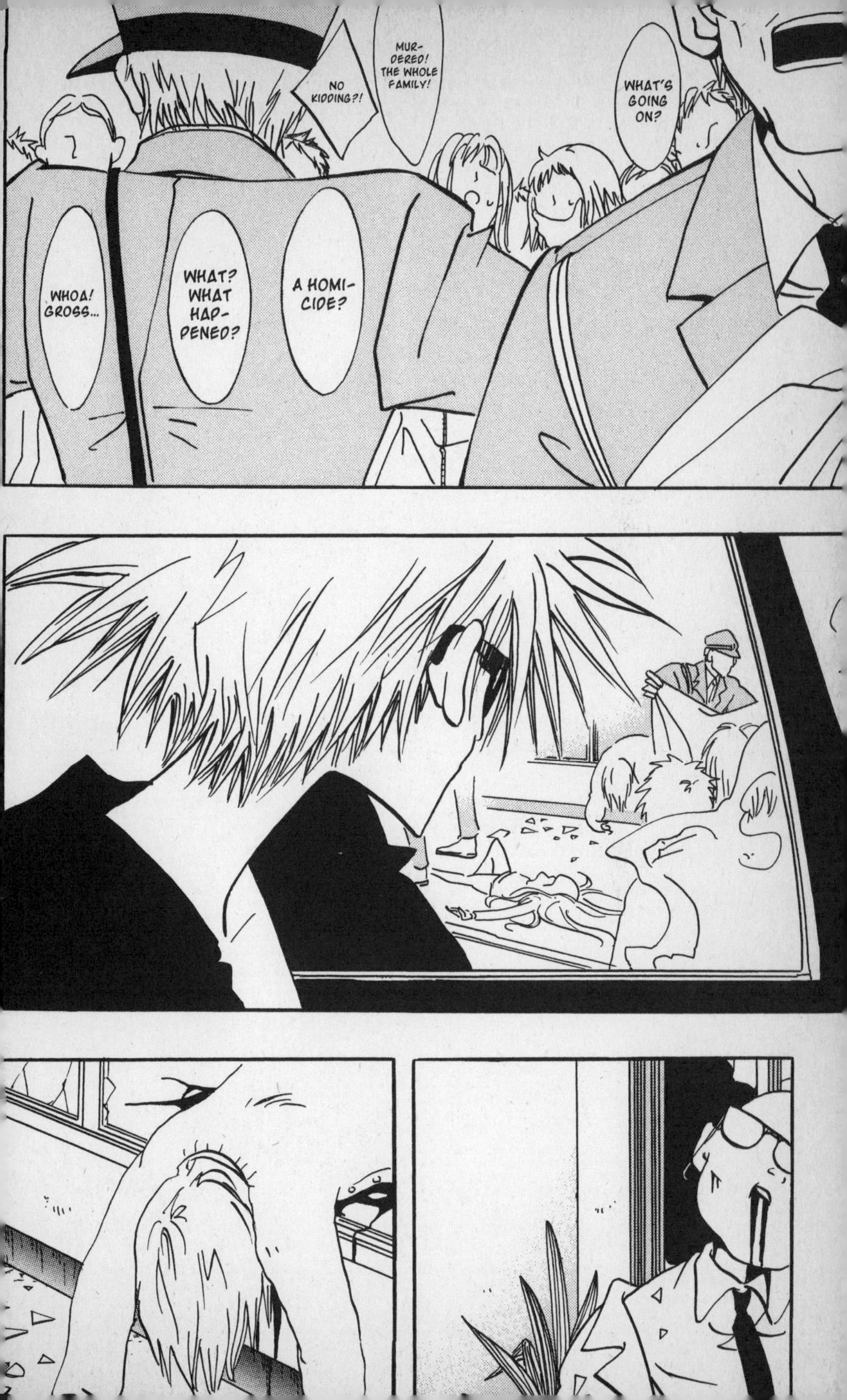
WHAT'S GOING ON?
MUR-DERED! THE WHOLE FAMILY!
NO KIDDING?!
A HOMI-CIDE?
WHAT? WHAT HAP-PENED?
WHOA! GROSS...

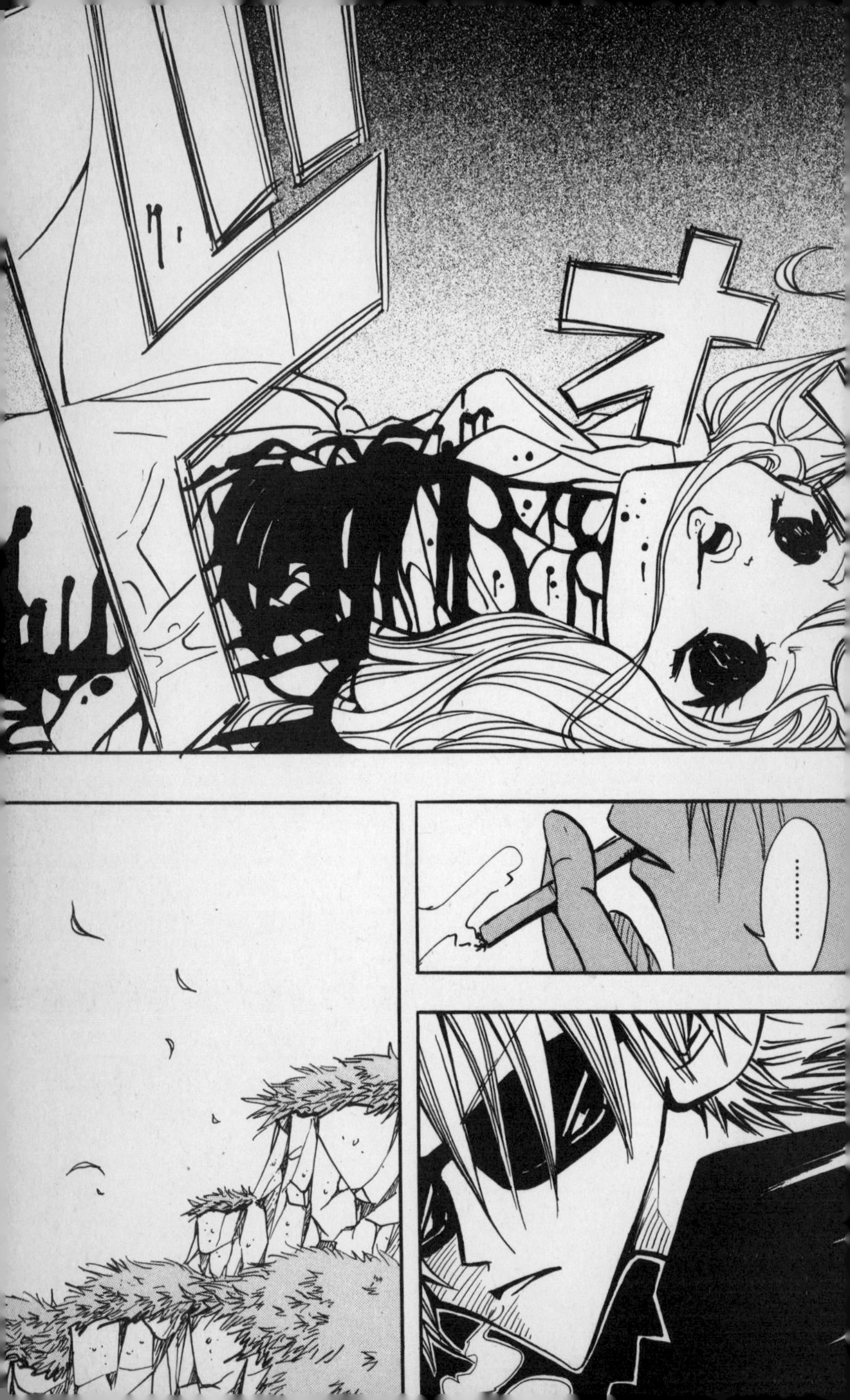

......

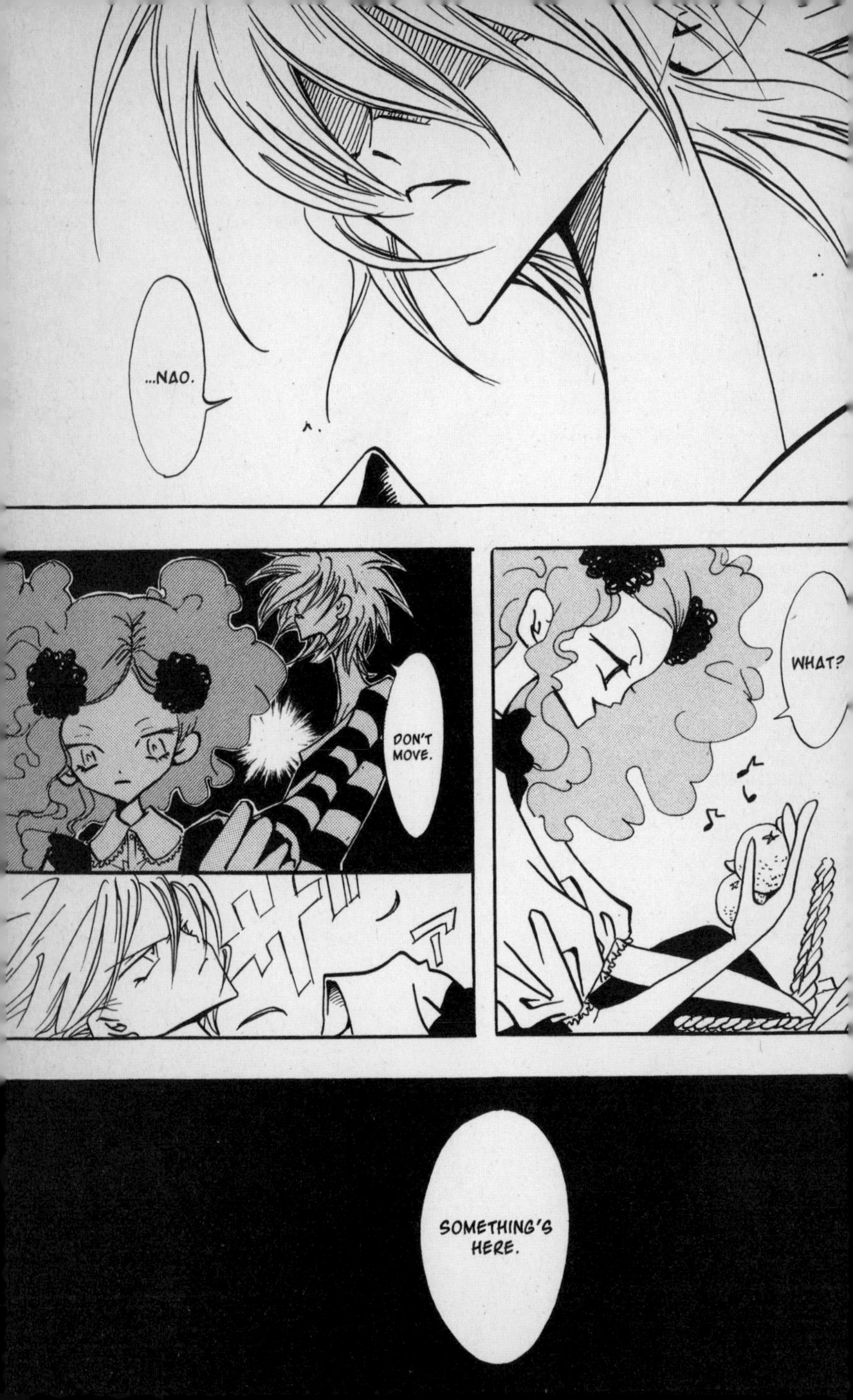
...NAO.
WHAT?
DON'T MOVE.
SOMETHING'S HERE.

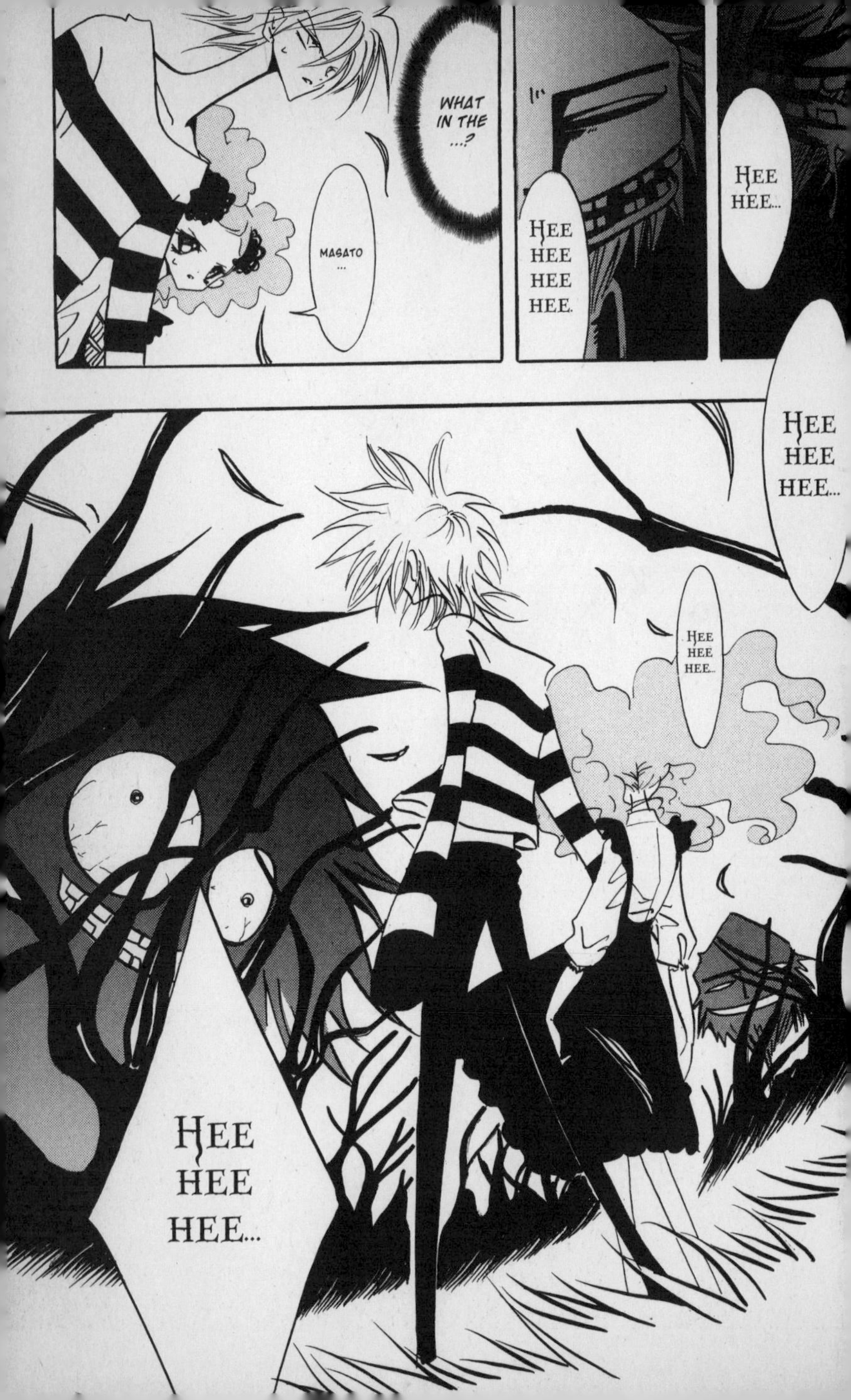
HEE HEE...
HEE HEE HEE HEE.
WHAT IN THE ...?
MASATO ...
HEE HEE HEE...
HEE HEE HEE...
HEE HEE HEE...

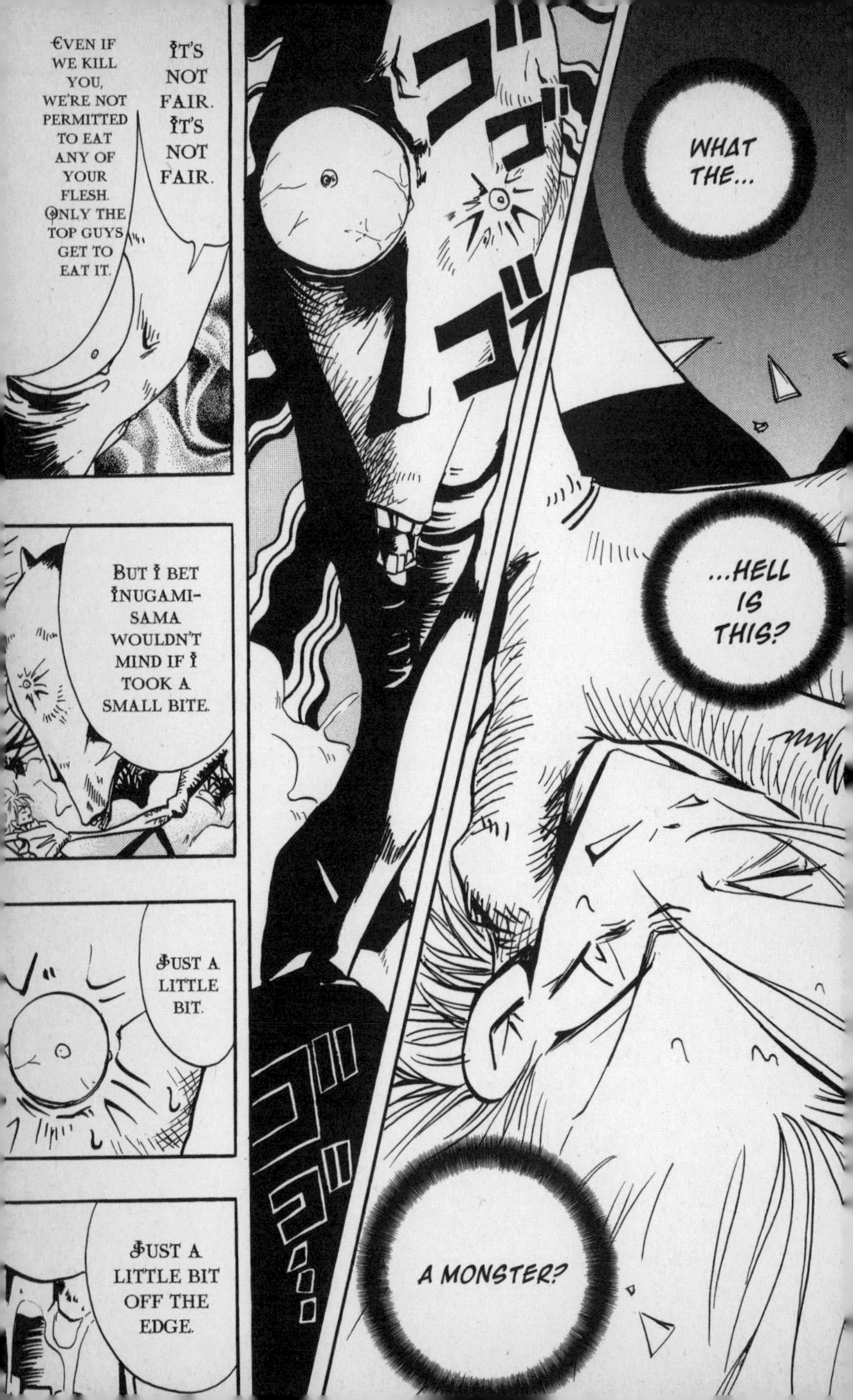
WHAT THE...
...HELL IS THIS?
A MONSTER?
IT'S NOT FAIR. IT'S NOT FAIR.
EVEN IF WE KILL YOU, WE'RE NOT PERMITTED TO EAT ANY OF YOUR FLESH. ONLY THE TOP GUYS GET TO EAT IT.
BUT I BET INUGAMI-SAMA WOULDN'T MIND IF I TOOK A SMALL BITE.
JUST A LITTLE BIT.
JUST A LITTLE BIT OFF THE EDGE.

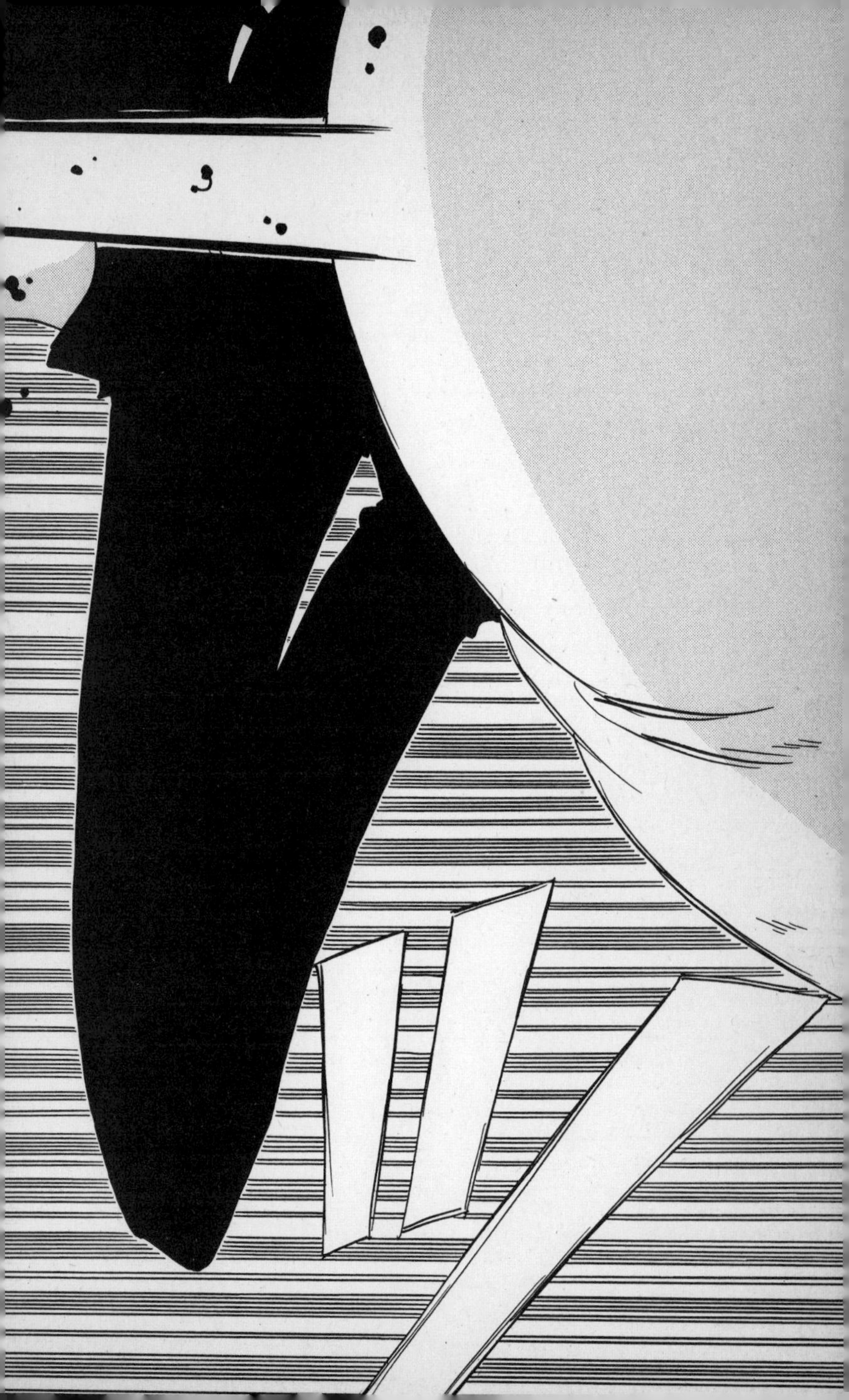

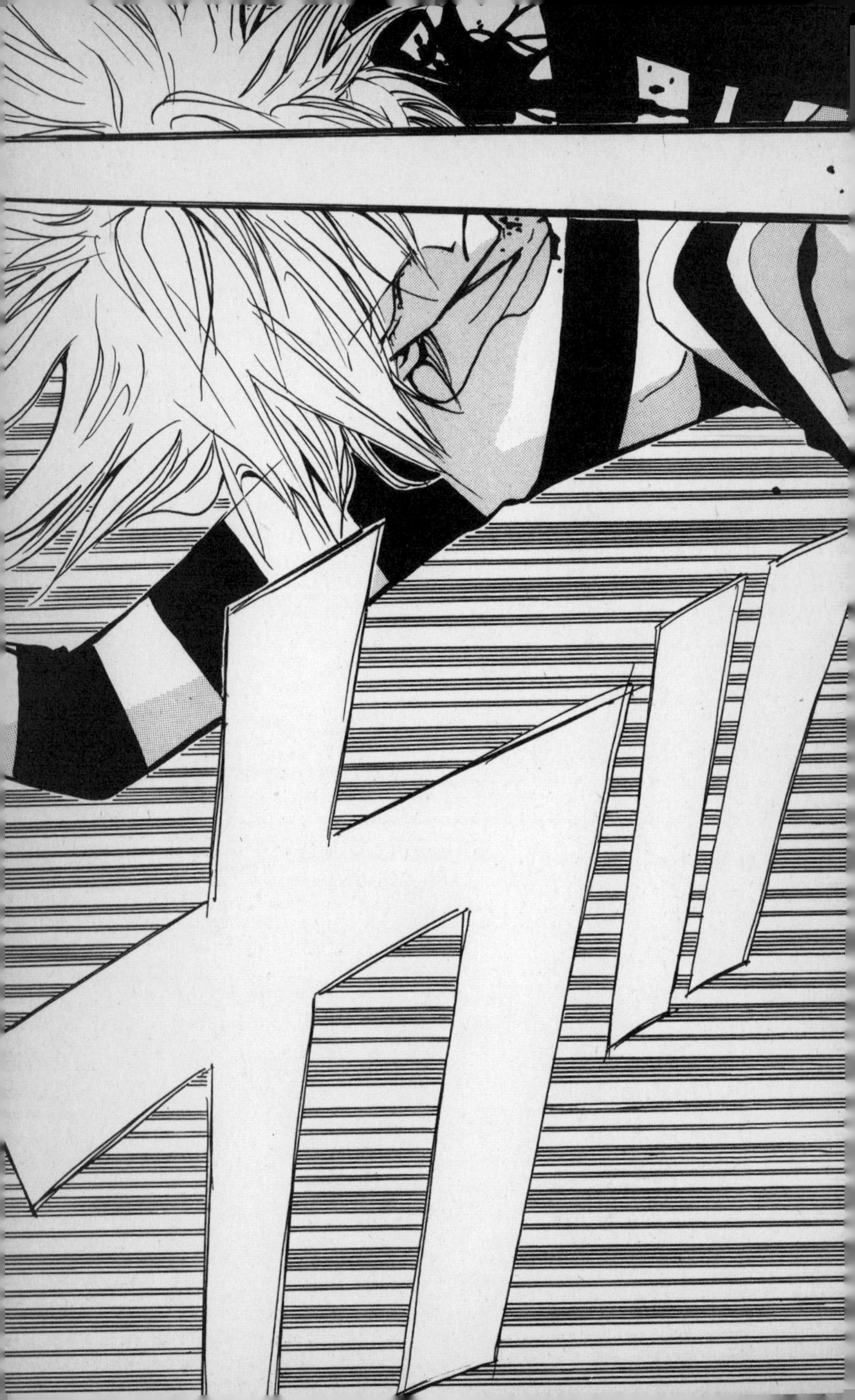

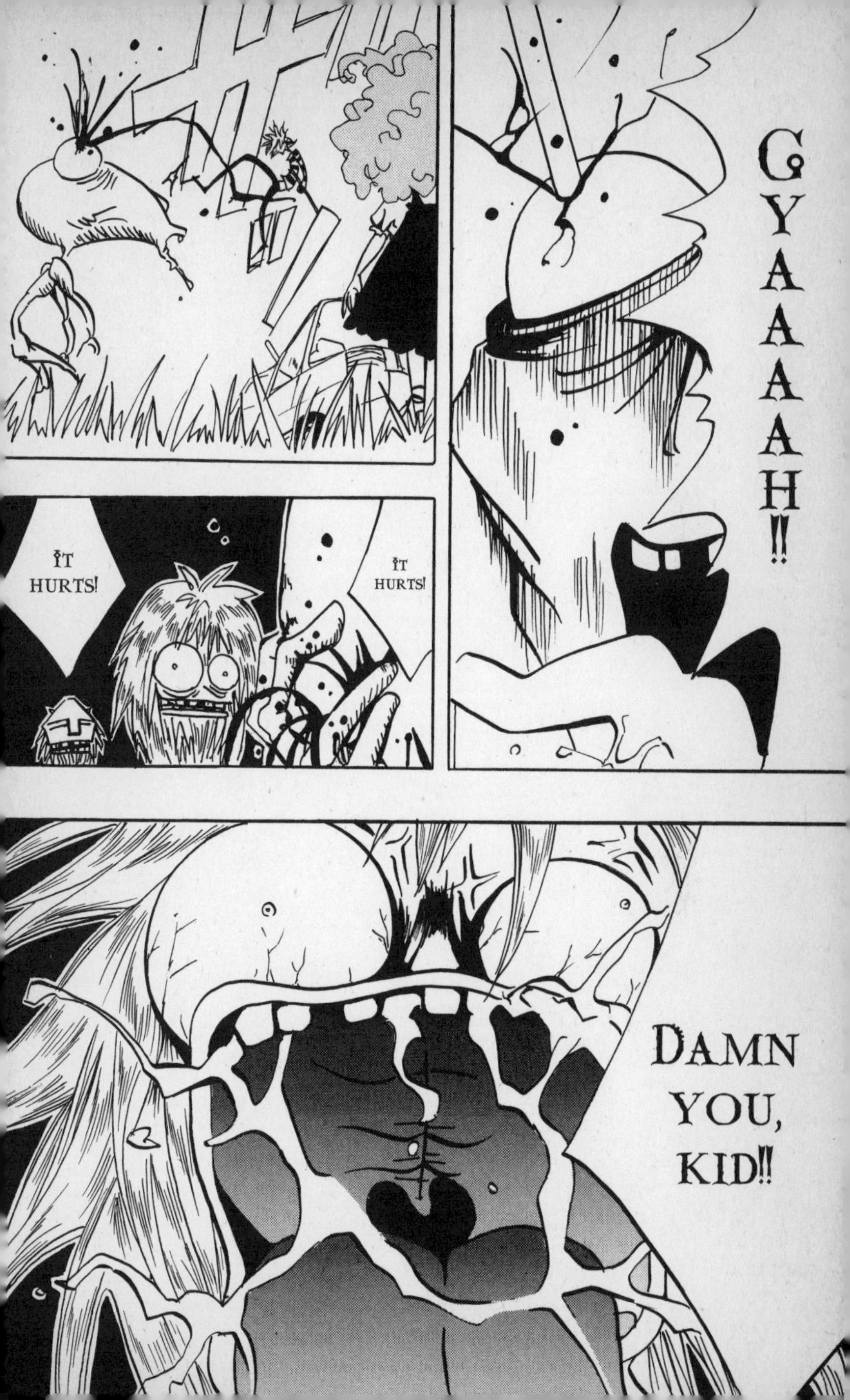
GYAAAAH!!
IT HURTS!
IT HURTS!
DAMN YOU, KID!!

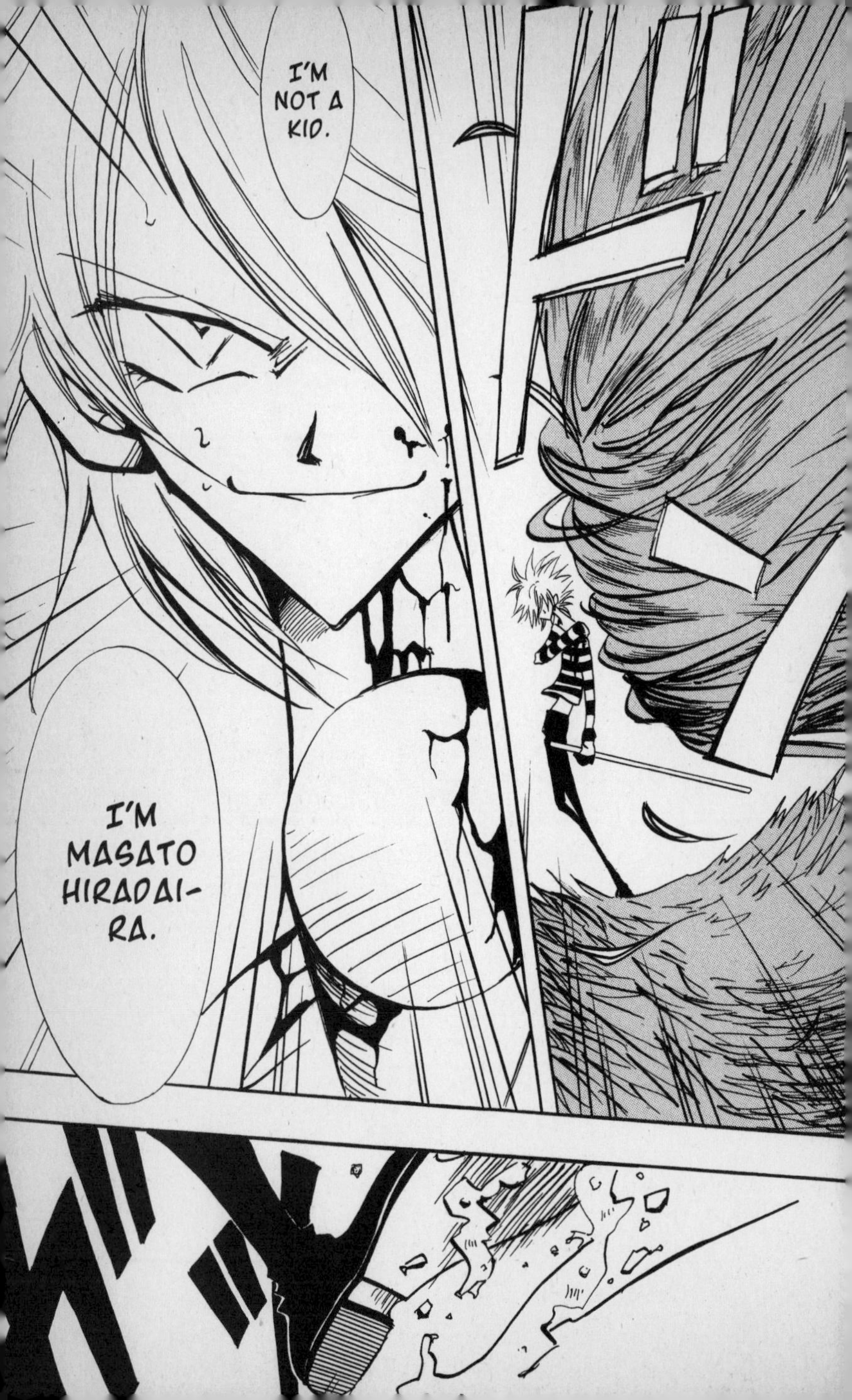
I'M NOT A KID.
I'M MASATO HIRADAI-RA.

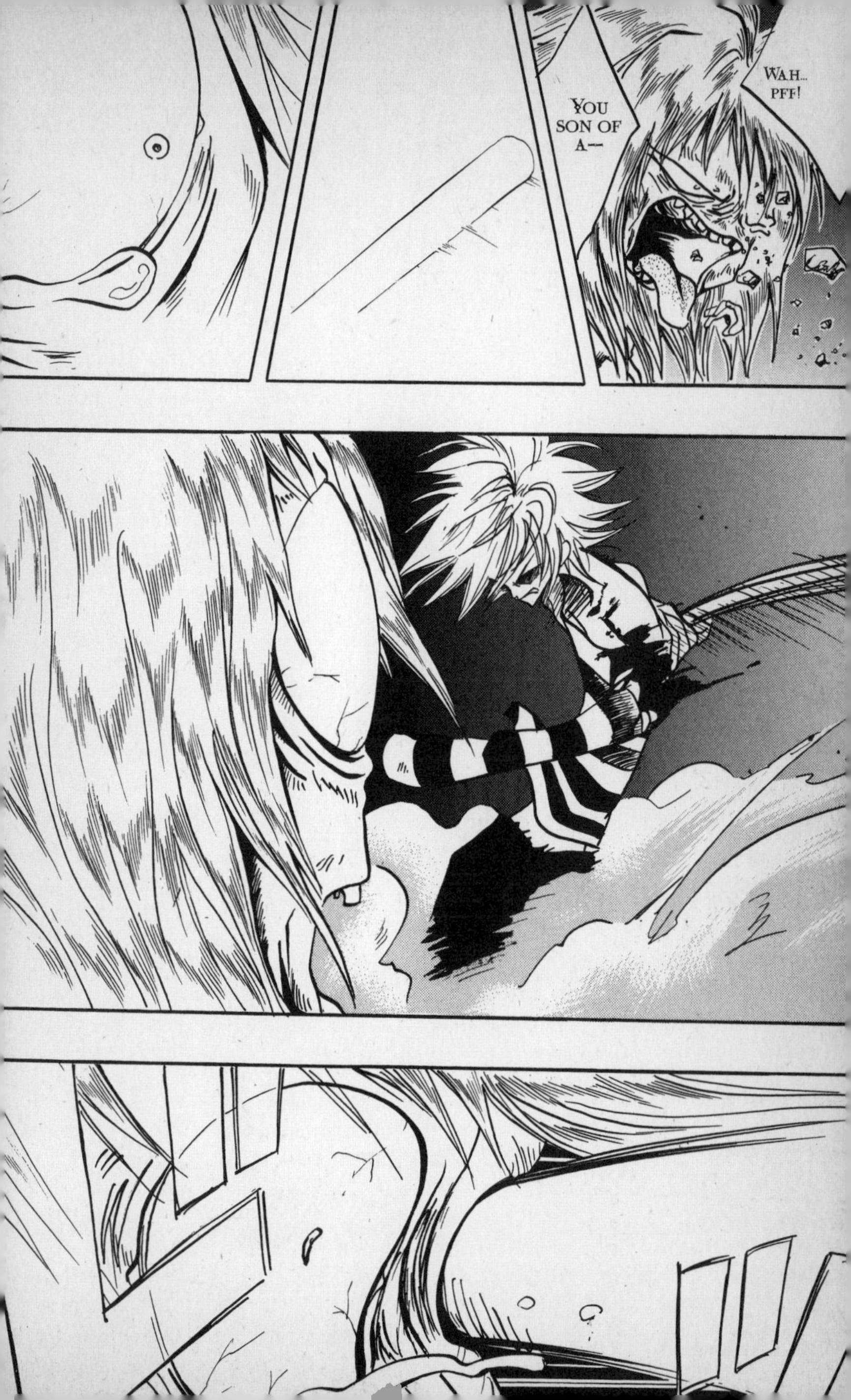
WAH... PFF!
YOU SON OF A—

IT'S NOISY HERE.

WHAT'S GOING ON?

OH, MAYBE THEY FOUND THE KURUIZAKI.

MAYBE HE'S REMEMBERING SOMETHING FUNNY.

WHY IS HE LAUGHING?

IN THIS SITUATION? I DON'T THINK SO.

HEE HEE HEE.

EEE HEE HEE HEE!

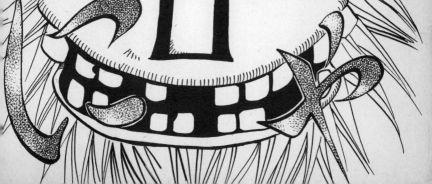

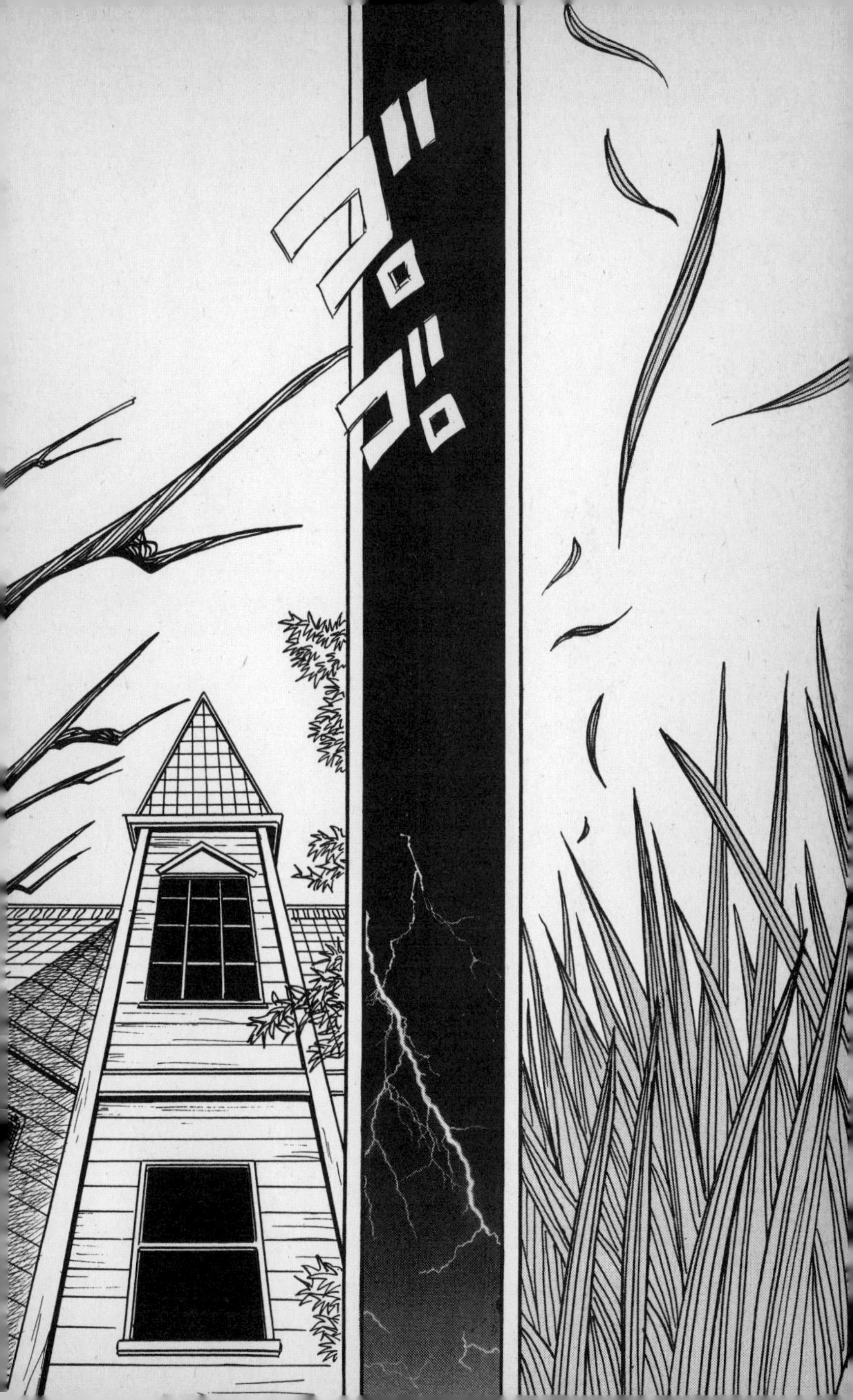
ゴゴ

WHAT?

YOU STAY IN HERE. IF YOU DON'T MAKE ANY NOISE, THEY WON'T FIND YOU. SO KEEP QUIET, OKAY?

Spurt Spurt

HEY ...

Hey, don't come out!

I won't...!

HEY! WAIT, MASATO!

MASATO!

NO! WHAT ARE YOU GONNA DO ALL BY YOURSELF?

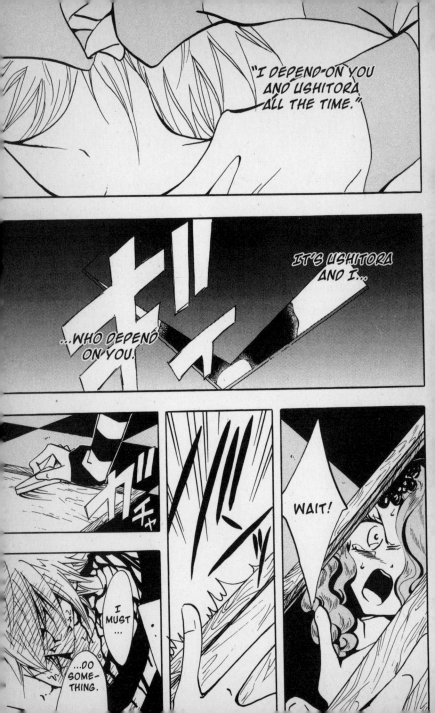

YOU'LL BE...
KILLED.

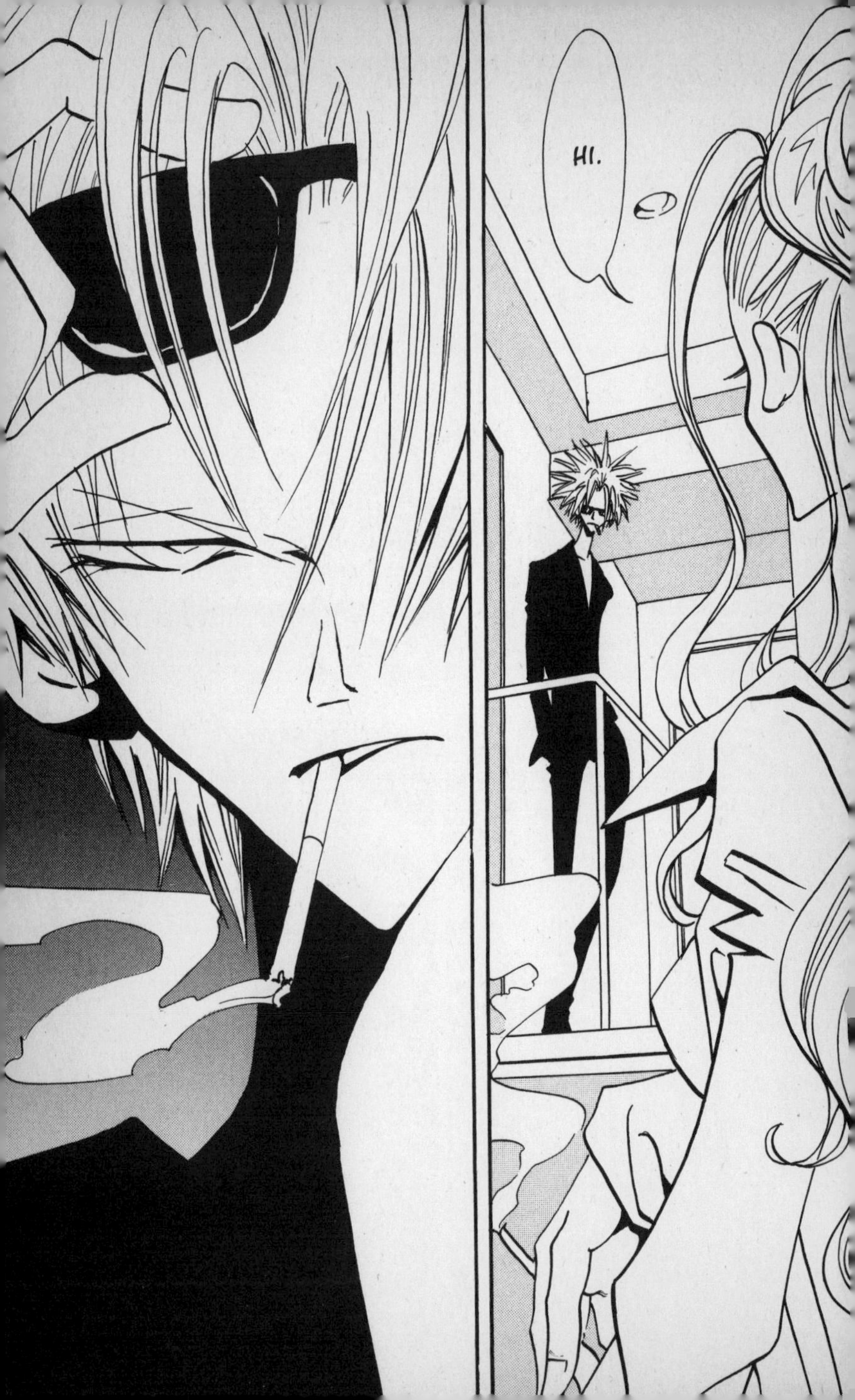
HI.

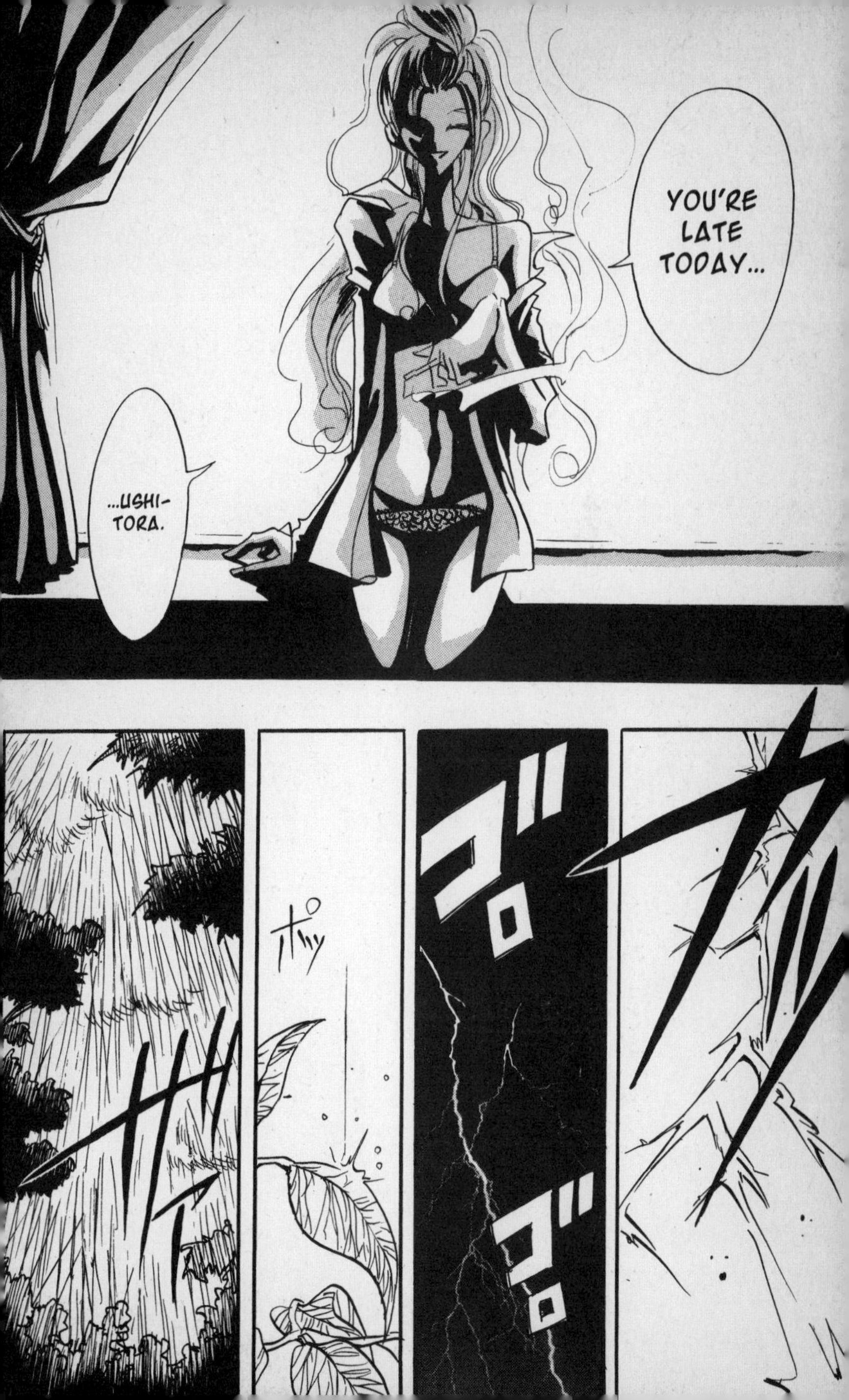
YOU'RE LATE TODAY...
...USHI-TORA.
ゴロ
ゴロ

NO.oo Dream

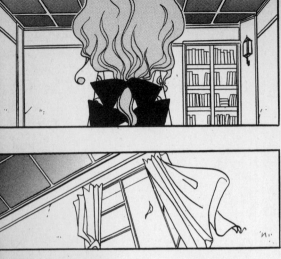

UGHI-
TORA?

I HAD A
STRANGE
THOUGHT...

...THAT THIS
LIFE I LIVE
WITH MASATO
AND USHITORA
MAY BE A
DREAM.

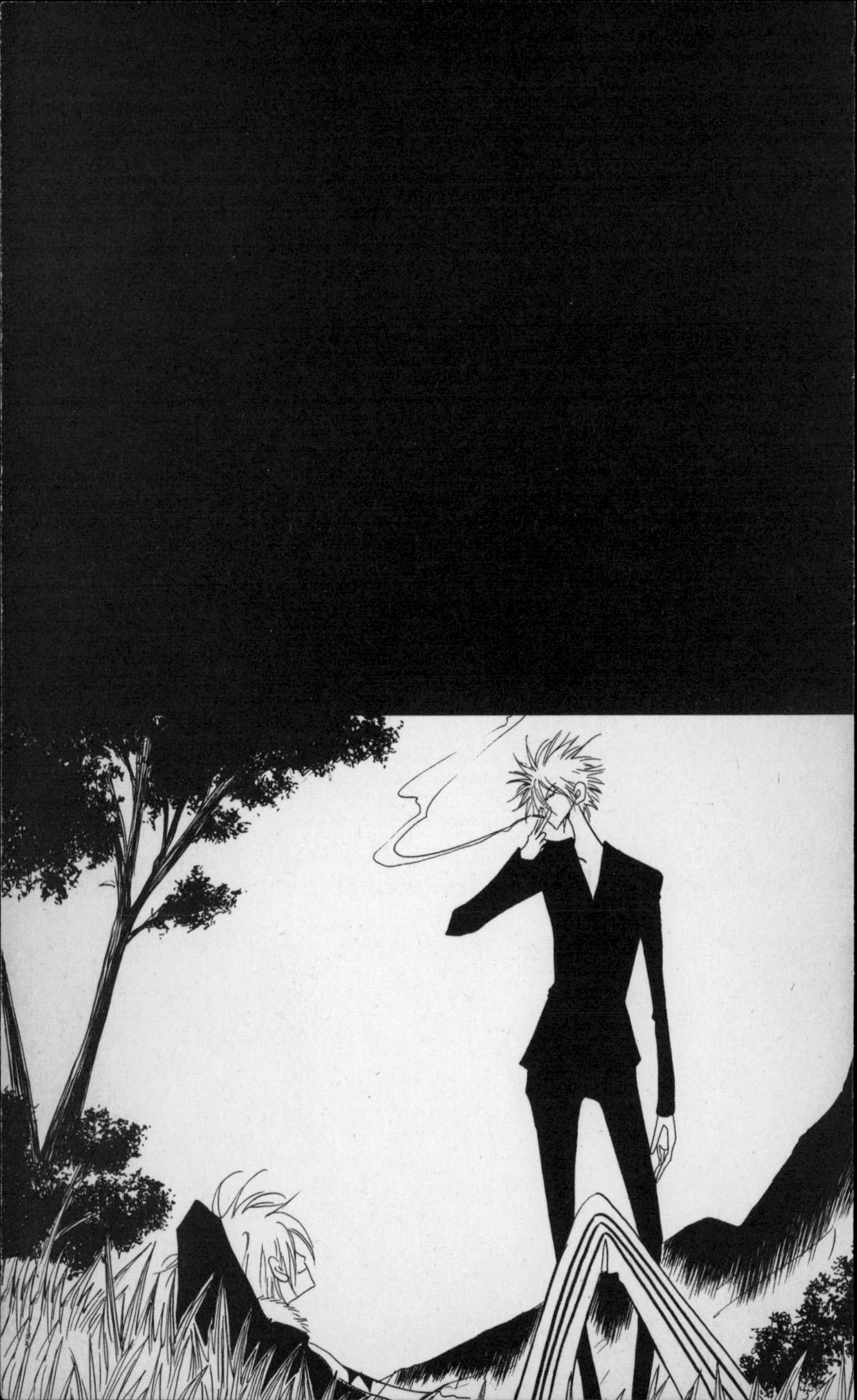

In the Next Volume...

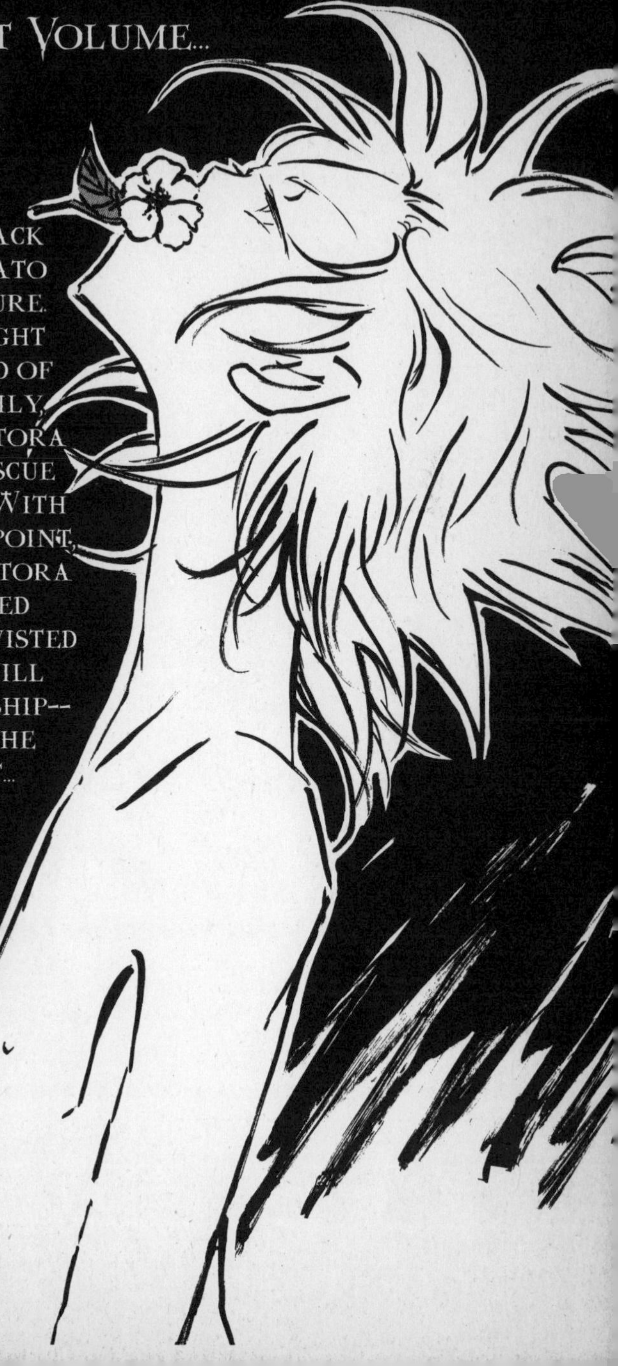

The demon attack results in Masato and Nao's capture. They are brought before the head of the Demon Family, Gold, when Ushitora storms in to rescue his companions. With Nao held at gunpoint, Masato and Ushitora are then forced o play Gold's twisted games, and it will ut their friendship--and love--to the ultimate test...

AVALON HIGH
CORONATION

VOLUME 1 • THE MERLIN PROPHECY

#1 New York Times bestselling author Meg Cabot's first ever manga!

Avalon High: Coronation continues the story of Meg Cabot's mega-hit novel *Avalon High*. Is Ellie's new boyfriend really the reincarnated King Arthur? Is his step-brother out to kill him? Will good triumph over evil—and will Ellie have to save the day AGAIN?

Don't miss *Avalon High: Coronation #1: The Merlin Prophecy*—in stores July 2007!

MEG CABOT

KING of THORN

YUJI
WAHARA

OT
OLDER TEEN
AGE 16+

CTION

WARNING:
Virus outbreak!

Kasumi and her
sister, Shizuku,
are infected with
the fatal Medusa
virus. There is no
cure, but Kasumi
is selected to go
into a cryogenic
freezer until a
cure is found.
But when
Kasumi awakens,
she must struggle
to survive in a
treacherous
world if she
hopes to
discover what
happened to
her sister.

From Yuji Iwahara,
the creator of
the popular
Chikyu Misaki
and *Koudelka*.

© YUJI IWAHARA

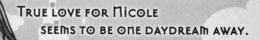

SAKURA TAISEN
BY OHJI HIROI, IKKU MASA AND KOSUKE FUJISHIMA

I really, really like this series. I'm a sucker for steampunk-type stories, and 1920s Japanese fashion, and throw in demon invaders, robot battles and references to Japanese popular theater? Sold! There's lots of fun tidbits for the clever reader to pick up in this series (all the characters have flower names, for one, and the fact that all the Floral Assault divisions are named after branches of the Takarazuka Review, Japan's sensational all-female theater troupe!), but the consistently stylish and clean art will appeal even to the most casual fan.

~Lillian Diaz-Przybyl, Editor

BATTLE ROYALE
BY KOUSHUN TAKAMI AND MASAYUKI TAGUCHI

As far as cautionary tales go, you couldn't get any timelier than *Battle Royale*. Telling the bleak story of a class of middle school students who are forced to fight each other to the death on national television, Koushun Takami and Masayuki Taguchi have created a dark satire that's sickening, yet undeniably exciting as well. And if we have that reaction reading it, it becomes alarmingly clear how the students could so easily be swayed into doing it.

~Tim Beedle, Editor

STOP!

This is the back of the book.
You wouldn't want to spoil a great ending!

This book is printed "manga-style," in the authentic Japanese right-to-left format. Since none of the artwork has been flipped or altered, readers get to experience the story just as the creator intended. You've been asking for it, so TOKYOPOP® delivered: authentic, hot-off-the-press, and far more fun!

DIRECTIONS

If this is your first time reading manga-style, here's a quick guide to help you understand how it works.

It's easy... just start in the top right panel and follow the numbers. Have fun, and look for more 100% authentic manga from TOKYOPOP®!